THE PALESTINIANS
BETWEEN
TERRORISM AND STATEHOOD

The Palestinians between Terrorism and Statehood

Pinhas Inbari

sussex
ACADEMIC
PRESS

First published in Hebrew in December 1994 under the title "Broken Swords"
by the Israeli Ministry of Defense, and the Miskal Library
of the *Yediot Ahranot* newspaper.

2 4 6 8 10 9 7 5 3 1
First published in English in 1996 by

SUSSEX ACADEMIC PRESS
18 Chichester Place
Brighton BN2 1FF, United Kingdom

Distributed in the United States by
International Specialized Book Services, Inc.
5804 N.E. Hassalo St.
Portland, Oregon 97213-3644
USA

British Library Cataloguing in Publication Data
A CIP catalogue record for this book is available from the British Library.

ISBN 1–898723 20 6 (hardcover)
ISBN 1–898723 21 4 (paperback)

Printed and bound by Biddles Ltd, King's Lynn and Guildford

Contents

———

Preface

This book provides the reader with basic information on the Palestinians' internal political system; the nature of the internal struggles within it; the arguments over the future of the Palestinian state; and the relations between the Palestinians and the Arab world, Israel, and the Western powers. The context, of course, is the Palestinians' transition to a sovereign state. The appearance of urban Islamic terrorism in the West *cannot be understood* without some familiarity with the internal Palestinan argument.

This book is the end-result of a long-term newspaper surveillance over the development of the peace process, so the presentation of the material is primarily journalistic. The spelling of Arabic names is based on the colloquial pronunciation customary among the Palestinians.

I would like to express my thanks to all those who have assisted me, with special thanks and gratitude to the translator, Judith Silver, who has brought the book closer to the English-language reader. The photographs appear by kind permission of Azzam Obed and Mahfouz Abu Turk.

Pinhas Inbari

Part I

Ides of March

1

The Revolution Devours its Children

On the night of 19 April 1988, Abu Jihad, Yaser Arafat's deputy in the PLO leadership, was absorbed in formulating the orders he was going to send to the Intifada's Unified Command in the occupied territories. Suddenly the phone rang, and a Fatah acquaintance in Rome informed him that Dr Fayez Abu Rahma, one of his relatives in Gaza, had been arrested by the Israeli military government there. The report was false, but it kept Abu Jihad in his study on the upper storey of a villa in the Sidi Busa'id quarter of Tunis. His wife Intisar, Umm Jihad, was in bed asleep with her small son Nidal, aged two and a half, at her side. At first Abu Jihad did not notice the strange sounds coming from the entrance foyer. When he did, he rushed out of the study, but it was too late.

Four men with their faces covered by grey-brown masks were standing at the bottom of the stairs. Abu Jihad fired first, and missed. He was cut down by automatic fire at the door to the room. Umm Jihad, who had taken a stand at his side at the top of the stairs, and little Nidal, escaped unscathed.

Less than three years later, on 14 January 1991, again in Tunis, Arafat's second deputy, Abu Iyyad, was dining with the officer in charge of Fatah's internal security, Hayel Abd al-Hamid, who was known as "The Sphinx" (Abu al-Hol) because of his extreme taciturnity. Suddenly one of Abu Iyyad's security men, Hamza Abu Zeid, burst into the room at Abu al-Hol's villa in a Tunis suburb and killed both men, together with one of Abu al-Hol's security men, Fakhri al-Umari, "Abu Muhammad."

In a relatively short period of under three years the Palestinian national movement lost two of its mainstays, each of whom had been considered, not without cause, to be Yaser Arafat's number two man.

Abu Jihad and Abu Iyyad represented two PLO extremes, with

each one striving to lead the organization in a different direction. Abu Jihad, the head of the PLO's military arm, favoured a continuation of the fight on Israel and the struggle with the United States. In contrast to him, Abu Iyyad pushed in the opposite direction: for reconciliation with the United States and the Palestinians' integration in a pro-American Middle East, with all that implied as far as acceptance of Israel was concerned.

It is impossible to understand the developments in the PLO, the struggles over the character of the Intifada, the appearance of the Palestinian delegation from the territories and the bitter struggles around it, without dwelling on the differences between Abu Iyyad and Abu Jihad which split not only the Fatah organization, but almost all the other organizations within the PLO.

To a considerable extent the two figures at the opposite extremes of the PLO, Abu Iyyad and Abu Jihad, were killed over words: an article that was published and a book that was not.

The Very Beginning

Dr Muhammad Hamza was one Abu Jihad's lesser known followers, possibly because he was not an arms-bearing PLO soldier or "general," but an editor of publications that reflected attitudes within the military wing of the PLO headed by Abu Jihad. A year after Abu Jihad's "liquidation," Dr Hamza published a book[1] eulogizing his commander, in which he revealed some of Abu Jihad's most closely guarded secrets and shed some light on the background to his assassination. Part of the description of Abu Jihad's murder is taken from that book.

Abu Jihad seems to have had many enemies, including within the PLO. Even though Dr Hamza does not link them directly to the killing, he does not leave much room for the imagination when he spells out the political background to the killing of the leader he adored. Abu Jihad appears to have been preoccupied at that time with fighting for the PLO leadership. On the day he was killed, there was a handwritten draft of a book he was working on tucked away in his chest of drawers. It was called "The Very Beginning" and was intended to be more than an autobiography describing Abu Jihad's central role in the establishment of the PLO. It was to specify the organization's original goals in such a way as to underline how far the organization

had since distanced itself from the essential motives for its existence.

It was just then that Abu Jihad was endeavouring to write the
book, because he realized that the central PLO stream was coming
closer to a political process involving the recognition of Israel. By
underlining the original ideological message of the Palestinian
revolution, his book was intended to give the Palestinians a sort of
Mao Tse Tung's *Red Book*, or Libyan Leader Muammar Qaddhafi's
Green Book.

When members of the elite Israeli unit (according to sources
outside Israel) burst into his villa, Abu Jihad was absorbed in
Intifada affairs. His connection with the Intifada went much deeper
than is generally believed, not only in its day-to-day administration,
but in having broken the ground for its outbreak.

It is customary to view the Intifada as a spontaneous event
that erupted over the genuine distress of two million desperate
Palestinians whose daily lives had been rendered insufferable by
the occupation and who could see no political solution to their
troubles.

The feelings of frustration and distress were undoubtedly the
major reason for the Intifada's outbreak. Toward the end of 1987,
however, several radical elements in the Middle East concluded that
the relative tranquillity in the Israeli occupied territories had to be
shattered, and began stirring a pot that was anyway about to spill
over. Abu Jihad was a major link between these elements.

The Intifada broke out on 9 December 1987, in the wake of a riot
in the Jabalia Refugee Camp sparked off by a road accident near
Ashkelon, in which an Israeli-driven truck killed seven of the camp's
workers. But the background to the Intifada was very much broader,
covering struggles throughout the Middle East. Eventually it was
these struggles that also led to the outbreak of the Gulf crisis.

Red Lines in Tripoli

Despite objective conditions, the Middle East had enjoyed many
years of relative stability, with no upheavals having disturbed its
principal countries for decades. Not everybody in the region, however, regarded this stability as a blessing. Some elements saw the
great emotions the Intifada aroused in the Arab world as a chance to
send shock waves through the Middle East. Furthermore, there are

indications that these elements actually encouraged the outbreak of the Intifada. An undercover struggle developed between those who also wanted to set a match to an Intifada in Cairo and Amman, and those who wished to keep it confined to Israeli–Palestinian relations, so that it would not cross the Jordan River eastward or the Sinai Desert southward. Abu Jihad was one of the leaders of those who supported turning the Intifada into a powder keg to ignite a pan-Arab revolution; this is why he was murdered. Abu Iyyad was murdered for the opposite reason; he wanted to turn the Intifada into a spur for political processes designed to bring calm to the Middle East.

When Dr Hamza declared that Abu Jihad had "crossed the red lines,"[2] he was referring not only to how Abu Jihad planned the Intifada's continuation – solely in the field of Israeli–Palestinian relations – but in a generalized Middle Eastern context, because "He was working toward a direction that conflicted with the process that had been agreed by the 'bosses', that of defusing the region, putting out its fires, and stabilizing the principle of military détente."[3] Dr Hamza himself drew the unavoidable conclusion. "This being so, there are many, and not only in 'Tel Aviv', who agree that the man who could complicate what the 'bosses' have agreed on has to be removed."[4] These people regarded Israel as a "works contractor" for a combination of international interests. I heard similar remarks in Abu Jihad's Tunis villa in October 1993. Abu Jihad's successors believed wholeheartedly that Israel was just a works contractor for an extremely broad system of international interests.

What did Dr Hazma mean by arguing that his revered leader had crossed the red lines? First, there was Abu Jihad's visit to Libya on 1 February 1987. Libyan Leader Muammar Qaddhafi was supporting international terror at that time, but Abu Jihad felt he was dissipating his efforts all over the world without giving the Middle East, particularly the Palestinians, the attention they merited. Abu Jihad went to Libya to "point [Qaddhafi] in the right direction."[5]

Up to that visit, relations between Libya and the PLO had been strained, because Qaddhafi was skeptical about the PLO's revolutionary nature. He was not prepared to receive Yaser Arafat in Tripoli. Strange as it seems, until that meeting Qaddhafi and Abu Jihad had never met face-to-face. The meeting was designed to unify the Middle Eastern terrorist forces to undermine the region's stability, and for this the most convenient tool to use was the

Palestinian problem. That conversation in 1987 laid the foundations for cooperation between Libya, Abu Jihad and Teheran, as well as with circles in Baghdad.

In order to understand Abu Jihad's and Qaddhafi's intentions to undermine the pro-Western Arab regimes a year before the Intifada, it is necessary to look at those governments' destabilization, under Iranian auspices, two years after the Gulf war, this time exploiting Islamic sentiments.

It did not take long for the results of these efforts to begin to be apparent in the territories. On December 9 the Intifada broke out and Abu Jihad's visits to Tripoli became more frequent. His last visit to Qaddhafi took place 10 days before he was killed.

Abu Iyyad: "Lowering the Sword"

Like Abu Jihad, Abu Iyyad was one of Arafat's deputies, but he represented a reverse development in the PLO. Abu Iyyad had come a long way since the time he commanded the Black September terror organization at the beginning of the 1970s. In the spring of 1990 he was honored by having one of his programmatic articles published in the prestigious *Foreign Policy* journal. Abu Iyyad was ultimately killed because of both what he wrote in that article and the circumstances in which he wrote it.

It was not Abu Iyyad himself who had initiated the article; it was an orderly formulation of responses to a detailed questionnaire the State Department had submitted to several PLO officials, headed by Abu Iyyad, designed to raise the level of the limping dialogue between the Americans and Palestinians. So as not to harm the delicate process of organizing an Israeli–Palestinian dialogue in Cairo, the US Administration did not contact Abu Iyyad directly, but gave the task to Richard Murphy, who had just retired from the foreign service. Murphy was accompanied by several Americans, including Charles Mainz, the editor of *Foreign Policy*. In addition to Abu Iyyad's own article in the magazine, Mainz also interviewed him. Most of the questionnaire can be reconstructed from his questions.

In fact, right from the start the Americans knew what Abu Iyyad would reply. This can be learned from the fact that Arab publications in Tunis knew the article's substance before it was published officially.[6] In addition, the State Department relied on the interview for some of the evidence it submitted to Congress in mid-March as part of its report on the dialogue with the PLO.

Abu Iyyad's article is entitled "Lowering The Sword." The title itself explains why the article pleased the Americans, but was frowned on by the "sword bearers" in Abu Jihad's camp. The article explains that with global changes, the existence of only one superpower and the end of the Cold War, new opportunities had opened up for peace. It outlines Israeli–Arab cooperation, with the Palestinians acting as a bridge. The Palestinian state would strive to open borders with Israel and cooperation with it in many areas, such as water distribution. For the first time, Abu Iyyad formulated the logic behind the pro-American approach, which accompanied the internal Palestinian debates following the exodus from Beirut and in the subsequent years. Similar debates were going on throughout the Arab world.

The London-based *al-Qabas*[7] reported that Abu Iyyad was asked fifteen questions, but gave details of only twelve: (1) The PLO's role in the peacemaking process; (2) the future of the peace process and its implications; what would happen if the current process were to fail; (3) the Islamic wing in the territories and its relations with the PLO; (4) the connection between the Intifada's Unified Command and the PLO; (5) the connection between Jordan and the PLO; (6) how did the PLO view the future of Jerusalem? (7) the PLO's position on Israel's refusal to negotiate with it; (8) the PLO's role in preparing an Israeli–Palestinian dialogue; (9) the Palestinian state; (10) conditions for ending the Intifada; (11) was the use of weapons a realistic option in the Intifada; (12) the impact on the Middle East of the changes in Eastern Europe.

Not all the answers were published in *Foreign Policy*. The main question concerned conditions for ending the Intifada. Abu Iyyad was also asked to outline his concept of a Palestinian state, or entity, and whether he saw peace only as a stage in a program whose real objective was the destruction of the State of Israel, or did he see a complete and final accommodation? He was asked to give his opinion on the Palestinian's right of return to their former homes in Israel and the desired nature of the relationship between the Palestinians and Jordan. But what later emerged as the critical question that led to Abu Iyyad's assassination involved his relationship with the violent groups within the PLO and whether he was aiming at a demilitarized Palestinian entity. If Abu Iyyad's answer to the Americans was that the Palestinian state would not have an army, it would mean that the military wing, Abu Jihad had taken such pains to construct, would have to be dismantled.

Abu Iyyad's responses did indeed give rise to satisfaction in Washington and concern among the arms-bearers. His full response on conditions for ending the Intifada did not appear in *Foreign Policy*, but his basic approach envisioned a diminishing of the Intifada and strict preservation of its public, non-violent, character. An "unarmed uprising" was the term he used, to the great suspicion of the military wing. His conditions for ending the Intifada were for practical steps – not just promises and statements – to be taken to materialize the solution of two states in the Land of Israel–Palestine, living beside each other in peace, with security arrangements.

As for the right of return, he maintained that the PLO must have a realistic approach. The right of return would not necessarily have to be implemented on the ground, but could also be implemented through compensation payments. In any event, the right of return could not be implemented at the expense of Israel's interests, but must take into consideration the situation created since 1948. Israel must accept the principle of the right of return. "We realize that a total return is no longer possible. We are not altogether unrealistic in our considerations on how to realize this right." The right of return, Abu Iyyad added, must not become an unbridgeable barrier.

The three remaining questions not reported by *al-Qabas* dealt with the demilitarization of the territories, how the PLO intended to impose its authority on armed groups, and how the Palestinians would safeguard their security in the event of demilitarization. At that time the PLO's political wing was beginning to demand international auspices for the territories, maintaining that such auspices would guarantee the Palestinians' security in the absence of an army. Abu Iyyad promised Murphy that he would work for PLO discipline to be imposed on the armed groups; and there are hints of this in *Foreign Policy*. Abu Iyyad said that some of the security arrangements would involve cooperation with Israel against border crossings by elements aiming at undermining any peace arrangements. He condemned those groups within the PLO that were already attempting to cross the border from Lebanon into Israeli territory in order to sabotage the peace process.

While Abu Iyyad's attitude toward cooperation with Israel was positive and he was prepared to come to immediate arrangements for cooperation and open borders, his attitude toward Jordan was chilly and he did not support entering into a confederation with it, unless it was in the wake of complex procedures. He was only prepared for confederation arrangements with Jordan if Israel were to become a third party. The leader of the former Black September terrorist organization had never forgiven Jordan for that month's bloody events. The Americans put tremendous efforts into persuading his successors to forget the past and establish relations of trust and cooperation with the Jordanians.

While Abu Jihad was coordinating all the anti-American forces in the Middle East, Abu Iyyad was becoming the principal pro-American force within the PLO, and just as Abu Jihad had crossed red lines by visiting Tripoli to shake Qaddhafi's hand on the eve of the Intifada, Abu Iyyad crossed red lines by shaking Murphy's hand in Tunis three years later. As Abu Jihad had gone to Qaddhafi to stir up the Intifada, so Murphy went to Abu Iyyad to seek a way to end it with a political solution. The *Foreign Policy* article did indeed encourage the Americans, and it seemed to have broken the ground for the level of contacts to be raised. The Americans had found someone in the PLO leadership who was willing to seek a political solution to the Palestinian problem based on principles acceptable to Washington. It is hard to say who really murdered Abu Iyyad, but it is quite clear that they came from those anti-American circles Abu Jihad had attempted to establish three years earlier. Abu Iyyad doomed himself by agreeing to a demilitarized Palestinian state, because the Palestinian fighters were unable to simply step down from the stage after having made such sacrifices for Palestine.

One of the major difficulties in understanding the developments within the Palestinian camp lies in attempting to perceive the internal struggles as though they were being waged between, not within the organizations. Ostensibly, it was the Fatah on one side and the rejectionists on the other, but actually, inside the Fatah, Arafat's two deputies represented opposite extremes which not only were unable to live together under the same roof, they were involved in a struggle over principles that ended with both of them eliminated. The correct way to read the political map of the PLO is to see a division that crosses all the organizations: on the one hand, those who favor integrating with a pro-American system and, on the other, those opposed to it. Abu Iyyad was with the Americans, Abu Jihad was against them. The very same question split all the organizations comprising the PLO: the Democratic Front, the Popular Front, the Palestinian communists. Even the fundamentalist movements, Hamas and Islamic Jihad, contained similar divisions. When the picture is presented this way, we are better able to understand developments among the Palestinians and in the Middle East as a whole.

"Gun Democracy"

In February 1986, a booklet intended to laud and exalt the memory of the PLO's martyrs, particularly those killed by the Israeli Mossad, was distributed in East Jerusalem.[8] What is noteworthy, however, is not the lament by its author, Abdallah Ghassan, for the many PLO martyrs killed by the enemy, but the mourning for those cut down by bullets fired by their Palestinian brethren.

> How sad, even painful and soul-destroying, it is that a large number of our young people and leaders have fallen to Arab bullets and, in some cases, to Palestinian bullets. It will do us no good to evade this truth . . . it is clearly truth – and as such it is painful and regrettable.
>
> When a martyr dies from an enemy bullet, we weep with pride, but when our martyrs fall to bullets [fired] by our own brethren, blood and tears flow in bitterness, anger and pain. This fact has been confirmed by Nabil Sha'ath, Arafat's adviser, when he said half the youthful Palestinian leadership were killed by the Palestinians themselves.[9]

The examples cited by the author do indeed involve Abu Nidal's murders of moderate leaders, but he hints at mutual assassinations against a deeper background – not by a fringe group like that of Abu Nidal, assassinating the leaders of the majority group – but of mutual acts of murder within the main body of the Palestinians, the Fatah itself.

> As for the differences of opinion among us . . . these are overt and healthy; after all, there is no way to avoid differences of opinion and arguments . . . but the dialogue [and there is no dialogue with Abu Nidal] must not develop into a bloody struggle that takes the form of bullets, murder and bloodshed.
>
> And there is no doubt that gun democracy, as our brother and commander Abu Ammar (Yaser Arafat) put it, is the most difficult model of democracy and it is the most dangerous and sensitive.[10]

The phenomenon of mutual acts of murder was an open sore in the PLO, but prior to the Gulf War it was very difficult for the

Palestinians to discuss it openly. They were prepared, at most, to acknowledge Abu Nidal's murders of people in the political wing of the PLO. The murderous tension between the Abu Jihad's people and the political wing that had gathered around Arafat gained no "recognition" by the rivals themselves, but one of the changes brought about by the Gulf crisis was the gradual lifting of this emotional barrier.

Although the fight was between the Jihadists and the Iyyadists, Abu Jihad's supporters, especially after his death, directed their main fury toward Chairman Arafat, while actually honoring Abu Iyyad. Judging by the leaflets they published, those qualities we think of as being Abu Iyyad's, namely: pragmatic compromise and moving toward the United States in order to strip the PLO of its military nature; were attributed by the Fatah military cadres to Arafat himself. There could be a dual reason for this: up to the Gulf crisis Arafat had indeed helped the Iyyadists against the Jihadists; or, without any connection with the fight between these two streams, Arafat was actually scared of the great power Abu Jihad had accumulated and his policy of mutual balances took a form that was necessarily detrimental to the military wing. The cadres did not remain silent, and after their leader was killed, the spirit of rebellion began to be sensed. They also began hinting that Arafat himself had had a hand in the internal killings – of Abu Iyyad and Abu al-Hol – that had set off an emotional storm in the PLO, or that at the very least he had benefited from Abu Jihad's assassination.

The Scars of Rejected Love

In the winter of 1991, one of the Intifada's most difficult periods of time, an official and definitely most unusual organization document was distributed among Fatah activists in the occupied territories. It was signed by Abd al-Aziz Shahin, a senior figure in Fatah's military arm, and for four months the Fatah activists tried to stop its contents becoming public knowledge. Eventually, however, the document was taken out of the cupboard that summer and stirred up a great storm, because in an official Fatah document Abd al-Aziz Shahin ("Abu Ali") was demanding Arafat's dismissal.

Shahin was not just another military wing commander. One of the Fatah's founders and revered heros, he had paid a heavy price for the Palestinian struggle. Shortly after the Six Day War, in October 1967, he was captured by Israeli security forces after a pursuit in the Tubas hills of Samaria. His squad comprised two men: himself and Yaser Arafat. Arafat managed to flee back to Jordan, and Abu Ali was captured. Abu Ali Shahin was sentenced to 15 years imprisonment, which he served to the full. He spent another two years isolated from Palestinians in the territories, under strict house arrest in Dahaniya at the southern tip of the Gaza Strip. He was then deported.

All through his years in jail he was the undisputed leader of the security prisoners and was responsible for organizing the PLO's military potential among the cadres Israel sent to the prisons. He was also responsible for conducting the PLO's fight within the jails against forces opposed to it, and Israel regarded him as its natural interlocutor in negotiations over deals for prisoner exchanges with Ahmad Jibril after the Lebanese war. Over the years, Shahin's health deteriorated seriously: he suffered from problems with his heart and eyes, his left leg was partially paralyzed, and he had spinal pains.

His reunion with Arafat after he was released from jail was potentially explosive. Shahin retained the original spirit of the fighting Fatah and could not bear the PLO's slick "diplomats" who stayed in luxury hotels, exploiting the sufferings and struggles of the fighting cadres.

Shahin was given command of Fatah forces in Southern Lebanon or, to be more precise, the forces loyal to Abu Jihad, but devoted a great deal of attention to the struggle, which took on aspects of actual warfare, against the forces loyal to Arafat: the contingent of force 17 in Lebanon. In 1987, just before the Intifada, Rasem al-Ghul, the Force 17 commander in Lebanon and Arafat's representative in Beirut, was killed. Shahin was accused of the assassination and jailed in Tunis. The episode was hushed up, so as not to provoke an overt explosion, and some time later he was freed.

The circular he distributed in the territories was an authentic expression of the depth of the rift between the Jihadist and Iyyadist wings. The main issue Shahin raised was the mutual assassinations, the "gun democracy," in Arafat's colorful language. Arafat is depicted for the first time as having benefited from the liquidations campaign, with heavy hints that he also had a hand in them.

All the world's national liberation movements have suffered from negative elements and are afflicted by many diseases. But what we see in our own revolution is something unique; what has weakened our revolution is that along its way it has become bogged down in an enormous amount of unusually negative manifestations, such as assassinations, and this great number of assassinations and murders of front-line leaders, the historical leaders of the founding generation . . .

It is impossible to conceal from anyone investigating the phenomenon and following our revolution that the scale of the conspiracies outside the revolution doubled the paralysis of the revolutionary action machine, and this fitted in with the efforts of the egoistical leadership [literally, personal leadership – a term of condemnation for Arafat] to build the presidential institutions on the shoulders of the privileged, from among those who have never combatted the Zionist enemy and most of whom have never fired even one shot on the national soil of Palestine.

According to Shahin, Abu Jihad's assassination was a clear example of how Arafat profited from the killings. In any event, it is important to remember that these were some of Shahin's more bitter thoughts and do not necessarily mean that Arafat was actually to blame. The PLO's military commander was first and foremost the commander of the "Western Sector," which ran its operations from Jordan, and this made it the most important of the military commands. Shahin claimed Arafat had begun plotting against the command of the Western Sector even before Abu Jihad's liquidation.

And even all this was not enough for him, he set himself the goal of shattering the Western Sector in order to establish his own private "Western Sector," that would not obey the apparatus of the sacred martyr Abu Jihad . . . and he appointed several of his men as his "Western Sector" and called it the "Supreme Military Council of the PLO," and poured a great deal of money into it while being tight-fisted with the men of the sacred martyr . . .

The sacred martyr, the founding commander, the victim of the revolution, Abu Jihad, had hardly gone from us when the work of destruction already began – the destruction of the Fatah organization's activities in the occupied land . . .

Fatah Veterans versus Arafat

About a year later, in January 1992, to mark Fatah Day a leaflet appeared, continuing Shahin's letter and signed by "Fatah veterans," those whom Chairman Arafat had "pensioned off." The leaflet carried even more pointed hints of the liquidation of the movement's leaders, and ran like this:

> When some members of the Fatah leadership began to discuss the internal situation in order to launch a confrontation of the type of Comrades Abu Jihad, Abu Iyyad and Abu al-Hol, the hand of fate suddenly swept them away, so that the situation would remain unchanged, in favor of the privileged gang [that is, Arafat's group].

For the first time, Fatah members tied up the chain of harrowing assassinations of the movement's leaders with the internal situation in the Fatah, implying that the killings of the famous personalities followed on from the killings of ground level cadre members, which did not gain international headlines. In essence, the circular accused Arafat of atrophying the Fatah military wing and abandoning it for the political wing.

Why Was Sa'ad Sayel Killed?

The mutual killings were not the result of increased internal tensions brought on by the Gulf crisis, but had roots that extended deep into the past. One of the old liquidations that had particularly upset the PLO was the murder of the PLO's operations officer in Lebanon, Amid (brigadier general) Sa'ad Sayel, "Abu al-Walid," immediately after the PLO's evacuation from Beirut, against the backdrop of the great split between Arafat and Abu Musa. Sa'ad Sayel was cut down in an ambush on 27 September 1982, when he was on a tour of PLO forces and their Lebanese allies in the Biqa' valley. It is customary to think that it was the Syrians who set the ambush. That, in any event, is what Mamduh Nofal, Sayel's colleague from that time, told me in Tunis in October 1993, but this explanation is not very logical, because Sa'ad Sayel was one of Abu Jihad's people and the Syrians had an interest in pulling him into the camp of those who were rebelling against Arafat. Abu Musa, after all, was a Jihadist, and the Syrians wanted to pull as many of that wing as possible over to their side. The Syrians' failure to pull Abu Jihad into their camp may have been of the reasons for the worsening of the relations between them in the following years and for the development of Abu Jihad's ties with Qaddhafi, of all people.

Dr Muhammad Hamza, Abu Jihad's biographer, does not believe

it was the Syrians who killed him. He does not reveal what he knows about this matter, but testifies that Abu Jihad was particularly distressed by the murder of "the hero of the defense of Beirut" in the Lebanese war, and as soon as he received the bad news he shut himself up in his apartment in Baghdad to write another chapter in *"The Very Beginning"*. Abu Jihad did not wish to reveal what he knew because "the time has not yet come to enter into these matters." Dr Hamza both discloses and conceals when he asserts that "Abu al-Walid's assassination is still one of the greatest political and security mysteries, enveloped in a thick fog, because it was one of the sharpest turning points in Palestinian history." All Dr Hamza was prepared to say was that several hours before Abu al-Walid left for the place where the booby trap had been laid, he had had a long telephone conversation with Abu Jihad. Arafat's deputy was scheduled to go to the Biqa' valley, but Abu al-Walid insisted on taking his place in order to let Abu Jihad escort Arafat on a visit to Saudi Arabia.[11] The unavoidable question is: why was there an argument over this? Was a visit to Saudi Arabia then considered to be crucial, as an expression of loyalty to the existing pro-US Arab regimes, while a visit to the Lebanese Bekaa would arouse suspicions of an intention to transfer more PLO forces to the anti-US rebels? Or was Dr Hamza trying to imply that the booby trap had actually been set for Abu Jihad, not Sa'ad Sayel?

Nevertheless, the assassins were almost certainly well aware of who they were shooting. Abdallah Ghassan provides another key to an understanding of the circumstances in which Abu al-Walid was killed, in remarks he had made when on a visit to Tehran, shortly before his death:

> The Palestinian organizations have agreed to halt certain activities, such as hijacking planes, but we will not give up the armed struggle . . . the Palestinian revolution has re-examined different methods for military operations and there is general agreement among the various organizations to halt certain activities, principally air hijacking.
>
> Our struggle has two faces: the first is military, the second aspect is political. On no account can we give up the armed struggle, or even agree to a tendency toward giving it up. All the PLO's achievements come from the armed struggle.
>
> We continue to adhere to the use of arms to achieve the goal of the establishment of an independent Palestinian state. We aspire to

launch fedayeen (guerrilla) activities inside and outside the occupied land.

After mentioning examples of operations in Israel's heartland, such as the Savoy Hotel attack and coastal road bus hijacking, Brigadier General Sa'ad Sayel continues:

> It is natural for us to continue to develop and escalate our operations. We cannot stop military operations against Israel until we achieve our goal . . . For twenty years now the solution to the Palestinian problem has been up to the Arab countries, without results . . . We will continue to escalate the armed struggle until it becomes a general uprising in the occupied lands.[12]

Abdallah Ghassan knew why these remarks should be mentioned as the key to understanding Sa'ad Sayel's assassination. Even then Abu Jihad's wing saw instigating an uprising in the territories as a result of the escalation in the armed struggle. Sayel went to Tehran because the Arab countries had let him down, and on that visit he crossed the red lines that Abu Jihad himself crossed six years later, by visiting Qaddhafi. In contrast to the PLO's political wing, the spirit of Abu Jihad's military wing was not far removed from the moods in Tehran and was already prepared to come to an understanding and enter into agreements with the Khomeinist revolution, even via the Syrians or Libyans; this being in basic conflict with the interests of the pro-Western Arab regimes with which Yaser Arafat had links.

In time, Arafat was to remind the Khomeini regime in Tehran that the Fatah had stood beside the Khomeini revolution's cradle and assisted it in its first days. This link was later to become a Fatah turning point – Abu Jihad's wing maintained that link and developed along religious lines that grew into the Islamic Jihad. Arafat abandoned this connection, thus causing sections of the military wing to rise up against him. Sa'ad Sayel's assassination pointed up the red lines for the Fatah; going to Tehran was considered to be crossing the red line. This may be why Abu Jihad, despite his sympathy for the Khomeini revolution, was careful not to go to Teheran. He was to cross that line some years later, however, by going to Qaddhafi.

The link eventually worked out between the Jihadist wing of the Fatah, the Khomeinist revolution in Tehran and Qaddhafi's Green Revolution was to be of great importance in laying the ground for the events that led the territories toward the Intifada, and was to have an indirect influence on the political developments in the entire Middle East.

The Night of the Hang-Glider, Arousing the Territories – from Words to Actions

The armed struggle, then, had a concealed goal about which there was not much talk; that of touching off a Palestinian uprising in the territories. The first objective was, naturally, to attack Israel; by both direct military action and also by setting fire to the imagination of the Palestinians in the territories, encouraging them to rebel. This was not talked about because there was another objective to inciting an uprising in the territories – that of rocking the general stability of the Middle East and also, fanning up an intifada in Arab countries against the existing regimes. The parties principally interested in this were the leaders of the Khomeinist revolution in Tehran, and Qaddhafi. The moderate, pro-Western Arab states followed the contacts between Palestinian terrorism and those regimes with great concern.

The Intifada has a Birthday, But When? Version 'A'

One organization of the entirely Jihadist model was, of course, that of Ahmad Jibril, the Popular Front for the Liberation of Palestine – General Command. This organization made a significant contribution to the outbreak of the Intifada. Jibril was the architect of the prisoner exchange deals in 1985, after the Lebanon war, and he insisted that, in conflict with what had happened in previous exchanges, many of the security prisoners would be permitted to return to their homes in the territories after being released.

The prisoners Jibril freed would later be among the main activists on the violent side of the Intifada. Moreover, a month before the outbreak of the Intifada, one of Jibril's men carried out an imaginative military operation when he used a hang glider to cross the northern border from Lebanon, attacked an Israeli army camp near Kiryat Shmona in Upper Galilee and killed six soldiers. Jibril's "night of the hanglider" and the Islamic Jihad's intensive activity in Gaza at that time had the same goal: to incite the Palestinians in the territories to rise up against the Israeli rule.

Israelis tend to see terrorist activities against them only in the direct Arab–Israeli context, finding it difficult to understand the internal Arab background. It transpires out that, no less than the desire to hit out at Israel, the Night of the Hang Glider had a pan-Arab background and the direct motive for Jibril's decision to carry out the operation was the Arab summit meeting in Amman shortly before that. Ahmad Jibril's journal, *Ila al-Amam* (Forward), comes right out with this in a comprehensive article by Muhammad Lafi on the Arab countries' obligations to the Palestinian problem, as expressed at various Arab summits.[13]

The article rules that the Amman summit was one of the reasons for the Intifada's outbreak, because it suffered from several basic drawbacks: first, the summit wanted to push the Palestinian question to the fringes of the Arabs' interests, to emphasize the importance of Arab reconciliation; this in an attempt to support Iraq in its war on Iran. This could have led to a cancellation of the 1974 Rabat Conference resolutions, which recognized the PLO as the sole legitimate representative of the Palestinian people. From the viewpoint of the article's author, what was so grave involved broad Middle Eastern contexts, not the purely Palestinian aspect. He noted that that conference had attacked revolutionary Iran and restored Egypt to the arms of the Arab world. The conclusion was: the Arab summits had furthered the political at the expense of the military option or, to put it differently, "reinforced the Arab reactionaries' defeatist trends."

The Night of the Hanglider on 25 November 1987 was designed to amend what the Amman Summit, which had concluded that month, had spoiled, by putting the Palestinian problem back on the top of the Arab agenda and restoring its violent nature, with all that implies regarding the development of the Arab world as a whole. Jibril and Abu Jihad, then, saw matters eye to eye. One worked out of Damascus, the other from Libya. A traffic accident at the Ashkelon intersection a few days later was the match that ignited the pile of kindling heaped up by Abu Jihad and Jibril.

Abu Jihad and Jibril began to be connected by a line of communications that tied them to Khomeinist Iran. Behind the hanglider operation, however, there was also a clear Syrian interest – to help its friends in Iran against the Arab world's trend toward siding with Iraq and foil the attempt to mobilize Saddam Hussein, who was then involved in a desperate defensive battle for Basra, to support an Israeli–Arab arrangement. At that time nobody knew where Saddam was finally heading. By renewing interest in the Palestine problem, however, and directing it to violent paths, Abu Jihad and Ahmed Jibril were trying to prevent the Arab world as a whole from devoting itself to peace with Israel and attack the US political effort in the Middle East from within Palestine.

The Collective Leadership around Arafat

The genuine political division in the PLO was not, then, between the organizations, but within them. Although marks of the Iyyadist struggle against the Jihadists can be found in most of the PLO organizations, it was particularly sharp and hard-hitting within the Fatah organization. Subsequently this division was to have a profound effect on the nature of the Palestinian delegation, deciding its fate. The classic PLO organizations found much more of a common language among themselves than could have been seen from the outside. The Jihadist wing of the Fatah was very close to the other organizations, and worked against an enemy shared by all: the Iyyadist, political wing. In the territories that wing was called the "national personalities," and on the outside: the "advisers." The organizations combatted the "personalities" in the territories from the Unified Command, and on the outside – in the various PLO institutions. The Palestinian delegation was finally established on the basis of the internal balances between the two wings. Each wing in the delegation had a supporter on the outside: the head of the negotiating team, Dr Haidar Abd a-Shafi from Gaza, represented the organizations. Faisal Husseini represented the "advisers" on whom Shahin had vented his fury.

The reason for the failure of the Palestinian delegation from the territories lay, then, in the internal balances between the two wings. Arafat conducted a policy of balances, which enraged both wings against him. Shahin demanded that Arafat's power within the PLO be reduced, but this demand only won a genuine public reverbera-tion after Abd a-Shafi put it forward in the territories in July 1993. In those years the organizations of Dr George Habash (the Popular Front) and Nayef Hawatma (the Democratic Front) demanded that the establishment of a collective leadership around Arafat. This was one of the major themes of their leaflets dealing with internal PLO affairs, and was the common denominator between the leftist organizations, the military wing of the Fatah and Abd a-Shafi from the territories.

The "advisers" came up with yet another danger as far as Arafat was concerned: the establishment of a new PLO within the territories, on the basis of Abu Iyyad's program. In the code-language of the internal struggles, this danger was called the "alternative leadership." Arafat's control over the PLO was also at risk from the Jihadist groups, and Arafat was far from denigrating this danger, but when he spoke of an "alternative leadership" from within the territories, he was referring to the Iyyadist challenge which was being formulated against him from within the Palestinian delegation.

The Jihadist wing, the organizations, demanded that Arafat back out of the political process that had, in their view, been dictated by the United States, and worked to surround him with a "collective leadership" of the organization heads. There was also danger to Arafat of another variety, from within the Iyyadist wing: pressure to disband the PLO as a whole, join the US circle and form the Palestinian institutions in accordance with a Western model, as part of the Western world. They did not demand Arafat's resignation, or surround him with a collective leadership, but that he "westernize" himself.

The various pressures can be described in another way: the military wing wanted to reinforce the PLO's revolutionary nature, both in its contents and in the composition of its leadership. The Iyyadist wing was constantly at work to blur the revolutionary, miltiary nature, even at the cost of the elimination of the PLO and its traditional leadership. Arafat's position was decided by his feelings about the United States' trends. When he authorized his personal Force 17 protection, he believed the United States had an interest in his survival and his protection against the Jihadist wing. After March 1990, however, Arafat began to be more afraid of the Iyyadist wing, since he feared that the United States wanted to replace him with Abu Iyyad, and afterwards, with his successors. Arafat maneuvered between the two wings, both inside and outside the territories: this time he was furious with one group, humiliating them, next time it was the other way round, until they both rose up against him.

One of the arenas of the struggle was the Fatah Revolutionary Council – an institution established in 1980 to represent the commanders of the combatant cadres of the Fatah – such people as

Shahin, or Fatma Barnawi, who planted a bomb in a Jerusalem movie house after the Six Day War. From this it can be seen that the Council was the Fatah's totally Jihadist institution. It met each summer, and was one of the most inconvenient institutions for Arafat. Even though he naturally chaired its sessions, there seemed to be no other PLO institution in which Arafat heard so many complaints and grumbles about having lost the original path, forsaken the revolution, and so on.

Arafat could not resign himself to the fact that there was a framework institution within the PLO that united the Jihadist force within it, and consistently worked to bring in Iyyadist representatives. Every summer the fight over the new appointments recurred; little by little, Arafat succeeded in insinuating into the arms-bearers' council such "advisers" as Nabil Sha'ath, the Al-Hasan brothers, or Akram Haniya, the deportee from Ramallah who, despite the combatant image he had acquired, was one of the most important people in the Iyyadist wing, and afterwards played an important role in support for the Palestinian delegation to be, Husseni's wing.

The Revolutionary Council may have lost something of its absolutely Jihadist coloring, but the recurring struggles with Arafat's leaning toward blurring the Council's combatant character only sharpened up the internal tensions and stepped up Arafat's image, as the Jihadists saw him, as a secret Iyyadist.

"Government" or "Executive Committee"; Some of the Signs of the Internal Argument in the PLO

From the very day the PLO accepted Arafat's leadership, it was afflicted with crises. The Palestine Liberation Organization was established not by Arafat, but by a Palestinian refugee from Acre, Ahmad Shuqeiri, on 28 May 1964. Shuqeiri exploited pan-Arab tensions, particularly those between Egypt under the leadership of Abd a-Naser and Syria, and between Egypt and Jordan. At first his path gained the PLO Egypt's support. Even then Egypt may have been showing fatigue with the Palestinian problem, and wanted to establish a Palestinian authority, to take away the burden of leading and representing the Palestinians.

Despite the paradox, Arafat, who is now identified as the PLO leader, began his career as an opponent of Shuqeiri's leadership and of the PLO. In its first years the Fatah organization, which he founded and headed throughout its history, articulated a radical line, highlighting the armed struggle idea.

There is a heavy fog surrounding the genuine reasons for the Fatah's establishment. The organization, which is the backbone of the entire PLO organization, was apparently born twice. Once was in the 1950s, in the Gaza Strip, as a cell of the Muslim Brotherhood, which was called "Al-Asifa" (the Storm), and this name accompanied the Fatah's military arm and adorned the leaflets of the military wing. In those years the people who were to lead the Palestinian struggle, such as Arafat and Abu Iyyad, were young students in Cairo. They headed the Palestinian students' cell in the Cairo University.

The Nasserite regime was not happy about the link between Arafat and the Muslim Brotherhood and that band of student activists was compelled to leave for Kuwait, where the Fatah organization as it is known today was founded. Here, too, there are several versions of the circumstances surrounding its establishment. In his book *Without Identity*, Abu Iyyad gave the date 10 October 1959 as the day of its establishment. The hidden pages of *The Very Beginning* by Abu Jihad, obviously give another version of the Fatah's establishment. Abu Jihad, in any event, accompanied Arafat to Kuwait. There other people joined this band, not necessary from Muslim Brotherhood circles, such as Faruq Qaddumi of the lefist tendencies; the organization's absolutely rightist nature began to blur and it became a broad movement with various orientations, as it has been known all through the years.

The Six Day War sent shock waves all through the Arab world, as well as among the Palestinians. More than ever the Arabs wanted to hand over the burden of defending the Palestinian rights to the Palestinians themselves, and the PLO was under the leadership of Shuqeiri, who was seen as a talkative, useless braggart and did not appear to the Arabs to be the appropriate man in view of the new era. The Arabs, then, encouraged the military organizations, with the Fatah at their head (at that time other organizations were established, such as the Popular Front, from which several other organizations, such as the Democratic Front, split off) to unseat Shuqeiri and take his place. Those Arab regimes defeated in the war may have hoped that, along with their release from responsibility for the liberation of Palestine, an exciting Palestinian guerrilla war would arouse new pride among the humiliated Arab peoples and distance the risk of undermining the internal stability. And indeed, it may have been thanks to this move that the regimes that had been defeated in the war gained many years of stability – in contrast to all the assessments.

In January 1968 representatives of the combatant organizations met in Cairo, and that July they took over the PLO. On 1 February 1969 Arafat was selected chairman. Although Arafat had acquired an image for himself – to a considerable extent, justified – as the omnipotent leader of the Fatah and the PLO, over the years he waged harsh struggles for control of the institutions. The Fatah organization is generally built on a general congress, a sort of arms-bearers' parliament, with three hundred members. Since Arafat's control over this body is not guaranteed, he does not often convene it. The General Congress is responsible for the Central Committee, with its twenty-one members, and the Revolutionary Council, containing eighty members.

Arafat's struggles revolved mainly around the manning of the Revolutionary Council, which is the interim body between the "parliament" and the Central Committee. The dominance that characterized this body over all the years did not fit in with Arafat's trend toward balances, and he was constantly bringing political figures into it.

The PLO is built in a similar form: the National Palestine Council is the parliament in exile which was first convened in 1964 by Shuqeiri, in East Jerusalem's Ambassador Hotel. The number of its members varies from session to session, moving between four and five hundred members. This body is made up in accordance with a key of representation for the military organizations, the independents, the representatives of the institutions, and so on. One third of the seats are designated for representatives of the territories, who have to date been unable to participate in the deliberations because of the ban imposed by the Israeli Government. Since the Palestinians say there are one hundred and eighty members of the legislative council in the territories, the optimal number of members of the Palestine National Council has to be five hundred and forty members.

As in the Fatah, a central council of some eighty members acts as an interim link between the parliament and the Executive Committee, which is the executive institution. The PLO Executive Committee comprises eighteen members. It is a sort of government, but the PLO has avoided calling it a government because of the armed struggle ideology. As long as the Israeli occupation continues, so do both the armed struggle and also the revolutionary nature of the Palestinian national movement.

This is actually one of the signs of the undecided argument in the PLO: it is no coincidence that the Iyyadists wanted to transfer to the format of a "government" and "parliament," while the military wing adhered to the existing descriptions, "committee" and "council."

2

The Islamic Jihad: Abu Jihad's Fingerprints

Speedily, sooner than expected, Abu Jihad's visit to Libya began to leave its mark on the occupied territories. In six months – that is, six months before the Intifada broke out – the dangerous fundamentalist underground, the Islamic Jihad, intensified its activity in the Gaza Strip and, after the breathtaking operation of the break-out from the most closely guarded jail in the Gaza military government building, perpetrated a series of acts of terrorism. The movement had its early roots in Gaza, but its dramatic appearance was on the eve of the Intifada. The signal was given on the night of 17 May: six of the most daring of the Islamic Jihad commanders, headed by Imad Saftawi, sawed through the bars of their cell, leaped into the yard, evaded the guards, and by the time the jail authorities had noticed their absence it was already too late. Israel began searching for the escapees in the direction of the Egyptian border and the naval escape routes, but the six decided to hide out in Gaza and, under the very nose of the Israeli rule, stepped up their attacks on Israeli targets. One of them was rapidly taken, but the Israeli interrogators did not manage to get any information out of him on his comrades' hiding place. These latter did not waste their time in hiding from the Israelis and throughout the period – up to the outbreak of the Intifada – they attacked Israeli targets in Gaza. By the inevitable flare-up in December the underground members' courage had dispelled much of the Gaza residents' fear of the rule.

The links Abu Jihad had established with Qaddhafi at the beginning of that year were indeed an accelerating factor (not a reason!) in the outbreak of the Intifada, but the PLO's military wing's extensive connections with Iran, which also involved the developments in southern Lebanon in the Lebanon war, were of no less major importance. It may be that from our current perspective more can also be learned of the circumstances surrounding the establishment of the Hizballah, on Iran's initiative, in 1983, from the Palestinian aspect: the PLO's military wing, defeated in the direct confrontation with the IDF, established a link with Iran and the Shi'ites under its influence in Southern Lebanon, in order to embark on a terrorist counter-offensive that to a considerable extent succeeded in attaining one of its major goals: that of dispelling the fear of Israel of the Palestinians in the occupied territories. It is no coincidence that some five years later Dr Fathi Shqaqi, the founder of the Gaza wing of the Islamic Jihad, settled in Lebanon with the Hizballah after having been expelled from Gaza. Shqaqi, who was born in Rafah in 1951, had studied medicine in Zaqaziq in Egypt. He was deported from Gaza in 1990, after four years in jail. When the circumstances surrounding the establishment of the Hizballah, the Shi'ite sister movement of the Islamic Jihad, are examined from this angle, the reason for the liquidation of the PLO man Sa'd Sayel, one of Abu Jihad's people, the year the Hizballah became consolidated, may be better understood. The Islamic Jihad, then, opened up the first crack in the IDF's deterrent capability, and did so twice: once in the Lebanon war, in the guise of the Hizballah, in the concealed link between Iran and the Fatah military wing; the second time occurred the year the Intifada broke out, in the concealed link between Abu Jihad and Qaddhafi.

In February 1993 Reuven Paz, a researcher of the Palestinian Islamic movement, said: "The Intifada broke out in textbook Islamic Jihad manner."[1] Paz saw the connection between the events the movement initiated in Gaza and the outbreak of the Intifada. This is also what a researcher of the Islamic movements in the a-Najah University, Dr Iyyad al-Barghuti, thinks: "The military operations the Islamic Jihad movement adopted as an operational path attracted the interest of both the Palestinians and the Israelis to an equal extent, and were . . . in addition to other factors, the preface to the outbreak of the Palestinian Intifada in December 1987."[2]

It is important to recognize the profound ideological link between the military wing of the Fatah and fighting Islam, but a distinction must be drawn between the movement's different origins. The Fatah's origins developed separately from those of Gaza, which is rooted in the radical Islamic groups of Egypt. It is no coincidence that the original group in which Dr Fathi Shqaqi was active in Egypt was also called the Islamic Jihad. Even before Shqaqi's return to

Gaza, there was a group bearing the same name in operation there, but he was considered the original founder and organizer of the group, which was active in Gaza on the eve of the Intifada. It was not founded by Abu Jihad and his people. Abu Jihad's Islamic Jihad was established in Amman by Hebronites and began its activity in Hebron, but there was a hidden string connecting them. Abu Jihad's success in allying himself with the group's Gaza branch from where he had settled with Qaddhafi was ultimately one of the most important reasons for the outbreak of the Intifada. The signs point to this having been Abu Jihad's intention right from the start, but he himself was taken by surprise when it actually did erupt.

The Intifada has a Birthday – But When? Version 'B'

The Intifada has several "birthdays." Its commencement is usually marked on 9 December 1987, four days after the most famous road accident in the history of the Palestinians, which occurred at the Ashkelon junction. The Islamic Jihad movement does indeed mark another date: 6 October of that year.

In August 1989 the Islamic Jihad movement published a leaflet giving its version of the circumstances surrounding the Intifada's outbreak, completely different from the chain of events the PLO, or even the Hamas, try to describe:

> On the evening of that same day the Islamic Jihad movement presented the Arab people with the war's martyrs, the heroes: Muhammad al-Jamal, Sami Sheikh Khalil, Ahmad Hillis and Fayez Qreiq'; several days earlier Musbah a-Suri gave up his life for the glory of God. [The reference is to an intensification in the Islamic Jihad movement's activity in the Gaza Strip, and the casualties, who fell in its aftermath]. Musbah was killed at an army roadblock. The martyrs of 6 October fell in an encounter with an army force in the Saja'ia neighborhood. In the days that followed, the movement circulated thousands of leaflets with pictures of the martyrs, and they covered the streets of the homeland. The leaflets called on the masses to confront the army forces in order to revenge the blood of the fallen. Those who issued this call were headed by the fighting Sheikh Abd al-Aziz Odeh who, from the pulpit of the Az a-Din a-Qassam Mosque, delivered the great sermon on "Death to glorify the sacred name," calling down shame on fear, false imaginings and hesitations, and for the martyrs' footsteps to be followed. He underlined the obligation to adopt the model of giving up one's life in war in a confrontation with the Zionist foe . . . and the movement published a booklet on the fallen . . . and signed it as the "Islamic Resistance in

Palestine." On 18 November a deportation order was signed against the fighting sheikh, Abd al-Aziz Odeh. The news of the deportation had hardly been learned before the masses proclaimed their refusal to obey it . . . a sheikh with his face masked mounted the pulpit of the Al-Qassam Mosque and delivered the historic Jihad Sermon. The mosque was filled with the masses, who had come from all over, and they wept because they could not see the sheikh's face. But the masked fighter's shouts from the pulpit were sufficient to spread the rage in all directions, and the masses went out into the streets in hysterical demonstrations, beating up anyone who stood in their way. They pounded the soldiers of the occupation, who fled before them. On 20 November 1978 the Islamic Jihad movement published a leaflet signed by the "Islamic Movement in the Occupied Homeland" calling on the masses to use force in opposition to the sheikh's deportation. The demonstrations continued, and the Islamic Jihad heroes carried out a military operation in the north of Tel Aviv [the reference apparently being to the stabbing of a Tel Aviv resident], and on 5 December one of the Islamic Jihad fighters succeeded in killing an Israeli settler in the heart of Gaza. Event followed event, and a Zionist settler driving a large truck ran over several Palestinians on the highway to Gaza from the north, killing four and injuring many of them. There is a prevalent rumor that the Israeli was the slain settler's brother and committed his evil deed as an act of revenge.

8 December was a milestone on the path of the Intifada, which was proliferating, watered each morning with the blood of the fallen. That same day . . . even before the news of the four casualties had been learned, the Islamic Jihad movement had prepared a leaflet for its further path and already taken it to the printers . . . and the printing was stopped, because the truck incident showed an escalation on the part of the enemy, and required a new and special approach, and the members of the Islamic Jihad were indeed the first to grasp its significance and for a long time they had already been prepared for action in the sphere of deeds; their senses were very keen when it came to understanding the significances and the symbols. They took the previous leaflet away from the printers and began to prepare a new text in accordance with the unusual developments. Consequently, the first leaflet on the Intifada's path was circulated on 9 December, although some say it was already on the 8th. In any event, the first Intifada leaflet was already in circulation by noon and it bore the signature of the Islamic Jihad movement. The leaflet called on the masses to revenge the blood of the four accident casualties and called for a strike, which was the first general strike with which the Intifada began.

Hadassa House, 1980: the Dress Rehearsal

There are many who disagree with this version of how the Intifada broke out, including the PLO, but one thing is clear: it was the Islamic Jihad, more than anything else, that broke the ground for it. Some six months before the organization's fighters were killed in the Saja'ia confrontation, the Gaza Strip was teeming with stepped-up, strenuous Islamic Jihad activity, and although no direct link can be indicated between it and Abu Jihad's visit to Tripoli at the beginning of the year, they were effectively tied together.

More than any other organization, the Islamic Jihad movement typifies Abu Jihad's true wishes and the secret of his power. Nor is the similarity between the names a coincidence, and it was not for nothing that Khalil al-Wazir selected the name Abu Jihad: "The father of the holy war." Abu Jihad may have maintained the link with militant Islam more than the entire founding generation of the Fatah, and he was the movement's genuine founder.

In the lecture he delivered at the Hebrew University in Jerusalem, Reuven Paz told of a conversation he had held with Dr Fathi Shqaqi, the head of the Islamic Jihad group in Gaza at that time, before he was deported. Shqaqi's description confirms what Dr Muhammad Hamza wrote in his book on Abu Jihad. Dr Shqaqi told Paz:

> They wanted to spark off a process that would shock the entire Arab world, tantamount to the first shot from a rifle, to shake the Arab regimes and accelerate the coming of the Islamic "Caliphate." We decided to act because of the passiveness of the Arab countries and the Muslim Brotherhood.

Shqaqi explained that he began feeling the need to work for Palestine after coming to the realization that in the Egyptian university, Zaqaziq, where he was studying – where the atmosphere was devoutly Islamic – Egyptian affairs were given preference over those of Palestine. He, as a Palestinian among Egyptians, felt alienated, and realized that to muster Islam for Palestine, Islam must be aroused in Palestine.

On 2 May 1980, Israel was shaken by a daring act of terrorism in the very heart of Hebron. A Fatah squad caught a band of settlers in crossfire opposite their stronghold in Hebron's Haddasa House, felling six of them and wounding sixteen. The tendency at that time was to regard this action as yet another act of "routine" terrorism by Abu Jihad, but, in retrospect, the Hadassa House action was the Islamic Jihad's debut.

Darwish Naser, the squad members' defense attorney, was later to write down the squad's story as he had it from four of its members.[3] Abu Jihad's name moves through the book like a leitmotiv in all the stages of planning and implementation. One of the men, Yaser Ziyadat from the village of Abu Na'im near Hebron, tells of his decision to join the Fatah on a religious impulse, because of his acquaintanceship with Abu Hasan, later to become one of the founders of the Islamic Jihad, and on his insistence that the action be carried out in Hebron, and against the settlers.[4]

Another member, Tayasir Sneineh, also from Hebron, made the move to Abu Jihad's Fatah from the Muslim Brotherhood. He had initially been hesitant, but was finally convinced, apparently after his recruiters let him know that they intended to develop the Fatah into a military religious organization in the future.[5]

Abu Jihad: the Romance with Jordan

Before Abu Jihad decided to tie his fate to Qaddhafi, he tried to establish a base in Amman. The basic conditions for the success of a PLO-Jordan link appeared promising. After President Sadat's historic visit to Jerusalem toward the end of 1977 and the opening of the peace process between Israel and Egypt, the Arab world got organized to thwart Egypt's unilateral political process. The spearhead was aimed at the occupied territories. The Arab world – headed by the PLO and Jordan – wanted to stop the Palestinians in the territories being carried away in the sweeping move in process between Egypt and Israel, lest they be severed from their links with Jordan and the PLO. This Arab effort took several forms, but the most important of them was the founding of the Joint Jordanian-PLO Committee in Amman, by virtue of the resolutions of the Arab summit that had convened in Baghdad toward the end of 1978. The Joint Committee received large amounts of money from Arab countries. It is estimated to have received a total of some half a billion dollars over its three years of activity. True, only part of the amount, possibly less than half, actually reached the territories, but this money enabled Jordan and the PLO to consolidate their political partnership in the territories. The PLO appointed Abu Jihad to head the Palestinian wing of the Joint Committee and, so as to reinforce and underline the link with Jordan, Abu Jihad moved his permanent place of residence to Amman.

The period when Abu Jihad was working out of Amman was

destined to be of great importance in the history of the territories since, because of the almost direct proximity to Nablus, Hebron and Gaza, Abu Jihad established a unique set of contacts with the internal political systems and familiarized himself with the military potential concealed in the territories. Abu Jihad did not keep orderly records and nobody in the PLO's upper echelons was able to trace the threads he spun in the West Bank and Gaza Strip. He kept everything filed in his head. Back then it was Abu Jihad, more than anybody else, who stood for the PLO to the Palestinians in the territories. Not only did he familiarize himself with the political system in the territories, he also learned how to recruit the Palestinians in the territories to the armed struggle. Underlying all this was the especially grave risk of his putting the terror potential in the territories at the disposal of international terrorism.

The fact that it was actually Abu Jihad, the "Palestinian chief of staff," who was appointed to coordinate the PLO's activity in Amman was of additional importance, in that the PLO's military wing gained an edge over the political wing, which was weak at that time in any event. In these conditions, in which the military wing controlled the stream of funds for the political activity in the territories, there was no chance of encouraging the political wing.

The War of the Two Committees

Abu Jihad's takeover of the occupied territories was not easy, and he never actually managed to completely secure his place. The hardest challenge facing him was the National Guidance Committee which had been established in the territories after the 1976 municipal elections, with its hard core of the mayors who had been elected in landslide victories in the polls, headed by Bassam a-Shak'a, the powerful mayor of Nablus. These mayors spoke in the name of the PLO, but were loyal to the other wings in the Palestinian organization; to be more precise, to the leftist radical organizations: the Popular Front and the Democratic front. Bassam a-Shak'a was even identified as a member of the pro-Syrian Ba'ath Party, and they had no wish to accept the rule of the Fatah organization in general and Abu Jihad's discipline in particular. The Palestinian Communist Party was also a partner in this committee, and it contained Fatah representation as well, for instance, Fahd Qawasma, the then-mayor of Hebron, but most of its members came from the leftist organizations, and it was also they who headed it.

Because the secret of their power was the populace, since they had been elected by the populace, the mayors declined to accept the superiority of the military wing, demanding that a Palestinian political struggle be conducted in the territories. They maintained that a military struggle would bring about the collapse of the power basis Palestinian nationalism had taken over in the municipalities and this struggle would be better operated in the open, from within the municipalities, not from the terror squads working undercover. Because these mayors were Habash and Hawatma's loyalists, the "political" approach won the paradoxical blessing of members of the Marxist PLO organizations, the "arms-bearers." In retrospect, we may say that the National Guidance Committee was the first active expression of the "Iyyadist" approach and it originated in purely pragmatic considerations, from right inside the leftist leadership in the territories.

From the very beginning Abu Jihad's approach was religious, but the fight against the competitive influence of the leftist organizations' National Guidance Committee made the connection of identification with religion even sharper and provided him with an incentive to strive toward seeking his allies against the left from among believers. Naturally, he selected people with affiliations to the Jihad values of Islam for his close aides in the "Western Sector" in Amman, and it was these people who organized the Hadassa House operation.

The Haddasa House operation was designed first and foremost to hurt Israel and get at the settlers. One of its objectives, however, at least from the aspect of its timing, was to put the National Guidance Committee in the shade. At that time Israel, willingly or because of the pressures exerted by the Qiryat Arba settlers, embarked on vigorous activity to settle Jews in the center of Hebron. The National Guidance Committee found it difficult to use methods of "public struggle" to cope with the challenge Israel had set it. That stormy night's salvo of shots at the settlers illustrated to the Hebronites that the political path followed by the Committee of leftist leaders was not the right way to combat the settlers.

In retrospect, that operation was indeed one of the factors in the the committee's weakening, and it gave Israel justification for deporting two of its mainstays, Hebron Mayor Fahd Qawasma and Halhul Mayor Muhammad Milhem. Although the National

Guidance Committee was basically leftist, Qawasma was at the extreme edge of the rightist wing of the PLO, and was at the center of the internal struggles between the Fatah and the leftist organizations within it. The National Guidance Committee rapidly exited the political stage.

Despite the importance Abu Jihad and his people in Amman attached to their fight on their Palestinian rivals, it should not be forgotten that their main target was Israel. In their use of violence to attack Israel they cut the ground from under the feet of the Palestinian left, which wanted to fight politically, not militarily. For quite a long time the fight on Israel focused on sporadic stabbings of yeshiva students.

Dung Gate, 1986: Premiere

Israel's security services maintained a state of constant alert, exposing squads while they were getting organized, but in 1986 Abu Jihad's Islamic Jihad could no longer be prevented from appearing in full force. On 15 October an Islamic Jihad squad ambushed IDF soldiers at the Dung Gate in Jerusalem, hurling grenades during a ceremonial march past they were holding and causing heavy losses to the soldiers and their guests: one killed and sixty-nine wounded.

The Hadassa House operation still bore the Fatah's name, but six years later Abu Hasan and his friends worked under the name Islamic Jihad; 1986 was marked by the consolidation of religious squads, and their strings led to the offices of Abu Jihad's Western Sector in Amman. Gradually the term Islamic Jihad began to find its way into Palestinian consciousness, particularly in the Gaza Strip.

"Hamdi"

In February 1988 three Palestinians met their deaths in Limassol, Cyprus, when starting up their car. It had been boobytrapped by an unknown hand. Two of them were known by their underground names: "Hamdi" and "Marwan," while the third was known by his real name, Abu Hasan Qasem. These were not rank-and-file terrorists who fell in some circumstances or other, but genuine founders of the Fatah's Islamic Jihad movement. "Hamdi" was their leader. His genuine name was Basem Sultan Tamimi from

Hebron. Hamdi had accompanied the establishment of the religious-terrorist infrastructure based in Amman, and was a member of the Palestinian committees from Jordan which were connected with the armed struggle, such as the "77 Committee," "Hebron Committee" and the "Western Sector." Since he came from Hebron, he devoted attention, such as the Hadassa House operation, to his town, but did not rest content with very impressive operations of this variety, but also initiated knife stabbings of Hebron settlers. If we want to trace the roots of the Islamic Jihad's "Knife Revolution" in the Intifada, this model, too, had already been tried out first in Hebron, under the inspiration of Abu Jihad's people.

Abu Hasan Qasem: the "Emir of the Jihad"

Abu Hasan Qasem, whose share in the establishment of the Islamic Jihad had not, indeed, been great, but who was more of a loss to the Gaza Islamic Jihad than others, also met his death together with Basem Sultan. As far as can be seen, Abu Hasan Qasem stood for another Islamic Jihad development – from a religious organization with its roots in the secular Fatah, to a genuinely religious organization.

Some two years after they were killed in their car, the Islamic Jihad organ, Al-Islam Wa Falastin, eulogized them thus:

> At the stage of the great spiritual soul-searching within our nation in the 1970s, the three martyrs were among the first heroes to cross over the space from . . . the left to . . . Islam, in their faith and in their commitment to the jihad . . . over more than two decades their struggle was part of the struggle of the Fatah, the founding organization of the Palestinian nationalist movement. Afterwards Abu Hasan and "Hamdi" played major roles in the establishment of the "Islamic Jihad Brigades in Palestine" as a framework unifying the normal military cadres . . . with their brethren in the Islamic Jihad movement in Palestine and the fighting Islamic movement. Together they confronted the criminal enemy in a series of campaigns, until they ignited the fire of heroism at the gates of heroic Saja'ia, which has set the homeland on fire from north to south, to this day . . . We who knew Abu Hasan all know that he was the most devoted and courageous of all his generation. We, those who knew him, know that he was a Muslim to the depths of his soul . . . Ever since completing his higher education he has known no profession but fighting. With all his senses and with the zeal given him by Allah, he tied his fate up with the fate of his fighting people, to death . . . he was a firm rock in days of distress and pain . . . Abu Hasan: Emir of the jihad.[6]

The Expulsion from Amman

Basically, Jordan was interested in cooperation with the PLO. Not just because the Arab world had committed it so to do in the 1978 Baghdad summit resolutions, placing considerable amounts of money at its disposal for this purpose, but also because this fitted in with its national strategy at that time and it was striving for a confederation with the territories. But the direction Abu Jihad wanted – that of mobilizing the fundamentalist potential for acts of terror – gave rise to emergent doubts in Amman. It was not just Israel's warnings that left their mark; Jordan's own interests demanded hyper-caution in using this dangerous potential.

Up to the end of 1986 Jordan exercised restraint, but for a different reason. Abu Jihad did not turn the religious military arm against Israel alone, but also against Syria. The Ba'ath regime in Damascus was dealing with a dangerous rebellion by the Muslim Brotherhood and one of the most important logistic bases was in the north of Jordan, operated by Jordanian intelligence and Abu Jihad. This activity gave rise to dangerous tension between Jordan and Syria, and when Jordan sensed that it was stretching the rope too far and saw that President Assad was succeeding in overcoming the Islamic underground, it initiated an appeasement with Syria. King Hussein appointed the pro-Syrian Zeid a-Rifa'i as prime minister and publicly admitted that he had helped the Islamic underground in Syria from his territory, and turned over a new leaf with Assad in their very turbulent mutual history. But Abu Jihad had to go. The dangerous development of the establishment of religious undergrounds, such as the failed underground in Syria, was also of concern to Israel; and after rioting broke out in 1986 in the Irbid University in northern Jordan, against a religious background, Jordan itself also had cause for concern.

At the beginning of 1987 Abu Jihad established ties with Qaddhafi; this was after it had become clear to him that he had lost his base in Jordan. In any event, it was also clear to him that after the reinforcement of his status with the establishment of the Islamic Jihad, an alliance with Qaddhafi suited him more than his alliance with King Hussein. The Jihadist wing, then, swung between Khomeini and Qaddhafi, and back then nobody could have guessed that it would actually be Baghdad that would suddenly appear as the stronghold of the genuine fight against both Israel and the United States.

3

Arafat Goes to Saddam

Fuller's Research

PLO Leader Yaser Arafat was waiting impatiently for the visit of Richard Murphy's delegation, not so much because of Murphy or the editor of *Foreign Policy*, as because of another member of the entourage, Graham Fuller, the former head of the CIA's Middle Eastern Affairs desk.

The Washington Administration was seriously concerned by the Intifada, not just because of the distress it was causing Israel, but especially from fear that the Palestinian rock might roll over the entire Middle East, undermining the pro-American Arab regimes; and this, as stated, was Abu Jihad's avowed intention. As was its custom, the Administration asked the US research institutes to study the problem and come up with suggestions. What the Administration wanted examined was how to put an end to the Intifada and reduce its damages as a factor undermining the stability of the Middle East. On more than one occasion the recommendations formulated by the research institutes had become official Administration policy. For instance, we know of the Brookings Institute's study in the 1970s recommending a Palestinian homeland and that its recommendations became the goal of President Carter's Administration policy.

Graham Fuller, who knew his way around the Middle East, was also asked to prepare a study on behalf of the RAND Institute and his research was one of the most encouraging to the PLO. This research, published in November 1989, was the only one to recommend getting the Palestinians to move out of the Intifada by supporting their demand for the establishment of a Palestinian state. Arafat realized that if Graham Fuller was being sent to Tunis, the Administration was curious to find out to what extent the ideas put forward in his research were acceptable to the PLO and might truly take the wind out of the sails of the uprising in the occupied territories. Arafat had grounds to believe that at the next stage of the dialogue the Americans would be ready to discuss the state idea and, before getting down to an official examination of the problem, they were discreetly trying to find out its significances. On the 25th of that month, the day the talks with Murphy's delegation opened, Arafat was still lavish with his praise for the US Administration and voiced willingness to help the US effort to convene the Israeli–Palestinian dialogue in Cairo. He said in Tunis that President Bush wanted to put an end to the conquest and that ultimately he intended to bring about the convening of a UN-sponsored international conference. The Israeli–Palestinian dialogue over which the Administration was then taking pains was supposed to be only a step toward the convening of the conference; this is how Arafat explained the meaning of his support for Bush and his efforts.

From High Spirits to Disappointment

Nevertheless, Arafat emerged depressed from the talks with the Murphy delegation. Not only did he halt the political effort, since the meetings in Tunis in March 1990 there had been a visible turn for the worse, and Arafat began to sabotage the US efforts, applying his energies to stirring up and intensifying the Intifada, in conflict with the main US effort.

In the end the Administration turned down Fuller's ideas, but this was not the reason for Arafat's fears of the political process: he looked on in amazement at how the US delegation was heaping honor on Abu Iyyad, concentrating its talks on him and honoring him in an interview in *Foreign Policy*, and inviting him to write an article for the prestigious journal. It was not only feelings of jealousy for his attractive deputy that were troubling Arafat. He feared that if the Americans were focusing on Abu Iyyad at the stage of clarifications over the establishment of a Palestinian state, they would seek a way to rid themselves of him. Since at that time Arafat's influence was uncontested in the Palestine National Council, the PLO Executive Committee and the other PLO institutions, fear of an assassin began to invade his mind.[1]

The truth is, Arafat had no need to go to such extremes to reach these conclusions, but could peruse the report the State Department submitted to Congress on 19 March, on the state of the dialogue with the PLO, in the very same days when Murphy's delegation was visiting Tunis. Abu Iyyad's article in *Foreign Policy* was already included in the State Department report and, altogether, the document's authors relied on what Abu Iyyad had to say and gave the interviews he granted the various media more weight than Arafat's remarks. Those who read the State Department report – and Arafat obviously did – could have formed the impression that even then it was Abu Iyyad, not Arafat, whom the Americans viewed as the man who articulated the PLO positions. The only quote from Arafat was the letter he sent to the Peace Congress in Israel, speaking in the spirit of what Abu Iyyad had said in *Foreign Policy*.

Incidentally, this State Department report is firm evidence of the genuine US trend on the Palestinian issue at that time, which was: finding a way to conclude the Intifada as part of the elimination of Palestinian terror. Almost the only criterion for examining the degree of success of the dialogue with the PLO was: to what extent it promoted the elimination of terror and end of the Intifada. This report should have aroused Arafat's satisfaction, because it found more achievements than failures in the dialogue. But this was not what interested Arafat. What did worry him was the discovery that Abu Iyyad had become the Americans' main source of authority in the PLO; and this did not please him at all.

"The Intifada – Jihad"

Arafat first voiced his dissatisfaction with the State Department report and Tunis talks a week later, on 7 April, in the deliberations of the Jerusalem Committee held in the Moroccan capital, Rabat. Arafat had forgotten what he had said in Tunis only the previous week. The optimism that had accompanied his remarks in Tunis was replaced by a gloomy vision of the dangers Jewish emigration posed, not just to the Palestinians, but to the entire Muslim world. In his speech in Rabat Arafat, for the first time, articulated the motifs he developed later, during the Gulf crisis; he said the Intifada was a jihad (holy war) and that the time had come to move from words to actions. Arafat deliberately played on the American's most sensitive nerve: he described the risks stemming from the immigration not just to the Palestinians, but to the entire Arab world, and called on all Muslims to go out on a jihad. In other words, Arafat moved over to a tone of speech befitting Abu Jihad, thus signalling to the Americans that he had thrown all his weight into the scales of fighting Jihadism, not compromising Iyyadism.

Abu Iyyad, then, met the Americans' expectations by moving toward them in their attempts to reduce the Intifada damages and the dangers it posed to their interests. In Rabat Arafat signalled to them that he was still the PLO leader and decision-maker. It was as though he was telling them that they were relying on Abu Iyyad in their attempts to moderate and stabilize the Middle East, but he, Arafat, would now toil to turn the Intifada into one big conflagration.

An "Accident" on the Way to Baghdad

Arafat's route to Saddam's trench was not obvious against the historical background of the relations between them. A severance had been created between Saddam and Arafat after Arafat took the side of the Ayatollah Khomeini in Tehran, the day of the return of the revolutionary Islamic leader, Iraq's sworn foe for many years. Even before this Iraq had opted to foster Abu Nidal at the expense of its relations with the Fatah, and also established a Palestinian organization, the Arab Liberation Front, which made inroads into Fatah's influence in Iraq and was able to recruit Palestinian youths from Iraq to its ranks, since they preferred to join the Palestinian–Iraqi organization. On 8 November 1990 *al-Majalla*, a Saudi Arabian weekly that appears in London, published an article by Hasan al-Alawi, an expert on Iraqi affairs, "The State of the Iraqi Organization and the Organization of the Palestinian State." The author noted that over the years Iraq had indeed followed a policy of deliberately weakening the Fatah organization, with Abu Nidal having murdered several figures in the moderate Fatah leadership. In the years when the Iraqi army was stationed in Jordan, from the Six Day War to the Black September events, Iraq made direct attempts to liquidate Arafat by staging an accident, al-Alawi does not give a specific date. This was when Arafat was staying in Jarash, near Amman. The Iraqis invited him to some function in Baghdad. When his car passed by the Abu Gharib military camp, a military truck came speeding toward it and smashed his car. Miraculously, Arafat was spared, but suffered serious arm injuries. He made a supreme effort to get to the event to which he had been invited, and everyone saw him with his hand bound up to his shoulder and his face distorted with pain. When asked what had happened, he replied: "Nothing serious. I was exposed to an Israeli attack when I was on 'feda'it' [giving up one's life in war] activity."

It is, of course, conceivable that this event really was a road accident, not an assassination attempt, but there is no arguing over the fact that Abu Nidal's pro-Iraqi organization carried out a series of assassinations among the political wing of the Fatah; accordingly, before the transfer to Saddam Hussein's side, Arafat ensured that Abu Nidal would be finally expelled from Baghdad. Abu Nidal's presence had been bothersome to Iraq even before this and in the course of the war on Iran, Iraq put restrictions on Abu Nidal's moves since it was in need of the Western powers' support. Nevertheless, the pact made between Arafat and Saddam Hussein in 1990 brought about an absurd situation in which Abu Nidal was, in principle, considered to be a member of the coalition against Saddam Hussein and the international terrorist himself was seen at the rally by the opposition to Saddam Hussein held in Beirut in February 1991.

Arafat in Baghdad: "To Be or Not to Be"

Saddam Hussein's wooing of Arafat presumably began prior to March 1990 and in those contacts Saddam Hussein must have tried to dissuade Arafat from helping Baker to promote the peace initiative of the "dialogue in Cairo." But it was only between that month and the dramatic end of that year that Arafat's frequent trips to Baghdad became evident. On those flights Arafat used the private aircraft he had been given by Saddam Hussein.

The milestone marking the "point of no return" apparently came between May and June of that year. In May Arafat met with Palestinian students in Baghdad at a mass rally attended by the heads of the rule in Iraq, headed by Prime Minister Taha Yassin Ramadan. Arafat did not leave much room for interpretation when he declared: "We are with Iraq . . . we have come here not for an exchange of compliments, but because of the bond of the struggle, for blood to embrace blood and hero, hero . . . to carry on the path from Fa'o (the site of the tough battle in southern Iraq for the Gulf coast, where Iraq repelled the Iranian Army) to Gaza, from Baghdad to Jerusalem . . . this is one battle and one fate."[2] In retrospect, in those remarks the Saudis and Kuwaitis could find proof that even then Arafat was in on the secret of Saddam Hussein's plans to invade Kuwait, since it was immediately after the invasion that Saddam issued his political program to link the Kuwaiti problem with that of Palestine, the linkage program, and this issue will be discussed later. So Arafat supported a linkage even then, long before Saddam talked of it officially. Arafat made his remarks not in hauteur, but from a feeling of distress and fear. "We are at the gravest stage," he said, "Our motto is: 'To be or not to be'."

One of the worrisome signs was the Fatah's Intifada headquarters' move to Baghdad. I happened to get hold of minutes, distributed by Jordanian elements, of the deliberations of one of the sessions, possibly from the days when Arafat met with the Palestinian students. According to testimony by one of the report's authors, some of the participants, all senior Fatah fighters, were appalled at Arafat's outspokenness, uncharacteristic at that period of time.

About then the possibility was taking shape of a large immigration of Jews from the Soviet Union to Israel and the Palestinians did not know what to do about the change that had taken place in the Soviets' position toward them. Arafat's decision was unambiguous: "I order you – shoot them! Today I am issuing my order to you to use violence against the emigrants and if anybody is negligent or dilatory – I will throw him into jail, and do not think I am just making a threat, I really mean it. From now on I will settle accounts with you and arrest anyone who does not follow my orders" (the same minutes).

Facing Arafat, appalled, sat members of the Revolutionary Council, from both its wings: in the Jihadist wing were such people as Abbas Zaki, the head of the Intifada Committee, Muhammad Jihad, the commander of the Western Sector, and, from the Iyyadist wing, Abu al-Hol. Neither of these wings was especially fond of Arafat; each for reasons of its own. Arafat, then, found yet another interest in the strong backing he was getting from Saddam Hussein: he could now re-impose his rule on the Fatah's fighting wing, which he had lost in the barren political process. The combat cadres could have interpreted his order for the military mechanisms to move to Baghdad as a deliberate move to negate their maneuvering capability. To a considerable extent, Arafat was putting them under a sort of house arrest with Saddam. And indeed, according to several other reports at that time, Arafat was picking a fight with the fighting cadres of the Fatah organization. As long as Saddam Hussein's star was in the ascendant and Arafat was enjoying his reflected glory, the Fatah fighters ground their teeth in silence. Arafat's differences of opinion with them were renewed one day after the war ended with the joint defeat of Saddam Hussein and Arafat. As will be recalled, Shahin's famous letter was circulated in the territories when the fighting died down in the winter of 1991.

In the same discussion with the fighting cadres of the Fatah, Arafat had another pointed message for them, which became even sharper after the crisis: he charged the Arab countries with abandoning the Palestinians, directing his remarks mainly at the Gulf oil barons. He preached at them that while they had sent 17 billion dollars to the Islamic underground in Afghanistan which was fighting the Soviets, they had given the Palestinians only two billion dollars in aid. He openly gave them a similar sermon in an interview with the London daily *al-Hayat*.[3] He said the Arab aid to the Palestinians was less than the minimum. They needed 100 million dollars a month and the aid they were actually receiving was very far from the amount required.

The Palestinians' sense of an economic blockade was not, then, the outcome of their position in the Gulf War, but preceded it. As soon as after the outbreak of the crisis Arafat explained his taking up a stand at the side of Saddam Hussein by the fact that he was the only Arab power who had not abandoned the Palestinians. It was not just the Saudi Arabians' financial stinginess that angered Arafat, but also the aid it was granting the toughest political underground to rise up against the PLO at that time: the fundamentalist Hamas movement.

4

The Threatening Sword of Hamas

Arafat had yet another reason to pin his hopes on Murphy's talks in Tunis and in this, too, he was to be disappointed. The Intifada was not only a surprise cooked up for him by Abu Jihad, Libya and also Iran, in activating the Islamic Jihad; it also produced the first real challenge to the PLO's hegemony in the Palestinian people's representation. On the one hand, the Intifada did indeed put the Palestinian problem back at the top of the Middle East agenda but, on the other, it actually set the PLO a knotty challenge in the form of the fundamentalist Islamic Hamas movement. The Hamas movement (acronym for the Islamic Resistance movement: Harakat al-Muqawama al-Islamiya) was founded immediately after the outbreak of the Intifada (according to the Hamas, the very day the Intifada broke out).[1] At first they wanted to call the movement Hams, but decided to add the other 'a' in the middle to give the organization's name a meaning: zeal. Its members came from the Muslim Brotherhood cadres in the occupied territories. As opposed to the PLO, which tried to lead the Palestinians from the outside, the entire Hamas leadership was on the inside and could claim to be more representative of the Intifada struggle than the PLO. The Hamas used its potential to undermine the PLO's position among the Palestinians, arousing the PLO leaders' genuine concern. Arafat invested tremendous efforts in trying to harness the Hamas to his own wagon or, at least, achieve a cease-fire with it, but all his efforts were in vain. He concluded that there was someone preventing a conciliation with Hamas, and he believed this someone was the United States. He became convinced that the Hamas was being used as a tool to pressure him to agree to the US formula of a dialogue in Cairo or, worse still, for a gnawing-away at the PLO organization's power, to the point of its destruction.

Carter Confirms Arafat's Fears

In actual fact, Arafat had no need to conjecture about the Americans' intentions for the Hamas. In April 1990, former President Jimmy Carter came to the Middle East for a round of talks and met, among others, with President Assad in Damascus. Assad asked for clarifications on the US position on the Hamas and Muslim Brotherhood movements, since Syria itself was having severe problems with that movement, and Carter replied that the Americans viewed the Hamas as a movement balancing out the PLO. Moreover, he believed that if were there to be elections in the territories, the Muslim Brotherhood and Islamic movements would win half the Palestine Council seats. "The US Administration thinks that this alone could block the PLO's influence and create a certain equilibrium to guarantee stability in the political equation."[2] In time, with Islamic lists' victory in the elections in Algeria in January 1992, there were several US statements instructive of the complexity of the Administration's attitude toward the Islamic movements and the fact that the United States did not totally dismiss them all. On 13 January, State Department Spokeswoman Margaret Tutweiler reacted to the army's coup, which had been made in the desire to stop the power being transferred to the Islamic blocs, by voicing concern about "interfering with the electoral process." When asked about the US attitude toward the Islamic movements in general, she replied that in a conception, many ways are used, through different people. It is important not to enter into generalizations on such a complex matter. It covers a broad variety of religious, political and social ideas, and there is no appropriate international movement. Tutweiler noted that for many years the United States has had excellent and fruitful relations with several Islamic, or very conservative, governments and parties, and we hope to carry on like this. Tutweiler mentioned Pakistan, Bangladesh, Saudi Arabia and "other" elements as examples. Arafat might have considered the Hamas to be among the "others." Yehudit Kipper, a US researcher from the Brookings Institute, advised the Administration to recognize election results in the Arab world, even if the Islamic movements were to come to power, to stop them going underground and developing in a radical direction. Administration experts drew a distinction between radical and moderate Islamic movements.[3] That is, based on the division of the Palestinian movements between the supporters and opponents of the United States, the Americans also distinguished between "Jihadists" and "Iyyadists" in the Islamic movements' political systems.

After the twin towers in New York were blown up on 26 February 1993 by the United States' "friends" in the Islamic world, the Americans' improper relations with the extremist wing of the Muslim Brotherhood, which the United States had used in the Afghanistan war, were disclosed. When that war ended, those fighters were left out of a job and began to act in the United States itself. Arafat might have suspected that the Americans were using the Muslim Brotherhood's services not only against the Communist government in Afghanistan, but also against him.

The War of the Fundamentalists:
Iran versus Saudi Arabia

In order to understand why Arafat might have suspected the Americans, the general structure of the Middle East on the eve of the outbreak of the Gulf War must be reexamined. The Arab world had begun to crystallize into blocs, with Egypt and Iraq as members of the "Club of Four," competing for its leadership, and Saudi Arabia heading the council of oil-producing countries in the Gulf. Saudi Arabia's suspicions fell on the Club of Four, and Egypt's disappointment with the struggle Saddam Hussein had compelled it to enter produced cracks in the Club of Four (Iraq, Jordan, Egypt, Yemen), which widened to the point of its general disintegration with the outbreak of the crisis. The internal struggles in the Club of Four led to an accelerated rapprochement between Egypt and Saudi Arabia, and this had an effect on many political spheres in the Middle East, as well on the crystallization of the religious parties which participated in the Intifada.

When the Intifada broke out at the end of 1987, the Muslim world was split between two fundamentalist extremes: Khomeinist, Shi'ite Iran, and the puritanical-Sunnite (despite its wealth) Saudi Arabia. Iran was fostering and encouraging terrorist groups of the Hizballah variety, because official Khomeinist ideology believed in "exporting the revolution," that is, undermining existing regimes so as to establish an Islamic government over at least the entire Middle East. Iran radiated fathomless hatred of the Christian West and its culture, regarding the United States, the leader of the Christian world, as the "Great Satan." In Palestinian terms, Iran was "Jihadist" (from the name Abu Jihad) and Islamic Jihad groups were indeed included in the pro-Iranian Hizballah's sphere of influence. From this aspect, in the final analysis Saudi Arabia was "Iyyadist."

Saudi Arabia also fostered a generalized Islamic movement, the Muslim Brotherhood. The Muslim Brotherhood movement was founded in Egypt in 1928, as an Islamic reform movement striving to revive the basic principles of Islam while integrating itself with the modern world so as to successfully meet the challenges of Christian Westernism. The Muslim Brotherhood did not maintain a unified character, but also developed combatant streams, and in Egypt the "Gama'at" groups, which highlighted the militant message. While the conservative religious establishment which had remained loyal to the government was generally identified with the Muslim Brotherhood, there were profound differences of opinion in the opposition bands, the Gama'at, over the question of peace with Israel and the demand to carry on with the jihad (holy war).[4] This, then, is the thread connecting the Islamic Jihad's groups in Gaza with their brethren in Egypt. The Muslim Brotherhood was generally linked to Saudi Arabia and the Gama'at, to Egypt's enemies, especially Iran, and for a long time, to Libya as well. Even though the Muslim Brotherhood's principles were actively anti-Western, the large amounts of aid it received from Saudi Arabia greatly blunted its militant sting. Saudi Arabia was, after all, one of the principal friends of the "Great Satan," the United States, and could not permit its protégé to turn its energies against the Americans, in the style of the Hizballah or the guardians of the spark of the Iranian revolution in Tehran.

The disappointing results of the war with Iraq did not deter the Iranian fundamentalists from continuing to "export the revolution," and after failing in the frontal attack on the Iraqi fortifications in Basra, they turned their energies toward undermining the Arab regimes from the inside. This is the reason for the Hizballah movement's establishment in Lebanon by the guardians of the Khomeinist revolution in Tehran. Against the Hizballah, Saudi Arabia and Kuwait adopted the Muslim Brotherhood movement as a world Islamic movement, designed to stem the dangers inherent in the Khomeinist Hizballah.

The confrontation between Saudi Arabia and Iran took the form of recurrent clashes involving pilgrims to Mecca, with the Khomeinist Iranians instigating riots designed to undermine the stability of the Saudi Arabian regime. During the pilgrimages to

Mecca much blood was shed in clashes between the Iranian revolutionaries and the Saudi Arabian security forces. This confrontation
took various forms throughout the Middle East, as well as in Gaza,
and in that densely crowded strip of land, it transpires, there were
also manifestations of violence which took a high toll in blood.

Saudi Arabia Intervenes in Gaza

Halfway through the 1970s Saudi Arabia decided to deepen its
involvement in Gaza. In 1978 the Islamic University was established
in Gaza on a local initiative, but with Saudi Arabian encouragement,
as the crowning glory of the energetic consolidation of the religious
groups connected with the Muslim Brotherhood within the framework of the "Islamic Alignment" (al-Mujamma' al-Islami).

Sheikh Yassin, who had been working for the Mujamma's establishment since the beginning of the 1970s, sent envoys to Saudi
Arabia to obtain its support for its establishment, and in 1973 he
obtained the Israeli license. Sheikh Yassin saw great importance in
the establishment of an Islamic university as part of the activity
toward the establishment of the Mujamma'. At that time there was
already a religious college active in Gaza: the al-Azhar college,
headed by Sheikh Muhammad Awad. At first the Islamic University
worked from inside the al-Azhar College, only afterwards moving
to a separate building. The al-Azhar College was Sheikh Yassin's
principal opponent, and represented the old generation of preachers.
The al-Azhar College also developed, becoming a university in the
course of time, so there were two universities active in Gaza: one
headed by Sheikh Awad and representing pragmatic moods and the
other, directed by Sheikh's Yassin's people, representing the Hamas'
radical mooods.

The Gaza Strip always differed from the West Bank in its leaning
toward religious orthodoxy. The suffocating atmosphere, the physi-
cal overcrowding, the old links with extremist Egyptian religious
groups and the high ratio of embittered refugees in the general
population; all these brought the hard-pressed, frustrated Gazaite
closer than his brothers in the West Bank to acceptance of the
Muslim Brotherhood slogan: "Islam is the solution." In the main,
it was militant Islam which was the principal factor motivating the
events which afterwards led to the outbreak of the Intifada.

The Islamic mood drew the attention of Saudi Arabia and Iran to the potential inherent in this pressure cooker, and since the Gazaite Sheikhs were also seeking external support, this is how Gaza's internal politics became part of the general Middle Eastern struggle.

Saudi Arabia preceded Iran in its involvement in Gaza and the threads extending from the Mujamma' ultimately led to Saudi Arabia. Islam had enormous power of its own in Gaza, but at an early stage Saudi Arabia's involvement in establishing the Mujamma' directed the religious potential into the Muslim Brotherhood. It is difficult to know why Saudi Arabia decided to intervene in such a backwater of the Arab world, but in retrospect it turns out to have been the right decision since, as the Intifada proved, developments in Gaza had important implications for the entire Middle East.

Toward the end of 1991, the Islamic University of Gaza published a book by Dr Atef Adwan praising the Hamas leader, Sheikh Ahmad Yassin. With all the problematics this type of book involves, many conclusions can nevertheless be drawn from it on the Hamas movement's roots and its early days, as well as the connection with Saudi Arabia. As far back as the time of Abd al-Nasser, the Saudi Arabians had seen to setting up links with religious circles in the Strip as part of their struggle against Nasserite Arab nationalism.[5] When the question of registering the Mujamma' with the Israeli Civilian Administration came onto the agenda, it had opponents from among the old Islamic establishment in the Strip, headed by the highly influential Sheikh Muhammad Awad. Awad headed several major religious institutions, such as the Shari'a courts and major religious educational institutions. In 1982 he went to Saudi Arabia, where the Muslim Brotherhood put pressure on him, and when he returned – he gave the enterprise his blessing.[6] When, immediately after that, the establishment of the university came up on the agenda, Sheikh Yassin's people brought in Dr Khairi al-Agha, a Saudi Arabian citizen who later acted as liaison between the university and the al-Medina University in Hijaz.[7] The Islamic University in Gaza was apparently established along the lines of its sister universities in Saudi Arabia.[8]

Eventually Sheikh Awad continued to maintain the conservatives' power and did not bow his neck before Sheikh Yassin. His power base was the al-Azhar University, a competitor of the Islamic University, which accepts the discipline of the Hamas Organization. Because of the struggle between the two sheikhs, Sheikh Awad leaned more and more toward support for Yaser Arafat and the PLO.

An examination of the situation in Gaza on the eve of the Mujamma's establishment shows there was no certainty that the main Islamic force would eventually join the pro-Saudi Arabian camp. There were many different religious groups in the Gaza Strip, many of them connected to those very Islamic circles in Saudi Arabia which, in Saudi Arabian terms, were in opposition to the regime. It is difficult to know quite how the structure of political forces in Saudi Arabia was built, and it turns out that there were religious streams with noticeably opposition character lines in their activities which were actually connected to the establishment, or to wings within it. The Hamas movement played off these power centers and was able to be seen as a pro-Saudi Arabian movement and, at the same time, ally itself with pro-Iranian Islamic streams, whose visiting cards were undoubtedly opposition to the Riyadh regime.

Up to the Saudi Arabian involvement in the Gazan cauldron, the political structure of the religious forces was confused and lacking in any clear character. Saudi Arabia established two institutions with the ability to impose central rule, enabling the Muslim Brotherhood, under its auspices, to organize the mingling of political and religious forces which had formerly existed without such order: the Mujamma' and the Islamic University.

The Turban Wearers

In addition to the Muslim Brotherhood movement, such fundamentalist movements as a-Salafiun, that is, "Those who follow the path of the first," were also active in the Gaza Strip. It had its center in Khan Yunis, in the south of the strip, and was headed by Sheikh Salim Shurab. This movement had links with a Saudi Arabian opposition group with the same name and believed in those extreme puritanical principles which guided the first Muslim generation. The group had a few hundred disciples, but they stood out in public because of their simple white garments and special turban with its tail, like the prophet Mohammad's attire. A branch of the same group was also active in Cairo. The fact that in 1970 it split over an argument on the turban's form – with or without a tail – is indicative of the group's special spirit.

In any event, these arguments did not amuse the Saudi Arabians, since it had been members of this group, under Juheiman al-Uteiba, who in 1979 tried to take over the Ka'aba by force of arms, and this was the most serious attempt to overthrow the House of Sa'ud. It may be in the Ka'aba events that an explanation can be found for Saudi Arabia's decision to take an interest in what was happening in the Gaza strip. And indeed, the Salafiun movement was actually an offspring of the Wahhabi movement which founded the Saudi Arabian kingdom, but was, however, unable to tolerate what it claimed was the life of luxury in which the Saudi princes revelled, thanks to the legendary oil riches which had fallen into their laps.

Despite their extreme puritanism, the Salafiun did not turn their energies against Israel, because they believed the struggle to "Islamize" the Arabs was more urgent. Just as Juheiman al-Uteiba aimed his revolutionary ardor against the Arab regime, so the Salafiun movement in the Gaza Strip aimed its activities against Muslim "infidels." In its attempts to impose the Puritan life-style it believed in on the residents of the Gaza Strip, it intervened with force against phenomena which appeared to it as immoral, terrorizing cafes and cinemas. It took over cinemas in central Khan Junis and Rafah by force, converting them to Muslim activity clubs and religious libraries.

"Khomeini: The Only Solution"

While the Muslim Brotherhood and the Salafiun were absorbed in arguments and struggles which to some extent reflected the clashes within religious circles in Saudi Arabia, the Khomeinist movement was established in the Gaza Strip in 1981 as an echo of the Khomeini revolution in Iran, on the basis of the ideological and administrative infrastructure already in place in the Strip. Its leaders were Sheikh Abd al-Aziz Odeh, the source of spiritual inspiration, and Dr Fathi Shqaqi from Rafah, the organizational brain; even from inside the Israeli jail where he was incarcerated. Sheikh Odeh was a preacher in the Az a-Din al-Qassam mosque in Beit Lahiya. Al-Qassam was a Syrian cleric who had headed the holy war (Jihad) against the British and the Jews in the 1930s, and his death in battle in the hills of Samaria was a source of inspiration to the religious groups fighting in Palestine; according to the Islamic Jihad myth, the call for the Intifada had been issued from the mosque that is named for the militant Sheikh.

Dr Shqaqi's biographical background is most instructive. He studied in the Zaqaziq university in Egypt, where he joined the extremist
Muslim groups, the "Gama'at" (bands). The political system of the
Egyptian religious circles was also divided between the violent
opposition, which opposed the regime, and its supporters. Generally
speaking, the Muslim Brotherhood did not jeopardize the regime,
while the Gama'at waged an armed struggle against it. The Gama'at
had connections with Libya and, after the Khomeini revolution, also
with Iran, while the Brotherhood were linked to Saudi Arabia and
Kuwait.

It was from among these Gama'at that President Sadat's assassins
came; after the murder Dr Shqaqi fled from Egypt, since he had
genuine connections with the squad which killed Sadat. He went to
East Jerusalem and worked in the Augusta Victoria Hospital on the
Mount of Olives. Some time later he returned to the Gaza Strip and
resumed his activity among religious circles connected to Libya and
Iran, soon finding himself in jail. Although he was not the group's
spiritual authority, he wrote an ideological book whose title says it
all: *Khomeini – the Only Solution.*

While the eccentric Salafiun people stood out from the community
by their strange garb, the Khomeinists of Sheikh Odeh and Dr
Shqaqi wore normal dress, and this had a significance that went
beyond the external appearance. When the difference between these
two extremes in religious activity in Gaza are understood, it is
easier to grasp the differences which would emerge in the course
of time between Gaza's Hamas and Islamic Jihad, which paralleled
the Hebronite Islamic Jihad movement of Abu Jihad's people in
Amman.

In Shi'a, since it was historically a persecuted religion, permission
was given not to wear clothes identifying someone as belonging to
a specific religion or sect. This principle was called "Taqiya," that
is, caution. Gaza's Khomeinists, although they were not Shiites,
nevertheless adhered to this principle, since their need to hide
resulted from their having being been the first to decide to organize
themselves into an underground to go out to fight Israel. They
absorbed much of the Shi'ite spirit of sacrificing their lives for the
cause on the one hand and, on the other, Dr Shqaqi's connections
with Libya, Iran and the Gama'at in Egypt created a very dangerous potential for radical activity within the Gaza strip. This
potential became increasingly realized when Abu Jihad's people
in Amman were seeking religious youths to be called up into the

ranks of Fatah's military wing, and like naturally called to like. This encounter took no organizational form; the Gaza wing organized itself separately and did not join the Fatah. The importance of the encounter between Basem Sultan (see the previous chapter for details of his activities) and his colleagues in the Fatah's Western Sector, and Fathi Shqaqi and his Khomeinist comrades, lay in the ideological cross-breeding. Abu Jihad's wing deepened the Gaza group's Palestinian consciousness and the Gaza wing deepened the Islamic Fatah's link with Iran and Libya.

Another dangerous combination also emerged: Basem Sultan and his people were Hebronites and their Islamic Jihad activity focussed on Hebron. The alliance with the Islamic Jihad in Gaza took the organization out of its narrow regional boundaries, Hebron and Gaza, and it became a general Palestinian organization.

The Hamas

Nevertheless, what was disturbing Arafat more than anything else in March 1990 was not the Islamic Jihad, but the Hamas. The Islamic Jihad was a movement possessing a dangerous ideological extremism, but the larger movement, with a broader public infrastructure, was that which was connected with Saudi Arabia: the Muslim Brotherhood. The fact that the Muslim Brotherhood had connections with oil revenues did not make it any more moderate. The Muslim Brotherhood was also anti-Israeli to an extreme and it, too, was unable to reconcile itself to the existence of a Jewish state in Palestine. It was not the extremist and uncompromising ideology, however, that dictated its daily activities, since it had an entirely different scale of priorities. While the Islamic Jihad saw the war against Israel as coming before all else, the Muslim Brotherhood believed there were more important things, primarily, to bring back to the faith those Muslims who had gone the way of the Christians and become Westernized. They believed that only after the Muslims had made a complete return to Islam would the way to the jihad, the holy war, be opened and God would give the victory to the Muslims, like a ripe fruit. The Muslim Brotherhood put all their efforts into education and religious preaching, distancing themselves from any violent activity. For instance, it was more important for them to overthrow the regime of the "infidel" Assad in Syria than to bring the Jewish occupation of Palestine to an end. On the basis of this ideological concept, in the early 1980s the Muslim Brotherhood was even capable of using Israeli aid against Assad.[9] Strange anti-Syrian cooperation, therefore, emerged between Israel, the Muslim Brotherhood, Abu Jihad's Western Sector in Amman, and Jordan.[10]

There was an echo of this cooperation in the Gaza Strip, when Israel did not interfere with the Muslim Brotherhood's extension of its influence through the construction of an enormous number of mosques throughout the Strip. It is incorrect to say that Israel supported the Muslim Brotherhood at that time. It did, however, turn a blind eye to the massive construction of mosques. It should be recalled that the Hamas had not yet been established, and the sheikhs who wanted to focus their work on religious preaching and education were not seen as a serious enemy, like the PLO. From the early 1980s to the end of the decade the number of mosques more than doubled, reaching 150. The mosque was not only a site for prayers, but also a center of educational, social and inevitably also political activity; because of their sanctity, the mosques acquired something tantamount to extra-territorial immunity. The religious parties took over the mosques, most of which came under Muslim Brotherhood influence. The Az a-Din al-Qassam mosque was, it will be recalled, the stronghold of the Islamic Jihad.

However, it turned out that Arafat had a special reason to fear not only the US–Saudi Arabian–Kuwaiti–Hamas plot to unseat him, but also to be furious because, surprisingly, he had actually made a great effort in Gaza to help the pro-Saudi Arabian forces in their fight on Abu Jihad and his genuine allies: the radical forces that wanted to rely on Iran, Libya and Syria. Arafat could have claimed the Saudi Arabians had returned evil for good.

Shahin could have testified to the many years when Arafat helped the Saudi Arabians in the Gaza Strip, and this was said in his famous letter to the occupied territories:

> [Arafat] supported the people of the religious stream [the future Hamas] . . . against the Fatah, on the basis of the opinion of the one and only leader [used ironically against Arafat] that the Fatah organization is not his organization, but that of Abu Jihad, and accordingly he has no alternative but to rely on the Muslim Brotherhood, his natural allies since his studies in the [Cairo] university until they moved [to Kuwait], and hundreds of thousands of dinars were poured out on them on the inside [that is, the territories] and the Gaza University received them, on the basis of his decision, signed by him, while he was tight-fisted with the Fatah organization when it was in the construction stage, giving it only a few thousand dinars.

This shows short-sightedness and was unreasonable, since it was in the occupied territories that he gained most of his popularity, and the man who helped him in this was the brother, the martyr [fallen in war] and symbol, Abu Jihad, by the decision he handed down that no picture but that of the "one and only leader" was to be displayed.[11]

Indeed, an examination of the budget of the al-Azhar University in Gaza reveals that one year before the Intifada, in 1986, it received the sum of over half a million dinars from the joint Jordan-PLO committee in Amman. This was also the total aid the university had received since its foundation in 1978. It is no coincidence that, according to Shahin, it was Arafat himself who signed for this enormous allocation, because Abu Jihad headed the Palestinian side in the committee and Arafat's special signature was needed, since Abu Jihad wanted to ally himself not with the pro-Saudi Arabian Muslim Brotherhood, but with the pro-Iranian Islamic Jihad. The joint committee did indeed receive most of its budget from Saudi Arabia, which is obviously also where Arafat's checks came from. This leads to a clearer understanding of the connection between Arafat and the Muslim Brotherhood institution. The Saudi Arabians also sent the university, directly, a sum amount of 200,000 dinars as "donations" from Saudi Arabia, and the PLO gave a similar sum, despite its difficult financial position at that time. (According to Israeli sources in January 1987. The sources expressed amazement at the PLO's massive direct aid to the university. Shahin's letter seems to explain the amazement.) From this we can see why Arafat was so upset when he realized that the forces with whom he wished to ally himself were not only turning their backs on him, they were actually trying to jeopardize his position. The PLO's support for the Islamic University in Gaza was stopped.[12] This was not the only expression of the confrontation in which, against his will, Arafat found himself in opposition to the Hamas and the Saudi Arabians.

Religious and "Reds" Fight over the University in Gaza

The aid the Saudis gave the Gaza religious university, either directly or via Arafat, led to a dizzy rise in the number of students and academic and administrative staff and, as a result, the university became one of the major, if not the most important of Gaza's political power bases. While in 1978 there had been 123 students, by 1986 this number had risen to 4,315, with the academic and administrative staff leaping from 11 to 326.

For various reasons, the Gaza Municipality, potentially the major secular institution which could have competed for influence with the university, was in Israeli hands, so the forces opposed to the mounting religious influence had no chance of putting up a barrier against the spread of the Muslim Brotherhood's power. This being so, the internal power struggles in Gaza were concentrated on those inside the university itself. To the outside observer the main struggle appeared to be going on between the PLO and the Muslim Brotherhood, but in fact this was not the case. Fatah was neutral to a considerable extent and the lines were drawn between the Muslim Brotherhood and the Popular Front for the Liberation of Palestine; the main leftist nationalist group in Gaza in pre-Intifada days.

As stated, Arafat supported the university, so the Fatah was neutral between the genuine rivals, the Muslim Brotherhood and the Popular Front for the Liberation of Palestine. The Fatah Organization was not as powerfully involved as the Popular Front. The only Fatah supporters who sided with the Popular Front were Abu Jihad's people, but in the main the Fatah's basic neutrality was an additional expression of Arafat's quiet support for the Muslim Brotherhood.

The Muslim Brotherhood did not deny the fact that prior to the Intifada their main goal had been to attack people from the Popular Front. They explained this as being because the Popular Front was headed by a Christian, and Sheikh Yassin could not bear the thought of a non-Muslim carrying the flag which should have been borne by a Muslim.[13]

In November 1984 the underground struggle came out into the open: an assassin shot dead Dr Isma'il at-Khatib of the Muslim Brotherhood, Rector of the Faculty of the Arabic Language. The assassin was identified as an emissary of Abu Jihad. Nevertheless, it was not on the Fatah, but on the Popular Front that the religious people vented their fury over the murder, and for more than two years they mercilessly persecuted the "red" organization, rioting in the homes of Popular Front members and stabbing and killing their activists. The "reds" knew how to hit back, especially the leftist female students, who introduced acid bombs into the fighting. The Muslim Brotherhood's edge, however, became increasingly conspicuous, particularly in view of the Fatah's neutrality. The attacks mounted throughout 1986, and several Muslim Brotherhood leaders such as Dr Ibrahim al-Yazuri, chairman of the Mujamma' council and, on the other hand, Dr Rabah Muhanna, deputy chairman of the Physician's Union, were hit. Bearded men set about the latter and, in a murderous beating, broke his arms and legs.

Yet the Popular Front had no chance. The Gaza Strip had always been religious, and the difficulties of life under the occupation strengthened the religious orthodoxy. The establishment of the Mujamma' and afterwards the opening of the religious university, provided the Muslim Brotherhood with a very efficient tool to spread their creed. The students' union elections in 1986 reflected a discouraging ratio of forces: two-thirds for the Muslim Brotherhood and one third for the Popular Front.

The fight on Islam weakened the people of the nationalist left and, with the outbreak of the Intifada in the Gaza Strip, they did not have the power to lead the masses; it was eventually religious people who headed the uprising.

Sheikh Ahmad Yassin: From "Majd" to the "Hamas"

There is one man to whom the Muslim Brotherhood movement owes thanks for the fact that the Intifada did not drag the religious youth of Gaza into the arms of the Islamic Jihad, and this is Sheikh Ahmad Yassin. Yassin was an ailing man, modest in bearing and appearance, who received his guests in a simple room, lying on a mattress, and could only get about in a wheelchair. He was born in 1932 to a poor but respected refugee family from the village of al-Jawra near Ashkelon, whose residents became refugees after 1948.

Ahmad was three years old when his father died and his elder brother, Abu Nasim, took over the burden of providing for the family, though he was only eleven. The 1948 War turfed the family out of its small village; first they wandered to Majdal, then to Gaza. They settled in the a-Shati refugee camp and Ahmad had leanings toward Islam from an early age. The Muslim Brotherhood were extremely active in the camp and their activities included sports. When still in elementary school, Ahmad competed with friends over who could spend most time standing on his head. His will power proved to be stronger than his body's capacity to endure, and he destroyed the marrow of his backbone. His legs became paralyzed and he lost the power to move his fingers. Because of his indomitable will, he succeeded in graduating from high school and was then given a position as teacher of Arabic in an UNRWA school.

He embarked on his genuine political activity at the beginning of the 1970s, and although loyal to the general Muslim Brotherhood framework, from his earliest days he tried to be independent, setting up a special framework loyal directly to him, not necessarily to the center in Saudi Arabia. This found expression in his attempts to give separate names to the group of activists whom he collected around him. Before joining together under the name of the "Hamas," Sheikh Yassin and his men were identified by various names, such as "The Islamic Direction" (al-Ittijah al-Islami),[14] "Majd,"[15] etc. He explained that in the fighting between the secular Arab regimes and the Muslim Brotherhood, Arab propaganda had succeeded in blackening the Brotherhood's name,[16] but this was a poor excuse, because in Jordan the movement was flourishing under its official name and under Jordanian auspices. Before beginning to act against Israel, Sheikh Yassin had to get rid of the older generation of sheikhs who preached in the mosques, whether they were sheikhs from the Muslim Brotherhood, who had grave reservations about the Israeli regime, but did not consider the time right to act against it, or sheikhs from the Waqf administration who were subject to the authorities and had become accustomed to patterns of co-existence with them. The latter were highly suspicious of Sheikh Yassin's pretensions, especially because of the various names by which he wanted to call his followers. They prevented his obtaining a job as preacher in the mosques and constantly thwarted his progress and, in order to cope with the problem, Sheikh Yassin found a brilliant solution: he turned his energies into mobilizing young people. The pressure the newly religious youths exerted against those sheikhs who were opposed to Sheikh Yassin proved to be efficient. Sheikh Yassin also changed the mosque's goals. It was no longer solely a place of worship, but a political and organizational center. Sheikh Yassin saw the period as identical with the days of Islamic expansion in the first generation of Islam, and for the mosque he designated the role the Prophet Muhammad had also intended for it: an actions base for political and military expansion.

In principle, up to the Intifada Sheikh Yassin had not disagreed with the Muslim Brotherhood's basic order of priorities: first of all, a return to religion, and only then a holy war against the Jews. Yassin did, however, disagree with how this was to be done. While the older generation of sheikhs did not turn to violence, but thought people should be brought back to religion through persuasion and peaceful methods, Sheikh Yassin turned to internal violence. On the eve of the Intifada, Sheikh Yassin's fights focussed on taking control of mosques and turning every new mosque into a center of activity. The Islamic Mujamma' and bands of youths who had united around him were his "soldiers" in the comprehensive expansion. The target of his pressures was the older generation of sheikhs; but at the same time he put pressure on drug merchants and owners of clubs and cafes, whose lives became a living hell. Against this background, even before the Intifada broke out he put pressure on collaborators with Israel, which was when the series of cruel liquidations began which later characterized the Intifada. When the Intifada broke out, with the establishment of the Hamas on the agenda, Sheikh Yassin already had the military infrastructure which he had initially used for internal struggles, and which he could now turn against Israel.

Sheikh Yassin commenced his political activity in the Shati refugee camp, as preacher in the new mosque which was opened immediately after the Six Day War, the al-Abbas mosque. Right from the start his style of preaching, so different from the norm, stood out. While the religious sermons were generally restricted to "folksy" explanations of purely religious problems, in his sermons Sheikh Yassin concentrated on clarifying everyday difficulties from the religious point of view. He was not the permanent preacher of the al-Abbas Mosque, but one of several, and when his name became widely known and connected with the mosque, the sheikhs began to work together against him and he was compelled to move to another mosque. The religious establishment already in existence there also looked askance at him and his method of joining with the youths in study circles, "Halaqat," a study method customary in the classic days of Islam. His discussions with the young people rapidly went beyond the elucidation of everyday problems in accordance with the way of Islam, expanding to discussions on the need to organize into a movement.[17]

On the Mattress in Jawrat a-Shams

There was an important milestone in the consolidation around Sheikh Yassin toward the establishment of the Hamas in 1973,

when his many disciples built a modest house for him in the Jawrat
a-Shams neighborhood in Gaza, on a plot of land donated to him.
It was from the mattress laid on the floor that this political genius
came up with and organized one of the most important Muslim
movements in the Middle East. It was from there that the ailing
sheikh ran the tough battles over control of the university and the
Islamic Mujamma' and on this mattress that the decisions to join
the Intifada and establish the Hamas were made.

Even though the Muslim Brotherhood did not lean toward the
pattern of violent activity, they did emit wave after wave of groups
of zealots, who tugged their activities toward violence. In 1980 the
Israeli security services exposed a wave of underground military
consolidation when it was still in the embryonic stage, which also
included Muslim Brotherhood activists in the central Israeli "Triangle" and the West Bank.[18] Sheikh Yassin's style of action presaged
the appearance of a new wave of violence and indeed, even before
the Intifada he had not followed in the footsteps of the Muslim
Brotherhood's theoretical mentors. What he envisioned was not the
models of the educational activities customary in his time in the
Strip, but that of the war waged on the communists by the Muslim
Brotherhood in Afghanistan.[19] Sheikh Yassin was arrested for the
first time in 1983, on charges of military organizational activities.
This activity was, it was true, aimed at the war on Israel, but also,
because of the Muslim Brotherhood's basic unwillingness to come
out on a Jihad at such an early stage, an appreciable part of the military energy was aimed against Arab collaborators, or drug dealers,
owners of clubs, etc. At that time these people were perceived as no
less dangerous than Israel and, as "corrupters of the youth," were
considered to be collaborators by definition, whether or not they
actually collaborated with Israel. The "collaborators" gained the
attention of Sheikh Yassin and his people, who attributed to them
the failure of the first military organizing in 1983. They thought
it was a Gaza arms merchant and collaborator who had ratted on
them to the security authorities after they had purchased weapons
from him.[20] One of the signs of the impending Intifada was, then,
an increase in the assassinations and attacks on collaborators, until
it became almost completely permissible to shed their blood.[21]

The Muslim Brotherhood's military activity at that time was
aimed first and foremost inward: the use of internal terror against
opponents, or residents considered to be corrupting the morals of
the youth; at the same time, Sheikh Yassin's attention was also

gradually diverted to action against Israel because from the very beginning his mood was very close to the concepts of the Islamic Jihad, despite his affiliation to the Muslim Brotherhood, but also because he drew operative conclusions from Israel's failure in Lebanon. It was not only the way the Shi'ite terror had hit the IDF that impressed Yassin, but also his evaluation that after the PLO's exit from Beirut and the blows it had taken from the Syrians in Tripoli, a vacuum remained which left room for the Islamic forces. Sheikh Yassin might also have been well aware of the internal struggles within Fatah, and believed that after the Lebanon war the status of the Iyyadists would be reinforced in relation to the Jihadists, and this would be the time for the Islamic forces to take up the flag of armed struggle which the Fatah had let fall. This is what Sheikh Yassin tried to explain to the Muslim Brotherhood people in Jordan, through an emissary he sent to one of their leaders, Parliament Member Yusef al-Azem, in April 1983. The Jordanian MP was impressed and sent Sheikh Yassin money to buy arms.[22] There is an interesting description of how the connection with the Muslim Brotherhood in Jordan was created. The envoy, Abd a-Rahman Hamraz, whispered a code word known only to the Muslim Brotherhood in al-Azem's ear; and the connection was made. On 7 January 1992, a source in the pro-Jordanian Muslim Brotherhood movement in the West Bank told me Sheikh Yassin had also received funding from the Egyptian Gama'at in Aswan.

Sheikh Yassin saw to setting up a link with the Muslim Brotherhood not only in Jordan, but also in the West Bank. According to Dr Adwan's testimony, it was Ismail al-Khaldi who made this link when he was touring the West Bank at the beginning of the 1980s. "The World Brotherhood Organization had not yet been created," Dr Adwan testified. Parallel with this, the Jordanian center also began taking an interest in what was happening in the territories, and when Amman heard that a Muslim Brotherhood man in Hebron had been elected to an institution, they sent a delegation to make his acquaintance.[23] In 1984, one year after the link was created between Yassin and al-Azam, Yassin was arrested and after a year in jail he was released in Ahmad Jibril's great prisoner and p-o-w exchange deal. When he returned to his home, the ailing sheikh picked up at the point he had left off on his arrest. Faithful to his custom of breaking out of the old patterns of Muslim Brotherhood activity, Sheikh Yassin also gave other names to the organizational activities of those years. The name of the organization that had

preceded the Hamas was "Majd" (glory), but it was composed of
an acronym which attempted to preserve some of the original
Muslim Brotherhood contents: "The Organization of Holy War
and Preaching" ('Munazamat al-jihad wa a-Da'wa). Even when
Sheikh Yassin tried to redirect the Muslim Brotherhood activity
toward a jihad (holy war), he had to include the matter of preaching
in the official name. Sheikh Yassin brought into the Majd two small
and violent organizations which had not found their place in the
Muslim Brotherhood framework, but nor did they want to join the
Islamic Jihad.[24] In time, the Majd organization would be seen as
the military wing of the Hamas. From this viewpoint, the Hamas
is viewed as the end of Sheikh Yassin's group's process of cutting
itself off from the old ways of the former generation of Muslim
Brotherhood preachers; the Hamas' foundation was also considered
to be the beginning of its acceptance of the ideological principles
of the Islamic Jihad, without joining the organization itself and
without linking up with Iran, keeping faith with Saudi Arabia,
and maintaining the spark of struggle in the PLO and the secular
nationalist groups.

The Foundation of the Hamas and the
Outbreak of the Intifada

Dr Atef Adwan notes that the Hamas organization was founded on
the very day the Intifada broke out; its establishment was accompanied by severe internal arguments.[25] According to the description
in his book, the Muslim Brotherhood people met at Sheikh Yassin's
home on 9 December 1978, the day when stormy demonstrations
broke out, and discussed the question of whether to officially join in
the mass overt violence against Israel. A different version was given,
in early November 1992, during an argument in Gaza between Fatah
members, and Hamas people. The Hamas people admitted that the
movement had not been established on the Intifada day.[26]

Unlike the competing organization, the Islamic Jihad, which not
only supported violence, but urged it with all its might, the Muslim
Brotherhood leaders had grave hesitations. The opponents claimed
that the forces behind the demonstrations were not Islamic (as
far as they were concerned, the Islamic Jihad was not considered
Islamic), and being dragged behind the events would take the
Brotherhood off the path it paved for itself and eventually harm

the movement. They also feared the new developments would bind them to entering into alliances with the street forces. If Israel did not succeed in overcoming the violent demonstrations, it might hand the Strip over to Jordan, and this development, the opponents claimed, conflicted with the interests of the Muslim Brotherhood.

Sheikh Yassin was enthusiastic about joining the Intifada. He failed to understand why alliances with other forces were to be feared; he thought returning to any Arab-Islamic rule was preferable to remaining under Jewish occupation. He detailed the corrupting cultural influences of the Jewish rule on the soul of Muslim youth; influences which would cease only if the Palestinians were to return to Arabic-Islamic rule. The sheikh's views were accepted, but they joined the struggle not in their old name, but under a new one – the Hamas – which was decided at that meeting. The Intifada and the Hamas were, therefore, born together, on the same day. On the 14th of that month the first Hamas leaflet was published,[27] and that was how the Palestinians learned that the Muslim Brotherhood was also participating in the struggle.

5

The Struggle for Control of the Intifada

The Islamic movements in the Gaza Strip were sufficiently powerful to inflame the masses and get them out into the streets, but the religious establishment lacked the organizational ability to control the outbreak of the masses and pilot them for its needs. The religious movements found it difficult to make the transfer from the stage of calling for the uprising to that of organizing and running it. They went on issuing inflammatory leaflets, but it was the secular forces that established the organizational framework that ran the Intifada, on the basis of the political frameworks they had set up in the territories in the years preceding the actual outbreak.

The Intifada had hardly erupted when the internal-Palestinian fight for its political control was in full swing and the internal logic of this battle cannot be understood unless it is examined in accordance with the fault lines already in existence between the approaches of Abu Jihad and Abu Iyyad. These lines were conspicuous within the Fatah organization, but spread over to all the organizations, including the religious movements. The struggles for control of the Intifada were tightly linked with the pan-Arab struggles over the nature of the Arab world in general, between groups from the anti-Western radical countries and the pro-Western, conservative countries.

The genuine division of forces was not between the secular and the religious, but between the forces who wanted to use the Intifada as a means to ignite a pan-Arab or pan-Islamic revolution, and those who wanted to restrict it to the territories, fence it in and use it as a lever for political arrangements. The insane race for control of the Intifada was important not just from the Palestinian viewpoint, but from a broad pan-Arab aspect, because the Intifada was also perceived as an internal danger to the Arab regimes – a little snowball that had begun to roll in the Gaza Strip. And where it would stop was anybody's guess. Abu Jihad's alliance with Qaddhafi meant the Intifada's mustering – and possibly even the very fact of its initiation – to shake the thrones of the Arab rulers. Abu Iyyad's alliance with the United States had the reverse meaning: as far as possible, holding the Intifada on the brink of violence and harnessing the energy contained within it, and taking advantage of the change that had occurred in the status quo, to steer the Palestinians onto the route of the political process. The Islamic Jihad was on the religious-Islamic side of the barricades, clearly siding with Abu Jihad, Qaddhafi and Iran. The Intifada, from their viewpoint, was perceived not only as an event that would bring about Palestine's liberation by force of arms, but as a pan-Arab and pan-Islamic event fitting in with Qaddhafi's revolutionary principles and the export of the Khomeinist revolution.

The Muslim Brotherhood encountered difficulties in the presentation of their genuine position. In principle, they were on the Iyyadist side of the map. They gained Saudi Arabia's support for the blocking of any radical, Abu Jihadist development. Up to the Intifada they had opposed the Islamic Jihad's tendency to put the fight against Israel at the top of their scale of priorities. But as soon as the Intifada broke out, they tried to stop the Islamic Jihad's takeover of the masses by joining in the radical line, that is, they tried to block the Islamic Jihad's spread from the radical potential itself, but they were unable to let their supporters know their genuine intentions. They held off the outbreak of Palestinian violence for as long as they could, but when they were forestalled by members of Dr Shqaqi's Khomeinist group and others, they had no choice but to give in to Sheikh Yassin's pressure, and established the Hamas. The Hamas Movement took a very active part in the Intifada, but where matters were connected with the strong pro-Saudi Arabian wing in Gaza, the Hamas did not ally itself with those forces in the Arab and Islamic world which aspired to bring about a pan-Arab revolution, to grow from within the Intifada. At a certain stage after the Gulf War Saudi Arabia was indeed happy to see Iran's effort to penetrate the Hamas, but it would take at least two years after the war before the Hamas could be defined as a pro-Iranian movement.

The "Intifada Constitution" for Pan-Arab Revolution

After the publication of Dr Ahmad Hamza's book on Abu Jihad there was no longer any doubt about which directions Abu Jihad wanted the Intifada to take. It must, of course, be taken into account that, in trying to glorify Abu Jihad's role in setting the face of the Intifada, Dr Hamza exaggerated in his description of the role he played in it, but there are no disagreements over how deeply the PLO's military commander, who was also the head of the "Supreme Committee for the Conquered Territories," was involved in anything to do with the organization of the uprisers' framework after the outbreak of the Intifada and the organization of the Palestinian political infrastructure in the territories even before that.

Even before the outbreak of the Intifada, Abu Jihad was busy organizing the Palestinian national entity and, inter alia, he took pains over the establishment of a widebranched network of "Youth Committees for Volunteer Labor," known in brief as the "Shabiba" (youth). For some considerable space of time this network was the basic infrastructure of Abu Jihad's supporters in the territories. So it is no surprise, then, that the first order Abu Jihad sent his personnel in the territories, as early as 20 December 1987, was to set up "Popular Committees" in every camp, town, neighborhood and village. These Popular Committees were supposed to take shape from within the Shabiba network, which was already widespread in the territories.[1]

On 27 March 1988 Abu Jihad texted the "Intifada Constitution" and crowned it with the title "We Will Continue with the Offensive."[2] The main order was to move over from the "War of Stones" to the "Fire War," the aim being to "take the enemy by surprise" and bring about a "constant escalation." Israel viewed with great gravity Abu Jihad's attempt to put the lessons of the IDF's expulsion from Lebanon into practice, that is, a gradual transition to live weapons and guerrilla warfare.

It was not just Israel, but also the pro-Western Arab countries who should have been concerned by Abu Jihad's "Intifada Constitution." And they did indeed conclude from the "Intifada Constitution" that Abu Jihad was aiming at a pan-Arab revolution.[3] By studying the Intifada leaflets we can keep track of Abu Jihad's order and trace which organizations kept faith with Abu Jihad's path and which organizations abandoned it.

Salah Khalaf: "Teacher and Fighter"

Against the background of all the above, the unbridgeable differences between Arafat's two deputies, Abu Jihad and Abu Iyyad, may be more clearly dwelt on. It is hard to find one point in common in their world views. Here and there some similar statements may indeed be found, but their comprehensive way of viewing the world was totally different.

Abu Jihad is totally steeped in the old Middle East. The violent revolution is an inseparable part of his personality. In contrast to him, Abu Iyyad regards the Middle East as part of the Western world and wants the Middle East integrated into the enlightened world. Furthermore, while Abu Jihad is a pan-Arab and pan-Islamic revolutionary in every fiber of his being, in Abu Iyyad there are glimmerings of heresies as far as the pan-Arab and pan-Islamic creeds and Arab nationalism in general are concerned. In "Lowering the Sword" he speaks clearly of the "non-military uprising" which is only a preface to the peace process. Not constant escalation, on the lines of Abu Jihad, but the reverse: a continuous thaw. Not the application of the lessons of Lebanon to the territories, on the lines of Abu Jihad, but a move away from terror toward patterns of Middle East cooperation, including with Israel, after sobering up from the intoxication of the pan-Arab ideologies and accepting the legitimacy of a non-Arab presence in the Middle East.

Just as Abu Jihad's liquidation produced the book by his admirer, Dr Hamza, after Abu Iyyad's murder a similar book appeared, from the Iyyadist side of the barricade; Da'ud Ibrahim's book *Salah Khalaf, Teacher and Fighter: His Life, His Struggle, his Death in War*.[4] This is a biography of Khalaf, containing chapters dealing with his political thinking and world view, at least as his supporters in the Fatah understood them.

Strange as it is, the differences of opinion between the two PLO wings are founded on one common denominator: disappointment with the Arab regimes. The difference lies in the conflicting conclusions each wing draws from this. While Abu Jihad harnessed himself to the service of the Arab oppositions, to overthrow the "rotten" regimes, Abu Iyyad was wary of this conclusion and speaks of his disappointment with the revolutionary regimes with whom the Palestinians made "strategic alliances" of the sort Abu Jihad was striving for. And, possibly more important: while Abu Jihad wanted the aid of the revolutionary Arab movements which were opposed to the pro-Western Arab regimes in order to combat Israel and the United States, Abu Iyyad opted to ally himself with Israel in order to shatter revolutionary pan-Arabism and disperse the PLO's military organizations.

Abu Iyyad admits the Palestinians suffered enormous frustration with the Arab regimes. "We made alliances with Arab regimes and explained that these were strategic alliances, and now, after having paid the price, we found that these alliances were transitory, very temporary."[5] Abu Iyyad discloses that the disappointment inflicted on the Palestinians by the Arab regimes gave rise to internal arguments and there were some who claimed the Palestinians could draw their power from the sympathy of the Arab masses, not the regimes. What this means is that there were PLO members who believed the Palestinians had to help the internal oppositions against the regimes, and thus Abu Iyyad cast suspicions on Abu Jihad. And indeed, "It is true that we sometimes maintained secret links with the opposition movements and, simultaneously, links with the governments, but matters reached public opinion in a manner that showed us up as following an opportunist policy."[6] Abu Iyyad reveals that the PLO decision to make the transition to political activity ultimately tied him up with the Arab regimes, not with the oppositions, and that decision had been unavoidable. This, of course, is in conflict with Abu Jihad's world view.

This argument inside the Fatah is the axis of the struggles for control of the Unified Intifada Command, and it is on the basis of this bone of contention that the directions of the developments and contents of the leaflets must be studied, as well as other matters that will become clear later.

The tendencies of Abu Jihad, toward supporting the Arab oppositions and Abu Iyyad, of supporting pro-Western regimes, restored the pattern of the struggles in Gaza over the Islamic Mujamma' (name given to the Gaza center of Hamas institutions) to what it had been previously: Abu Jihad supported the Islamic Jihad; Abu Iyyad supported the Hamas. This was not given direct, overt expression. Officially, the Jihad and the Hamas dismissed the Unified Command, but behind the scenes Saudi Arabia supported Abu Iyyad's efforts to take over the Unified Command; Iran and Libya supported Abu Jihad.

The significance of the revolutionary change brought about by the religious streams in the territories was understood not by the cumbersome Fatah, but by a small, alert organization which was attentive to the subtleties of the moods of the Palestinians on the "inside." This organization was the Democratic Front for the Liberation of Palestine or, to be more precise, the members of Yaser Abd a-Rabbo's wing.

The Democratic Front for the Liberation of Palestine – Pragmatism or Opportunism?

Just as the Fatah Organization was divided between the Iyyadist and Jihadist approach, almost all the other large organizations were divided in their views; this dispute was manifest in Nayef Hawatma's Democratic Front for the Liberation of Palestine.

Hawatma founded the Democratic Front for the Liberation of Palestine in February 1969, from within George Habash's Popular Front for the Liberation of Palestine. The two organizations are the offspring of the pan-Arab ferment that was aroused in the Arab world in the days of Egyptian President Jamal Abd al-Naser. Their mother organization was the Beiruti *al-Qawmiyun al-Arab* (the Arab Nationalists). Hawatma left Habash's auspices because of both personal quarrels and ideological arguments. Hawatma was more a dogmatic Marxist and less an Arab nationalist and right from the start he set up a link with Moscow and tried to persuade the Soviets to recognize him and his movement as the genuine Communists. Moscow did not accept him as a Communist because he was not prepared to lay down his rifle, continuing to favor the armed struggle. Hawatma was a pioneer in putting forward formulae for a relatively pragmatic solution to the Palestinian problem and broke the ground for Palestinian recognition of Israel.[7] With all the pragmatism he displayed against the tough positions of George Habash's Popular Front, Hawatma found it hard to cross the borders of the Jihadist world view.

The shock the PLO suffered in the Lebanon war accelerated pragmatic processes which Hawatma had embarked on in the Democratic Front, but lacked the spiritual forces to carry on.

In July 1991 the Democratic Front convened a general congress in Syria and one of the major issues discussed there was the clarification of the internal disputes that ultimately led to the resignation of Yaser Abd a-Rabbo, Hawatma's deputy. Afterwards Hawatma's loyalists collected the minutes of the deliberations and

published the documents relevant to the internal argument.[8] One of
the documents details all the contentious points between Hawatma
and his deputy on the political problems,[9] and it emerged that the
reason for the rift was to be found in the argument that sprang
up in the PLO after the departure from Beirut, the "Paradise
Lost" (of the Jihadists), as the document phrases it. The group
calls itself "pragmatist," but Hawatma's people prefer to call it
"opportunist." The lesson they learned from the departure from
Beirut was that from now on they would turn toward the United
States. In order to tighten the link with the Americans, the group
was even ready to concede the right of return. Later, in Tunis, I
met Mamduh Nofal, one of the leaders of the Abd a-Rabbo group,
and he maintained that Israel should compensate the Palestinian
refugees while the Arabs should compensate the Jews of the Arab
countries. Nofal did not, indeed, speak in terms of a return.[10] When
the PLO became fully aware that there was nothing for it but to
adopt Security Council Resolutions 242 and 338, this sparked off an
internal argument: whether to accept the US demand and adopt the
resolutions as they were, or as a package deal, along with all the UN
resolutions. Abd a-Rabbo's people wanted to sever the link, and the
internal document discloses the reason: to come closer to the United
States. The document does indeed present the positions of the Abd
a-Rabbo group from the viewpoint of the Hawatma group, but
the reality proved the justice of their claims: Abd a-Rabbo headed
a PLO delegation to a dialogue with the United States. On the issue
of the right to return, toward the fourth round of talks with Israel, in
February 1992, the delegation drew a distinction between the right
to return of the 1948 refugees and the right to return of the refugees
of the 1967 war, with the aim of resolving the 1948 problem through
compensations and resting content with the actualization of the
right to return of the Six Day War refugees. Abd a-Rabbo's people
played a major role in establishing that delegation and forming its
concepts.

The Starting Point: the Lebanon War

The Lebanon war is, then, the starting point in any attempt to
gain an understanding of the argument in the PLO. While the
pragmatists left Beirut with the lesson that the military struggle
chapter must be brought to an end and the political work got

down to seriously, the Jihadists (including, in this context, Sheikh Ahmad Yasin of the Hamas, despite the Hamas' basic attachment to the conservative camp) actually drew encouragement from the long guerrilla war that had compelled the IDF to pull out of Lebanon, viewing it as a precedent for similar activity in the occupied territories. From the perspective of some years back it may be possible to rule that the difference in the lessons both wings learned deepened the differences toward the outbreak of the Intifada: while the Iyyadists' main impressions were of the expulsion from Beirut, the Jihadists were impressed mainly by the partisan war the Hizballah waged on the IDF in its retreat from Lebanon. The Iyyadists' lesson was to come closer at any price – including giving up the right to return – to the United States, while the Jihadists' lesson was to move the Hizballah-type guerrilla war into the territories themselves. The Hizballah's terrorist combat against the IDF was, then, an introduction to the terrorist combat the Jihadist Palestinians waged on the IDF in the Intifada. Dr Hamzah specifically determines that: "Most of the Hizballah's leaders are graduates of Abu Jihad's school of thought . . . and they were the bridge for field coordination between Abu Jihad . . . and the Hizballah leadership."[11]

Dr Hamza also explains the Intifada's roots in the Lebanon war:

The Intifada's genuine path actually began in Abu Jihad's brain, when he had made up his mind to amend the basic situation up to then, which was reliance first and foremost on the "outside," not on the "inside," as the focal point of the Palestinian national activity, and made a firm decision to amend the situation in which the PLO relied on military activity at the expense of organized political activity. Accordingly, after the exit from Beirut in 1982 and the departure from Tripoli in 1983 [meaning the results of the war between the PLO and Syria and its Palestinan loyalists in the north of Lebanon] Abu Jihad finally decided to go back to activity in the occupied territories: to the conquered Palestinian lands. And in the course of five full, rich years of activity and grinding effort and profound, silent work, Abu Jihad succeeded in blazing the Intifada trail. He established the infrastructure, capable at the first stage of standing firm (Sumud) against the occupation so that at the second stage it would be able to confront the occupation and, at the third stage, carry on with and escalate the confrontation.[12]

Dr Hamza rightly comments that this strategy conflicts with "what the great ones agreed between themselves," that is, not just Israel, but also the superpowers and the pro-Western Arab countries. When Abu Jihad speaks of political work he does not mean the political process toward a peace involving compromise, nor just the recruitment of squads for military raids, but the establishment of a political wing to provide such activity with political backing.

The "Paradise Lost" of the Democratic Front

It is against the backdrop of the lessons Abu Jihad learned from the Lebanon war that the document of the Democratic Front for the Liberation of Palestine must be re-examined. The document articulated the argument not just in the Democratic Front, but in the entire PLO in the period following the departure from Beirut: whether to move to the pro-US camp and accept Washington's terms for a solution to the Palestinian problem, with all it implied, including a practical solution to the refugee problem that did not insist on the actualization of the right to return, or to continue with the old wars the PLO had waged from within the "Paradise Lost" as though they had not in the meantime been expelled from there and as though nothing had happened in the international arena, for example, the collapse of the Soviet Union.

For Moscow's sake Hawatma was prepared to weaken his links with the radical Arab nationalists, but no more. When relations between Washington and Moscow improved, this did not lead Hawatma to draw the conclusions reached by Yaser Abd a-Rabbo in the aftermath of the Lebanon war trauma. In July 1988 Abd a-Rabbo submitted a paper to the Democratic Front's politbureau, demanding that it move toward the US requirements and channel the Intifada in that direction, "to qualify the PLO to be an acceptable party in talks."[13] This is a clearly Iyyadist position. Hawatma's personnel put forward their Jihadist position: the Intifada must be escalated and armed to be a lever for the PLO's "return to Beirut", that is, the PLO, with all its power, brought back to the armed struggle. It is impossible not to identify the bone of contention between Abyu Jihad and Abu Iyyad in the internal arguments that split the Democratic Front.

There was no need for anyone well-informed in the details of these arguments to be surprised by the fact that the man Arafat appointed to head the Palestinian team in the dialogue with the United States was Yaser Abd a-Rabbo. Nor can the circumstances

of the establishment of the Unified Intifada Command be understood without dwelling on another aspect that distinguishes the
Democratic Front from the other organizations, which is the special
emphasis the Democratic Front had always put on the importance of
making progress in political activity inside the territories as opposed
to activity "outside."

From the National Guidance Committee to the Intifada's Unified Command

When comparing the resolutions of the Democratic Front's general
congresses with the resolutions made by other organizations, it is
difficult not to notice the Democratic Front's detailed attention to
what was happening in the occupied territories. The interest this
organization displayed in political life in the territories and the
senior status of its activists in the territories in comparison with
the status of activists from the other organizations is undoubtedly
conspicuous.

Prior to the Intifada the Fatah Organization, the largest of the
Palestinian organizations, was unable to give major weight to what
was happening inside the territories. Basically, its leaders were
disturbed by what was happening in the Arab world and the
burden of the political preoccupation was shouldered by members
of the political apparatus in Europe and Arafat's political advisers
who, like him, were nomads in almost all the world's capitals.
The dominant Jihadist wing was for the most part absorbed in
the "armed struggle," and although Abu Jihad's involvement in
political life in the territories was profound, particularly after the
exit from Beirut, his interest was nevertheless given over mainly
to the Arab world. His involvement in the territories was not from
the political, but the military aspect and he always gave preference
to the considerations of the "armed struggle." George Habash's
Popular Front was also deeply involved in what was happening
in the territories, but he, too, devoted his energies mainly to the
"armed struggle" and pan-Arab politics. The Democratic Front, in
contrast to this, especially Abd a-Rabbo's supporters, invested their
energies mainly in what was happening in the territories. What
was unique about the Democratic Front was not just the special
attention it devoted to day-to-day politics in the territories, but also
the fact that it preceded the Fatah in understanding the importance

of putting down political roots among the Palestinians under the occupation.

The Unified Intifada Command was not the first framework organization in the territories. It was preceded by the National Guidance Committee, with its nucleus of the mayors who had been elected in the 1976 elections, and was headed by Nablus Mayor Bassam Shak'a. This committee based itself on activists from the Palestinian left and although the committee head did not come from the Democratic Front, but was closer to Habash and Qaddhafi, nevertheless major personalities in it, and almost certainly those who had come up with the idea of establishing the committee, were members of the Democratic Front and the Communists, to the dissatisfaction of the Fatah organization, mainly because it had traditionally opposed the establishment of a major political center inside the territories. Bassam Shak'a, despite his basic loyalty to the Jihadist wing, also disappointed his patrons on the other side of the border, conducting a policy that was basically Iyyadist and very close to the Communists. Abu Jihad, in any event, was unhappy about the leader of the National Guidance Committee and there were many confrontations and disputes in the relations between them.

The National Guidance Committee was the first attempt to move the weight of the scales of Palestinian politics from outside to inside the territories, the steering wheel being held not by the Fatah organization, which mainly represented the Palestinians abroad, but by members of the leftist groups, especially the Democratic Front. This committee failed because neither the Fatah nor Israel wanted it. But the lessons from its failure were deeply etched in the memories of Yaser Abd a-Rabbo's supporters, since they were the first in the secular wing to grasp the significance of the change that had occurred in the religious circles in the basic concepts of political life in the territories. The National Guidance Committee disintegrated at the beginning of the 1980s over internal disputes, accompanied by the Fatah Organization's subversion, and was finally officially dispersed by Israel on the eve of the Lebanon war. The Democratic Front activists, however, particularly Abd a-Rabbo's people, did not give up their dream of reviving the major institution in the territories in the form of a National Guidance Committee in which they would have decisive influence.

For this reason it was actually the Democratic Front members who were more attentive to the moods in the territories and before

Arafat and his personnel had managed to digest the occurrences, Yaser Abd a-Rabbo's group was the first in the territories to try to direct the stream into its own framework.

The "Organizations versus the Personalities": the Secret of the Internal Struggle for the Intifada Leadership

At the beginning of 1993 Bassam a-Salhi, a leftist Intifada activist, published a book on the political leadership in the territories at the time of the Intifada.[14] The book's importance lies in the fact that the undercover Intifada leadership is, for the first time, described from the inside. A-Salhi himself is a member of the Communist "People's Party" and, as he testifies, wrote sections of the book during the years he spent in the jails for his participation in the Intifada. He naturally exaggerates in his description of the Palestinian Communists' share in those stormy events. A-Salhi differentiates between two types of leadership: the overt leadership, which he calls: the "Corps of Personalities ("Hay'at a-Shakhsiyat") and the covert leadership: representatives of the organizations within the PLO framework (the "Tanzimat"). The "Personalities," those familiar representatives such as Bethlehem Mayor Ilyas Freij, *al-Fajr* editor Hana Siniora and such well-known activists from the central stream as Attorney Ziyad Abu Zayyad, Radwan Abu Ayyash, Jamil a-Tarifi from al-Bira, Sa'id Kan'an from Nablus, Fayez Abu Rahma and As'ad a-Saftawi from Gaza, were generally unacceptable to the PLO since the organization feared they would develop along the lines of the 1970s National Guidance Committee. In October 1993 a-Saftawi was indeed murdered by the Fatah organization, in circumstances that will be discussed later.

After the disappearance of the National Guidance Committee, the PLO tried to stop these figures organizing themselves into a common framework. Their activity focused on the formulation of delegations of figures to meet with diplomats and statesmen abroad: no more. According to a-Salhi's testimony, the PLO saw to tying up each of the figures to a separate source of support abroad, which were known contemptuously in the territories as: "stalls" ("Dakakin"). That is, the PLO linked personality "X" in the territories to personality "Y" in the PLO, and other personalities in the territories to other personalities abroad; not to the PLO as the central institution. Another measure used by the PLO was to employ the figures from the territories in "information," that is, the PLO directed their public activity not into getting organized in political frameworks, such as parties or movements, but into press offices. Thus the "personalities" were kept busy not in political organization, but in a flow of praise and eulogies for the PLO, the source of their incomes.

A-Salhi reports that the major battle for the Intifada's leadership was between the "personalities" and the "organizations." The PLO weighted the scales on the organizations' side and took the "personalities" out of the decision-making circle. According to his report, with the exception of the famous activists from Yaser Abd a-Rabbo's group, the other Unified Command members were low-grade representatives of the different organizations and their role focused on coordinating positions and leaflets, not leadership guidance and decision making; the PLO wanted to keep these for itself. In days to come Mamduh Nofal, one of Abd a-Rabbo's group, was to confirm this description to me.[15]

From the Palestinian National Front to the Labadi and Zaqut Brothers

A-Salhi states as a fact that over all the years there was a continuous struggle between the "inside" and "outside" over the leadership of the occupied territories. This struggle, the circumstances surrounding the establishment of the Palestinian delegation, and the determination of its composition cannot be understood without some familiarization with the basic element in this struggle, the Palestine National Front, which was established in the territories at the beginning of the 1970's by representatives of the left, particularly Hawatima's people in Ramallah (from the nucleus of activists from among Abd a-Rabbo's supporters, who later left the organization), such as Ramallah Mayor Karim Khalaf. Their partners were Palestinian Communist party members and Habash's personnel. The very fact of the organizational activity was designed to cancel out the PLO's senior status in running Palestinian affairs in the territories, although this could not be openly admitted. It was from this front that the National Guidance Committee was afterwards established. The driving force was the Democratic Front members and after the split among them, Yaser Abd a-Rabbo's people took over the seniority in the territories. While the National Front was a secret organization, the National Guidance Committee was an overt one which based itself on people who had been elected in the elections to the municipalities and different organizations in the territories.

In retrospect, it was thanks to their alertness and alacrity that the Fatah organization was later also able to congratulate itself on the fact that the Intifada did not spill over into the frameworks of the religious movements. The activists who brought about this situation were a family from the Gaza Strip and the Jerusalem region, Jamal Zaqut and the brothers Muhammad and Majed Labadi; all three were deported at the beginning of the Intifada for the major role they played in publishing the first Intifada leaflet; they later participated in struggles over the texting of the other Intifada leaflets and spurred the secular organizations on to accelerate the establishment of the Unified Intifada Command.[16] The Labadi brothers were active in the trade unions, the Democratic Front's preferred sphere of action; and this is evident in the texting of the first leaflets, which carry a conspicuous call for workers' activity, almost to the point of placing the main burden of the struggle in their hands.

From "Palestinian Forces" to "Unified Command"

The first leaflet, written by Muhammad Labadi, does not yet bear the stamp of the Unified Command, but that of the "Palestinian Forces". The leaflet is indeed loyal to the PLO, but mentions the PLO only once, and not in the title. This leaflet does not yet speak of the establishment of the Command, but does contain a call to the other organizations to lose no time in organizing themselves into common frameworks in order to institutionalize the Intifada leadership in the hands of the secular forces and take the control out of the religious parties' hands. Ten days later, on 10 January 1988, the first leaflet of the Unified Command had already appeared.

Like the Palestinian Forces leaflet, which was not a PLO leaflet and gave the PLO only a passing mention, so the second leaflet in which, for the first time, the Unified Command is named, was also not on behalf of the PLO and gave the PLO only a mention. The leaflet's heading and signature bore only the name Unified Command. It was only from the third leaflet on that the PLO was mentioned as being behind the leaflets' appearance, with the

Unified Command subordinate to it, or tantamount to one of its arms. This phenomenon may be interpreted as a struggle between Labadi and his colleagues and the PLO–Tunis, that is, Abu Jihad, for control of the Unified Command. When Hawatma's people, in arguments with the Abd a-Rabbo group, claimed they were actually striving to topple the historical PLO from its status and establish a new PLO to be founded on activists in the territories, they were able to use the struggle underway over the headlines of the first Intifada leaflets to prove their claims.

When the PLO "outside" compelled the Unified Command to be its arm, the struggle with the "inside" was not yet over. The activists on the "inside," who bore the burden of the genuine fight, made attempts to better the status of this "arm." Leaflet No. 10, dated 11 March 1988, dismisses the importance of the role played by that "arm," defining it as nothing more than the "organizational arm"; for instance, the Intifada activists were simply organizational officials doing the work of the Intifada's architects abroad. The field activists, those who bore the Intifada's burden, were not at all pleased with the denigration of their value and in the leaflet that followed, No. 11, dated 19 March, they were already calling themselves: "The Struggle Arm and the Political Arm."

The Labadi brothers and Zaqut were not prominent, charismatic leaders like their predecessors, the members of the National Guidance Committee, the mayors of the large towns. They were trade union functionaries and preferred to remain in the shade and work in secret, both because, had their identities been discovered, they would not have succeeded in getting the the masses to follow them, and also because they had learned the lesson of their predecessors' failure. These latter had become known and pulled fire down on themselves from both Israel and the PLO. At one time Abu Jihad was personally involved in the fight for the National Guidance Committee to be disbanded. The Jewish underground which, in June 1980, planted bombs in the cars of the mayors who were committee members, resulting in their being gravely wounded, was actually doing Abu Jihad's work.

Abu Jihad speedily identified the fingerprints of the Palestinian left in the new Command and from the text of the first Unified Command leaflet he could see that if Abd a-Rabbo's people were to take over the Unified Command, the affair of the National Guidance Committee in the territories would recur and the Committee would try to stop him setting a violent Intifada in motion, one that would be guided by his own handiwork: the alliance between the military wing of the Fatah and the Islamic Jihad. Through this alliance he wanted to help Qaddhafi and the Iranian revolutionaries in Tehran further the fulfilment of their dream of an Arab-Islamic revolution sweeping over the entire Middle East.

It is against this background that Abu Jihad's lessons after the collapse of the armed struggle strategy, based in Beirut, must be understood. From the Democratic Front's attempt to establish the National Guidance Committee he learned the importance of political consolidation in the territories themselves, but this was in order to lay the infrastructure for military organizing. After the loss of the military base in Beirut, he considered the need to follow in the footsteps of the Democratic Front, consolidate his power and attain his goals from within the territories. When Abd a-Rabbo's people forestalled him with the establishment of the fledgeling Unified Command, he could not remain inactive, but worked to man the Command with those people he saw as preferable: representatives of the actual military organizations, not "politicians" or functionaries like the Labadi brothers and Zaqut.

This differentiation was to be of great importance when the Palestinian delegation to the peace talks was established. Although it was composed of quite different people, ideologically it carried on the original activity of Abd a-Rabbo's people in the original Command, not that of the representatives of the organizations who manned the Command later. The struggle over the image of the delegation began with a fight over the manning of the Unified Command which was actually over the nature of the basic PLO policy: armed struggle or peace process. On one side were the political echelons and public functionaries and, on the other, the fighting cadres who had difficulty in putting their weapons aside.

The fight between Abu Jihad and the Abd a-Rabbo group left its mark not just on the different definitions of the internal, "executive and organizational" or, accordingly, "political arm," but in an overt attempt by the "Corps of Personalities" to impress their stamp on the chain of developments in order to retain their grasp on the end of the reins before it was finally taken away from them and moved into the hands of the organizations. The "personalities'" rule of the Command meant the Intifada was piloted toward a political process; control by the "organizations" meant an escalation of the military struggle.

On 14 January 1988, about a month after the outbreak of the

Intifada, the "Corps of National Personalities" called a news conference in East Jerusalem at which they officially issued the "Iyyadist"
demands for halting the violence. They asked to meet with Defense
Minister Yitzhak Rabin, but were turned down. This was the "Fourteen Point Document" for negotiations with Israel. It took five years
of the Intifada for Israel to consent to discuss these points with the
Palestinian delegation, the successor to the "Corps of Personalities."
Later this document was to serve as the basis for the various papers
the Palestinian delegation submitted in the course of the peace talks,
mainly on matters of human rights and an exchange of confidence-
building gestures between the parties to the negotiations.

The main demands the "personalities" made of Israel were: to
release security prisoners, cease the deportations policy, bring back
deportees, stop the demolition of houses, honor the various Geneva
Conventions on human rights in the conquered territories, pull the
IDF forces out of the urban centers, stop the settlements, lift the
restrictions from political and economic activities and change the
taxation policy.

The National Personalities versus
the Unified Command

Abd a-Rabbo's group was small, but extremely influential. This is
because the great Fatah organization was under Abu Jihad's control
at the time. Abu Iyyad was neglecting the occupied territories,
so to some extent the difference in the territories between the
Iyyadists and Jihadists was unclear, since there were groups, such
as Abd a-Rabbo's people and political figures in the Fatah, with
Iyyadist traits, but they had no organizational framework such as
the one Abu Jihad had established for his loyalists. The group in
the territories was not organized and there were great differences
between its different components. Abd a-Rabbo's people differed
from the circles close to them in the Fatah and the Iyyadists in
the Fatah, such as Siniora and Husseini, were also involved in
personal power struggles between themselves. Although we put
them all in one group, it is doubtful that in those times they saw
themselves as all being tightly bound into one framework. But we
may say in general that on the eve of the Intifada the "Corps of
National Personalities" was intended to develop into the Iyyadist
source of authority in the territories. When the Intifada broke out,

the Jihadists, with the aid of the long arm of Abu Jihad from the outside, managed to expel the Iyyadists from the Command they had established in order to put their people in it.

The Palestinian delegation-to-be was created at that stage when the "Corps of National Personalities" headed by Husseini's wing succeeded for a short time – thanks to the Gulf War – in taking over the Unified Command. It was the struggle between the two approaches that characterized the texting of the various Intifada leaflets. The method of texting the leaflets was for the lead to be given to a different organization in each "cycle" of leaflets, which explains quite a few of the internal contradictions between the leaflets but also, to no less an extent, the internal struggle in the Fatah between the "national personalities" from among whom the Palestinian delegation was destined to emerge, and the representatives of the military organizations. One of the internal arguments sparked off by the texting of the leaflets was over the future status of the military cadres, Abu Jihad's people, whom Abu Iyyad wanted to eliminate.

Abu Jihad: "To Burn the Ground from Under the Feet of the Zionist Conquerers"

Abu Jihad immediately identified the fingerprints of Abd a-Rabbo's people on the "National Forces" leaflets, realizing that this band, which had already in the past gained experience in the technique of political consolidation in the actual territories, intended to steal the show which he, together with the Islamic Jihad, had worked so hard to stage. With the second leaflet began the fight over the texting of the Intifada's contents, particularly military, which would be won only after his liquidation. The second leaflet already carried the battle slogan texted by Abu Jihad, who imposed it on the leaflets' authors: "To Burn the Ground under the Feet of the Zionist Conquerers." A plague of incendiarism in Israel's forests, which was begun spontaneously by frustrated Palestinians imbued with the fighting spirit, received encouragement and guidance from Abu Jihad and his allies in the Islamic Jihad. The slogan's importance, however, lay elsewhere. Abu Jihad wanted to stop the Intifada developing in the political direction and this was the first step on the path to military escalation.

Even at the time of the National Guidance Committee an internal argument was in process: where did the border lie between the public, political struggle – "the struggle of the masses" – and the armed struggle. As far as actual weapons are concerned matters are clear, but it was not clear how the Molotov cocktail was to be regarded. Those who wanted to highlight the political nature of the Palestinian struggle in the territories rejected the Molotov cocktail, but those who wanted to retain the option of armed struggle for the future included the Molotov cocktail among the permissible weapons. It is difficult to point to a division between organizations in this argument. The Popular Front and those to its left favored the Molotov cocktail; in the other organizations there was an internal argument. The Communists rejected the Molotov cocktail, but among them, too, there was no unanimity. Abu Jihad's battle slogan was intended to determine, right from the beginning, the fact that the Intifada was retaining the military option. Abu Jihad saw to it that the fire and blood motif was included in the Intifada leaflets. "Burning stones" and "rivers of blood" were phrases that permeated the Intifada leaflets in order to, as far as possible, give it the nature of an armed struggle.

The major issue of interest to Abu Jihad at that stage of the Intifada was that of maintaining the status of the arms-bearers, members of the military wing, in all developments in the future. He accordingly opposed the various formulations, in the PLO and among the activists in the territories, on a demilitarization of the territories and international forces, not PLO fighters, to guard the Palestinians' safety. Retention of the military option and the "beating committees" development into an emergent army were intended to guarantee the status of the PLO's fighting cadres, that is, to guarantee the status of Abu Jihad's personnel. What can be learned from this is that the organizations attributed great importance to being members of the Unified Command and removing the status of the "personalities."

Beginning with the second leaflet, 10 January 1988, the task of defending Palestine was handed over to the Palestinians themselves; this was the first leaflet texted by Abu Jihad, which stated:

All the highways will be blocked to the armies of the occupation. The cowardly soldiers of the occupation will be stopped from entering the camps and major population centers by setting up Palestinian barricades and burning tires. Palestinian stones will land on the heads of the soldiers of the occupation and those who collaborate with them.

The demand for international auspices had to wait until after Abu Jihad's liquidation. Leaflet No. 20, from the end of July 1988, did not give the task of defending Palestine to the Intifada youth, but to the international community and, for the first time, one of the main motifs of Abu Iyyad's concepts found its way into the Unified Command leaflets:

> Accordingly, the Unified Command emphasizes the immediate goals: to guarantee our people international protection in the occupied lands, have international observers sent to supervise the implementation of the UN resolutions, hold municipal elections under international supervision, honor the Fourth Geneva Convention, the charter dealing with the protection of civilians under military rule in conquered territory, on the following issues: protection of civil rights in wartime, the army's withdrawal from the population centers, the release of the detainees, the closure of the Nazi detention centers, the deportees' return to their homeland, a stop to the deportation policy and honoring the principles of human rights.

In April 1992, at the peak of the political process, there were Iyyadists in the Unified Command. This can be gathered from the fact that the formulators of Leaflet No. 81 "forgot" to mark the fourth anniversary of Abu Jihad's liquidation.

These struggles later determined the form of the Palestinian delegation and were at the basis of its failure. Arafat was not neutral in these struggles. After March 1990 he was disturbed by the rise in the Iyyadists' power, and in the work of internal balancing he tipped the scales in favor of the military wing; without giving it overmuch reinforcement. It was as a result of this that on the outbreak of the Gulf crisis he found himself in Saddam Hussein's court.

It must be recalled that Abu Jihad was murdered before the political process began and it is hard to guess what his stand would have been had he lived after the Gulf war. His widow (upholding his will), Intisar al-Wazir (Um Jihad) supported Arafat in the peace process. And with all this, Abu Jihad's departure was one of the factors enabling the appearance of the Iyyadist delegation from the territories, headed by Faisal Husseini.

6

Faisal Husseini and the Palestinian Delegation

The Palestinian delegation to the peace talks was a direct outcome of the inter-Arab disputes, having been born on the dividing lines between Saudi Arabia and the Gulf states on the one hand and, on the other, Jordan and the PLO. From the Saudi Arabian point of view, the delegation was designed to undermine both Arafat's leadership and the Jordanian–Palestinian connection, which had turned out to be so dangerous to the Saudi Arabians during the Gulf crisis.

It is no coincidence that the delegation's establishment could only be actualized after the Kuwait crisis. It was established thanks to the efforts invested by Secretary of State James Baker. Saudi Arabia helped after becoming aware that the Americans had goals of their own and were striving to bring about good relations between it and Jordan. The US–Saudi Arabian intervention in the establishment of the delegation from the occupied territories was important, but it should be recalled that the Palestinian leadership in the territories had their own interest in maintaining their status against the old PLO.

Saudi Arabia and Kuwait had an interest in the political process and in the consolidation of political arrangements between Israel and the Palestinians, both out of gratitude to President Bush for having rushed to their aid, but also from practical considerations: a desire to make a contribution to the overall effort to calm the Middle East and dissipate the tensions there, so as to put things back on a "normal" basis and stabilize the situation. The Gulf crisis had unequivocally proved how dangerous a continuation of a state of instability would be to them, since it was an actions arena for such dangerous people as Saddam Hussein, Qaddhafi and various Palestinian groups. To the Saudi Arabians and their Gulf allies, stopping the Intifada and calming down the Palestinians' revolutionary ardor appeared to be essential conditions for Middle Eastern stability.

In the Arabian Peninsula, the Gulf crisis and the alignment of Arab forces it involved not only sharpened up the need for comprehensive calm in the Middle East and, of course, on the Palestinian matter, but also the need to get Arafat and Hussein, two of Saddam Hussein's most absolute allies, off the stage.

The "Husseini Group": The Jihadist Beginning

Abu Iyyad's connections with Saudi Arabia and the Gulf Emirates were, therefore, natural. First, because of his increasingly close links with the Americans; both overtly and covertly, they expressed his concepts: the need to eliminate the PLO's military wing and get the organization to move over to a "civilian" track, in order to incorporate it in the political process as part of the US circle of influence.

From the viewpoints of Saudi Arabia and the Gulf States, however, the connection with Abu Iyyad was important from another aspect: his traditionally anti-Jordanian positions, which went back to the days of Black September, in 1970. It will be recalled that he reiterated these positions in "Lowering the Sword," which is his basic position paper on his relations with the Americans. The reports on his contacts with the Likud over the realization of the "Jordan is Palestine" formula only improved his status in Riyadh.

Accordingly, Saudi Arabia's involvement in the Palestinian issue was not restricted to fostering the Hamas. It also began to undermine the PLO leadership identified with Arafat by means of the Iyyadist wing, which it tried to promote through the gaps the Intifada created between the PLO/Tunis and the PLO/territories. The Intifada brought about a fundamental change among the Palestinians. The Palestinians in the territories took the torch of liberation out of the PLO's hands, overshadowed the PLO's military wing and proved that wonders could be wrought through non-military means in the struggle on Israel.

This development was not to the PLO's liking and, as Intifada leaflets testify, the PLO made constant attempts to dwarf the role of the Intifada's heroes and compel the Unified Command in the territories to define itself as a "PLO arm," not as an "internal leadership." For a long time the Unified Command was not a permanent framework of actual personalities, but an expression of coordination among the various PLO factions. Little by little, however, a group constituting the nucleus of the future Palestinian delegation began to consolidate around Faisal Husseini. It was a sort of "mini-PLO," in that it represented the different PLO organizations: Faisal Husseini represented the Fatah; the women's activist Zahira Kamal represented the Abd a-Rabbo's wing of the Democratic front; Ghassan al-Khatib represented the Palestine Communist Party, which became known as the People's Party after the collapse of the USSR; and Riad al-Malki represented George Habash's Popular Front. The Hawatma wing was missing from the Husseini group forum and did not have a representative in the "mini-PLO." The main reason for this was apparently that the Hawatma wing was not prepared to sit down under the same roof with Abd a-Rabbo's people, who had far-reaching rights to steering the Intifada into the Unified Command frameworks in its earliest days. Even though Husseini headed this group, when the PLO/Tunis looked at the very fact of its organization and the conspicuous representation for the leftist organizations, especially the active participation of Abd a-Rabbo's people, it could not shake off the memory of the National Palestinian Front and National Guidance Committee of the 1970s, which posed a challenge to the PLO from within the territories.

Husseini's leadership gave the "mini-PLO" a special extra touch, for he was the son of Abd al-Qader al-Husseini, the leader of the Palestinian fighting force in the Jerusalem region, "The Holy Jihad," who fell at the Qastel in the 1948 war. At the same time, in 1989, when the initiative for the Cairo dialogue was developed, Faisal Husseini's group had not yet accumulated sufficient power to form the delegation from the territories. Furthermore, the PLO itself opted to send Abu Ayyash and Jamil Tarifi from Ramallah and their people to Cairo, not Husseini and his "mini-PLO" group. This was not because the Husseini group was not yet sufficiently powerful to be introduced as the Intifada's leadership or Unified Command, but because the PLO had begun to identify the core of an alternative leadership in it. This had no definite exterior signs until after the Gulf crisis; in conflict with Abu Iyyad's line, the year prior to the Gulf war Husseini organized a boycott of the United States, parallel with the tension that had arisen between Washington's friends and enemies, and in his public statements he refused to either condemn or express reservations over the murder of collaborators. He was thus expressing an outright Jihadist approach. Boycotting the US Consulate and the US envoys to the territories was an old Jihadist line, from as far back as the time of Camp David.

At the end of July 1986, Husseini, undoubtedly on direct orders from Abu Jihad,[1] initiated a general strike in East Jerusalem against George Bush, who was then the US Vice President, organizing congresses and texting wall slogans against those Palestinian personalities who, despite the Jihadist boycott organized by Husseini, went to meet Bush. These personalities were headed by Hanna Siniora, the editor of the *al Fajr* daily, who represented the most absolutely Iyyadist line in the territories at that time. This is noteworthy because he then held the title of member of the Palestinian delegation, as did Attorney Fayez Abu Rahma from Gaza who, although related to Abu Jihad, also voiced Iyyadist positions. They had both been appointed members of the Palestinian delegation in its first version (July 1985) by Arafat, as a sign of goodwill toward the United States.

Husseini was still carrying out Abu Jihad's orders two years later, when US Secretary of State George Shultz was trying to promote his political initiative, a variation of the traditional US line, whose main point was self-rule for the Palestinians, with a link to Jordan. A Unified Initifada Command leaflet dated 21 February 1988, called for a boycott on Shultz, and it was indeed in vain that the US Secretary of State did indeed wait for the Palestinian delegation in the American Colony Hotel to tell them of his political program. The humiliated Shultz read the TV crews the message he was to have delivered to the Palestinian envoys at a meeting which never took place.

The gravity of the activity by Husseini and his colleagues in the territories can be learned from the parallel effort Abu Jihad made on the "ouside." Abu Jihad timed his military activities to thwart the US political efforts, as Dr Hamza himself admits.[2] The coastal road operation, in which Israeli bus passengers were murdered in 1978, was designed to thwart the talks between Israel and Egypt; sending the terrorist ship "Atavarius" with an armed squad on board, which was to have broken into the Tel Aviv Defense Ministry after a massacre in the city streets of Tel Aviv coast, was aimed at foiling Murphy's mission to hold a meeting between Israel and a Jordanian–Palestinian delegation in 1985; and three years later, while Husseini and his friends were organizing the strike against Shultz, Abu Jihad was readying a terrorist squad to break into the atomic reactor at Dimona, not just to thwart Shultz and his concrete initiative, but to rock the internal stability in many Middle Eastern countries, since this had the potential to bring frenzied masses out on the streets. This would have produced not just a shock to the constant US effort to reinforce the existing stability; it could have led to internal deterioration in many states, which was the genuine goal of Qaddhafi and the Iranians, Abu Jihad's supporters at that time.

The Son Who did not Take After his Father

Tunis, accordingly, was apparently unimpressed by the Jihadist orthodoxy of Husseini and his people in their first days. First, the Iyyadist wing, and Arafat himself, who was closer to the Iyyadists than to the Jihadists at that time – as Abu Ali Shahin's letters testify – did not take kindly to this orthodoxy, because Abu Jihad's great power in the territories and the dangerous direction of his activities was disturbing the rest of many of his Fatah colleagues. As Dr Hamza testifies, Tunis, too, looked askance at Abu Jihad's independent activities, and there was a profound sensation of unease over his unchallenged hold on the territories. Husseini's obedience to Abu Jihad's orders also did not make much of an impression on Tunis, for the reverse reason: Tunis did not believe that Husseini's support for Abu Jihad was genuine. They interpreted this support as a necessary compulsion. At that time Abu Jihad's hold was too strong to be challenged by any organization. In retrospect, the strength of the organizational structure Abu Jihad established in the territories can be learned from the fact that it lasted for quite some time after his liquidation. This applies even more to the difficulty involved in realizing the Iyyadist potential in the territories in his lifetime. Abu Jihad ruled the roost in the territories, because he was the genuine commander of the Western Sector and headed the Intifada Committee. His many years of relatively good relations with Jordan gave him a base there, which he used for a profound involvement in all the Palestinian institutions in the territories. What is more, he himself had established many of them, and there was hardly a Palestinian institution in the territories not bound by links with Abu Jihad, whether or not he had founded it. Dr Hamza specifically mentions Husseini's institution, the Center for

Arab Studies, as one of Abu Jihad's institutions at that time, along with journalistic and other bodies, noting that these institutions' links to Abu Jihad were the reason Israel saw fit to close them down for long periods of time.[3] Abu Jihad encouraged institutes of research, journalism and information, because they glorified the PLO and did not act as a focus for the consolidation of an internal leadership. This is one of the reasons why Husseini's first institute was not genuinely political, but intended for academic and research documentation. Another, no less important reason, was that Israel would not have given its agreement to the activity of a political institution headed by him from East Jerusalem.

In contrast to him, Abu Iyyad, because of both the mutual hostility between him and Jordan and his objections to the development of the classic PLO apparatus, was unable to compete with Abu Jihad's profound influence on the political system in the territories. He did not even try to do so. An Iyyadist system could only develop in the territories after Abu Jihad's elimination, the gradual atrophying of his military attack apparatus and the dying down of the power of the military wing's pressure. Abu Iyyad did not have the logistic back-up Jordan had placed at Abu Jihad's disposal.

Faisal Husseini began his career as an outright Jihadist, even before the differences surfaced between Abu Jihad and Abu Iyyad. In the Six Day War he served in the artillery in the Palestine Liberation Army in Syria. Immediately after the war he hurried home to Jerusalem, and as soon as October 1967 he was arrested by the Israeli security forces in the course of a hunt for PLO leader Yaser Arafat, who was trying to bring about an armed Palestinian uprising against Israel from within the bases he was attempting to set up in the West Bank. At the time he was hiding out in caves in Samaria, the Nablus "Casba" and a house in Ramallah just across from the headquarters of the Israeli military government. Among others, he contacted Husseini. During the hunt for Arafat two machine guns which Arafat had given him personally[4] and a large quantity of ammunition was found in Husseini's house. In March 1968 he was brought before a military judge, who was lenient with him and sentenced him to one year in jail. He worked first as a tractorist, then as an X-ray technician. In 1977 he went to Beirut, returning two years later. After the Lebanon war he established the Institute for Arab Studies in East Jerusalem, which became the base of his political power during the Intifada.

Faisal Husseini did not, then, follow in his father's footsteps. To imagine what he would have had to do in order to be faithful to the tradition of his forefathers, it is worth looking at his younger brother, Ghazi Husseini. Not only did the younger Husseini become part of the Fatah military apparatus, he entered its Islamic wing, the Islamic Jihad, deep inside Abu Jihad's apparatus. From this aspect, Abu Jihad was the genuine successor of the Mufti of Jerusalem, Haj Amin al-Husseini, and the Islamic Jihad is the continuation of the Husseinis' "Holy Jihad" battalions in the 1948 war.

In his book Dr Hamza expands on the profound influence Haj Amin al-Husseini had on Abu Jihad's thinking. Abu Jihad was preoccupied by the model of the "all-Palestinian" government Haj Amin established in Gaza after the 1948 war; he endeavored to learn the reasons for the failure of this model and gave considerable thought to how to amend it.[5] Abu Jihad began his career as one of the Muslim Brotherhood's men in Gaza, with the memory of Abd al Qader al-Husseini's "Holy Jihad" battalions setting fire to his imagination.[6]

As it happened, two of his teachers in the "Palestine" secondary school in Gaza were volunteers from the Muslim Brotherhood movement in Egypt, who had come to the Palestinians' aid in the 1948 war: Muhammad Foda and Salah al-Bana.[7] Not only did these two teachers deepen the young Khalil's militant religious consciousness, they also actually brought him in on the secrets of the underground military industry. Ghazi Husseini carried on the family tradition under Abu Jihad's auspices. His brother Faisal, however, parted ways with the family, and instead of turning toward militant religious activity in the appropriate framework – the Islamic Jihad – he took a new path, that known by the name of Abu Iyyad.

The Professors

In general, the PLO had no interest in the development of any consolidated leadership in the territories, even if it were to be entirely loyal to the "outside" leadership. The extreme proximity to Israel and to the Western consuls in East Jerusalem, particularly the US consulate, developed a potential for isolationism. The Intifada, the brunt of which was born almost solely by the Palestinians in the territories, sharpened up these basic PLO fears; this was the real reason for the imposition of constant new boycotts on US diplomacy, using all sorts of pretexts. This is why the completely Jihadist nature of the activity by Husseini and his collagues when they were setting out did not made much of an impression in Tunis. What did concern the PLO more than anything else was the actual formulation of a "mini-PLO" in East Jerusalem, not so much its fears about the style and contents of its activity and the routine declarations of loyalty to Tunis.

It was the highly prestigious Palestinian lobby in the United States which was free of Jihadist pressure. Surprisingly, the Intifada in the territories generated an Intifada among them, but while the Intifada in the territories was overtly directed against Israel, the Palestinian leadership in the United States declared an Intifada on the old PLO. The PLO Tunis leadership feared the emergence of a link between the two Palestinian groups which had begun to awaken outside Tunis: in East Jerusalem and in Washington, between Husseini and his colleagues in the territories and the Palestinian lobby in the United States. The PLO was eventually to fail in this goal because the Palestinian delegation was in the main the connection between Husseini's "mini-PLO" and the Palestinian intellectuals in the diaspora, which had difficulty getting along with the classic PLO's slogans of the "Palestinian revolution" and reinforced the delegation from the territories with creative brains with a clearly Iyyadist approach.

When discussing the system of balances between the PLO/Tunis and the PLO/territories, it must be taken into account that there was no clear division between the two wings. There were important forces in the PLO/Tunis that supported Husseini and the internal Palestinian crystallization in the territories, and these came mainly from the Iyyadist wing of the Fatah, and powerful forces within the Husseini group which supported the "classic" PLO, such as, for example, Riad al-Malki of the Popular Front.

However, upsetting the balance in the ratio of forces between the PLO and the leadership in the territories gave rise to another important result: it was not only the balance between the classic PLO in Tunis and the PLO in the territories which was upset, so was that between Tunis and the Palestinian intellectuals in the diaspora. The renowned Palestinian professors who gathered in a pro-Palestinian lobby in the United States, such as Edward Said, Ibrahim Abu Lughd, and Hisham Sharabi, raised their hands in despair at seeing the old PLO, which was incapable of translating the Intifada into terms of political success. Moreover, it was a factor that was holding the Palestinian leadership in the territories back from taking a stand against the Israelis to actualize the achievements.

One of the hallmarks of the Palestinian delegation from the territories was to be its close ties with the Palestinian intellectuals in the diaspora. The Palestinian professors manned many of the think-tanks and advisory committees, even representing the Palestinians in the official committees of the multilateral track.

To understand the nature of this link, it is necessary to go back to January 1990. Professor Hisham Sharabi, one of the most important of the Palestinian activists in the United States, published an article in the pro-Saudi London daily *a-Sharq al-Awsat*, entitled: "A call for an 'Intifada' within the PLO, to create a genuine opposition and a united national front."[8] Professor Sharabi, a refugee from Jaffa, born in 1925, achieved great success in American academic life: he was a lecturer in history and political sciences at the University of Georgetown in Washington and afterwards head of the Faculty of Arab Studies in the same university.

The Iyyadist basis of his approach stems from the demand that the PLO improve its relations with the USA and make a fundamental change in its image, sharpening up the Intifada messages, that is, stepping up the role of the Palestinians in the territories. In his article he spoke specifically of the PLO's failure to realize the Intifada's achievements and the feelings of frustration and rage against the PLO which this failure aroused among the Palestinians in the diaspora. These angry passions gave rise to a need among the diaspora Palestinians to declare an Intifada within the PLO, so as to completely change the organization's organizational and political infrastructure through encouraging self-criticism. Sharabi hints at the need to establish a new PLO to replace the classic PLO, and he mentions names of alternative personalities for the Palestinian framework when the reforms he demands be carried out are complete: a Palestinian government-in-exile, or "united national front." In a clear hint of the difficulties between the PLO and the leadership of the Intifada in the territories, Sharabi writes the following:

> The Palestinians and their supporters among the American Arabs are not convinced that these reforms wiil indeed be carried out, and in their opinion the result depends, to a considerable extent, on their ability to coordinate their efforts among circles in the Palestinian diaspora which are levelling criticism at the PLO . . . and to exert sufficient pressure to compel the PLO to adopt the proposed reform

movement – but the decisive factor in this entire move depends to a great extent on the Intifada itself and the way in which, through it, the connection between it and the PLO leadership will finally be consolidated.

Sharabi's main message was the need to implement reforms to alter the PLO's image from 'A' to 'Z', to the point of its actual elimination and the establishment of a new Palestinian framework. One of the immediate reasons for this call was directly involved with the relations which developed between the PLO and the United States. Sharabi charged the PLO leadership with its inflexible policy having left the political arena to Israel and the Israeli lobby in Washington, thus leaving the United States as Israel's main supporter, despite the Intifada. It is not surprising, then, that it was Professor Sharabi who made this point, since he headed the US Arab lobby, something which also makes his criticism so important.

Unlike AIPAC, the pro-Israel lobby which remained loyal to any government that happened to be in Jerusalem, the pro-Palestinian lobby had no hesitations about coming out against the PLO leadership and intervening in the internal Palestinian struggles. From the style of Sharabi's remarks it is not hard to guess that, in the main, the approach of the Palestinian intellectuals in the diaspora was Iyyaddist. They feared for the future of relations between the Palestinians and the United States, and rejected Abu Jihad's approach of a constant, worsening confrontation with the Americans.

In his article Professor Sharabi did not deny that US policy was indeed pro-Israeli and hostile toward the Palestinians, but he opposed the concept prevalent among the Palestinians, that there was nothing that could alter the US positions on Israel:

> There is nothing permanent in politics, and these positions may be changed, and it is not inconceivable that one of these days the United States will alter its policies on Israel, but such a change will not occur automatically . . . a policy of flexibility, moderation, and maneuverability in the shadow of these conditions is a crucial need to prevent Israel reaping the fruits of Arab and Palestinian rejectionism. *It is, therefore, crucial to establish a significant link with the United States.* [emphasis added]

It is noteworthy that Professor Sharabi was speaking not for himself alone, but for the entire diaspora. And indeed, even though not all the Palestinian leaders in the United States supported these approaches, they undoubtedly enjoyed broad support, including that of the two most famous Palestinian personalities, Professors Edward Said and Ibrahim Abu Lughd. Immediately after the Gulf war, these two figures, along with scores of other Palestinian intellectuals, participated in laying the foundations for a new PLO, which would be connected with the Palestinian delegation.

Professor Said had actually preceded Sharabi in criticizing the PLO, although not in the harsh terms characterizing Sharabi's article. On 7 October 1989 he published an article in two important Arab papers, *a-Safir* and *al-Qabas*. He focused his criticism on the PLO's ignorance about anything involved in US policy, pouring scorn on how the PLO was conducting its dialogue with the Americans.

Professor Said frequently repeated this criticism, but in an interview with the East Jerusalem daily *al-Quds* on 28 October 1992, he added a special touch by ruling that the diaspora and the territories had a common denominator, in their opposition to the Tunis leadership:

> The Palestinian leadership in Tunis did not attach any importance to the US intentions and never tried to obtain the assistance of the Palestinian exile in the United States, and the result, accordingly, is near-disastrous, and everyone is angry, here and in Palestine.

These remarks do indeed focus on only one of the many aspects Sharabi had included in his criticism, but it is actually the main one: relations with the United States and all the implications stemming from them, such as the need to alter or eliminate the PLO, which is the crux of the great argument between the two wings of the PLO: the Jihadist and the Iyyadist.

Professor Said noted that his remarks had been made with the agreement of Professor Ibrahim Abu Lughd. In effect, it was these two who had launched the overt dialogue between the United States and the PLO when they met with US Secretary of State George Shultz in Washington on 27 March 1988. This was the first time an official US figure had met with members of the Palestinian National Council.

Professor Said is not just any Palestinian professor in the United States, but one of the most important, if not the most important of the PLO's ideologues. Many of his formulations turned up in official PLO resolutions, and the Palestinians made use of many of his arguments in their struggle against the Zionist ideology. He is a Christian, born in Jerusalem in 1939. He is a Harvard graduate and professor of English literature in the University of Columbia in New York. He was a member of the Palestinian National Council since 1964. In 1977 he served in the PLO delegation to the United Nations.

Professor Ibrahim Abu Lughd, born in Jaffa in 1929 was one of the PLO's major figures in its world information. He was a member of the PLO delegation to the UN in 1975 and for many years edited the important Palestinian journal *Shu'un Falastiniya* (Palestinian Affairs), as well as enjoying great academic success, working as professor of political sciences at the North-Western University near Chicago.

On the eve of the Madrid conference, toward the end of 1991, the two professors who had launched the dialogue between the US Administration and the PLO announced their resignation from the Palestinian National Council, thus severing the threads still tying them to the classic PLO. This enabled them to visit Israel and the territories, which they did frequently in the year following the Madrid conference. Abu Lughd eventually established his center in Nablus. The internal opposition to Arafat, from the diaspora and the territories, was able to ally itself with the Husseini group, from which the Palestinian delegation was later to emerge, under the auspices of that same Iyyadist wing of the Fatah which saw an essential need to change the PLO's image and eliminate the historical PLO.

The Right to Return: in Conflict with Palestinian Nationalism?

The appearance of the Palestinian lobby in the United States as an independent political force is of importance, not just from the aspect of how it pushed the PLO toward the United States, but also because it expressed Iyyadist positions on the issue of the right to return.

After the Madrid conference, the connection between the representatives of the Palestinian diaspora in the United States and the delegation from the territories became reinforced and senior representatives of the Palestinian lobby took a hand in the delegation members' attempts to persuade the Palestinians in the territories of the justice of the delegation's policy. In August 1992 two members of the delegation's advisory committee, Professor Rashid al-Khaldi and Dr Kamil Mansur, visited Gaza and devoted a great deal of time to discussing the right to return and, for the first time, sowed doubts on the traditional Palestinian views on this sensitive issue, hinting that the literal realization of the right to return would conflict with the Palestinian national interest. Their approach was of great importance, because they both represented the Palestinian diaspora which was demanding the right to return, and it was no coincidence that they concentrated on Gaza, because it contained one of the densest concentrations of refugees. Professor Khaldi made it clear that the Palestinians' return to Israel would obligate them to become Israeli citizens, insinuating that this was incompatible with the national interest in reinforcing the Palestinian people. He added:

> We must adhere to the right to return but, in the leadership's opinion, this right is restricted to Resolution 194, which determines return or compensation. Return means the refugees will come back to their homes and live in peace with their neighbors, and this term can only be construed as meaning that they will become *Israeli citizens* [emphasis added] living under the shadow of Israeli law. In other words, anyone returning to Haifa, which is under Israeli rule, will have to become an Israeli citizen. There are several questions involved in the issue of return or compensation. Will it be a return to the future Palestinian state, or to all sections of Palestine? The compensation: will it be collective, or will each individual be compensated for his property and losses? There are no clear answers to these questions. In my opinion, if we demand the right of return for anyone who wishes to return to Jaffa or Haifa, this must, after all, be negotiated, and the chances of Israel's being prepared to accept two million returnees are extremely minimal.[9]

Professor Khaldi was accompanied by another representative of the Palestinian diaspora, Dr Kamil Mansur from Paris, who was also a member of the delegation's diaspora wing. He added another dimension to this challenge to the traditional concept of the right to return. Of Professor Khaldi's distinction between personal and collective compensation (the compensation to be received by the Palestinian state), he said that, in his view, the national interest should be given preference, that is, no personal compensation should be provided.

In an article in *New Outlook*[10] Professor Khaldi expanded on these concepts. He said that after the declaration of a Palestinian state there would be three limitations to the implementation of the right to return: (1) the emphasis would move from an actual return, to the payment of reparations; (2) those refugees who opted to return to their homes would have to accept Israeli citizenship and abide by Israeli law; (3) the refugees would be permitted to return only to the Palestinian state territory, not to Israel. He said that a senior figure in the PLO, Nabil Sha'ath, believed this was the case, as did Faisal Husseini. The PLO, Khaldi reported, had not yet made up its mind on this problem. This last comment was, of course, of great importance in tracing the thread tying together Husseini, the PLO wing containing such figures as Nabil Sha'ath, and the Palestinian diaspora in the West.

In an interview in *Al Hamishmar* Husseini said the Palestinians would have to abandon their demand for the realization of "absolute justice and full rights," and act within the framework of "international legitimacy," which, according to Husseini, meant the establishment of two states in Palestine, "even if this harms absolute justice and the realization of the Palestinians' full rights."[11] That is, in Husseini's opinion, a full return to within Israel would conflict with the concept of two states in Palestine. According to Professor Khaldi, "international legitimacy" in this matter means adopting UN General Assembly Resolution 194, that is, return or compensation. In the same edition of *New Outlook*, journalist Michal Sela reported on Husseini's behalf that, in his opinion, the Palestinians would not even actualize their right to return to the Palestinian state. In the view of the Iyyadist wing of the PLO, the basic component of the delegation, the Palestinians, would have to demand Israel's recognition in principle of the right to return, but this right must not be used to injure Israel, since the Palestinians wanted to realize the principle of two states in Israel/Palestine.

Arafat did not accept this concept; not overtly, in any event. On 17 June 1995, following the establishment of the Palestinian authority in Gaza and Jericho, in its "Refugees' File" program, Radio Palestine reported that in 1985–86 Richard Murphy had tried to persuade the Arab refugee-hosting countries to settle the refugees in their territories, in return for economic aid. "The Palestinians" – that is, Arafat – "rejected the Murphy Initiative because it was a position that the United States had taken over from Israel." These remarks may contain yet another hint at why the March 1990 Murphy–Arafat talks had broken down.

A Change in the PLO

The creation of a positive link to the United States, with all that implies, especially the adaptation of the right to return to criteria Washington could accept, were the ideas which delineated the ground where the Palestinian delegation could flourish. Another important idea was that of altering the image of the PLO in such a way as to enable Israel hold to talks with it. It was not only the leaders of the Palestinian lobby in the United States who thought like this, but also that wing in the Fatah which supported them, even though the leaders who were settled in Tunis were unable to express their positions with the same freedom as their colleagues in the wealthy diaspora in the United States.

On 30 January 1990, the PLO leadership met in Tunis for two days of discussions on the Baker initiative, ahead of the meeting in Cairo between the Israeli delegation and a Palestinian delegation from the territories, to prepare for elections there. In the end the Cairo meeting did not take place. Most of the leaders of the organizations, headed by PLO leader Yaser Arafat, his adviser Abu Mazen and other major Fatah figures such as Hani al-Hasan and Jamal Surani, participated in the Tunis talks. From the rejectionist organizations, in addition to Hawatma and Habash, their senior advisors also participated, as well as even more ouright representatives of the rejectionist organizations, such as Abu al-Abbas, whose Nitzanim operation in the spring of that year was to put an end to the US–Palestinian dialogue.

In substance, the remarks made at that meeting have not dated and they well reflected the PLO's basic dilemmas. It was then that Baker asked the different parties questions that would enable a basis for a dialogue to begin, and the PLO hesitated over whether to respond to Baker in the affirmative. This is what Arafat said:

> If only we could tell Baker: no. And, to elections: no. Accordingly, we say to elections: yes, but . . . and we shall tell Baker: yes, but . . .
> I cannot avoid "working" with the Baker plan, because it "works" with me; but I am well aware that it is constructed to improve Israel's position. I constantly attack the United States and receive threat after threat, that if I continue to adhere to my positions, I will lag behind those of the Arabs. [Prior to this Arafat had complained that the Arab foreign ministers had not addressed any of the letters he sent them].
>   I have to "work" with Baker, despite all the maneuvering, so that they will not slaughter me like a beast, because what they want

is to put an end to the PLO, since only it means a state . . . Just imagine, one of the "rulers" [a denunciation of an Arab leader, apparently from the Gulf] said to me: Why are you sticking to Jerusalem? And then he told me: Why are you sticking to the PLO – to rule?

Arafat's conclusion was that the unity of the organizations had to be safeguarded, because "Through Palestinian unity we have thwarted plot after plot." Ostensibly, Arafat was speaking against the United States, but his remarks were aimed at someone who had spoken before him, his adviser Abu Mazen. Mahmud Abbas (Abu Mazen) had made remarks of no less importance, the significance of which was to become clearer with the passing of time, and they grated on Arafat. After stressing the need to sit down with the Israelis, Abu Mazen explained: "It is difficult for Israel to recognize the PLO, because the PLO's structure is the reverse of Israel's. The Israelis understand this better than others, and this is why they are refusing to sit down with us." Abbas maintained that since it was hard for the Israelis to accept the PLO as it was, it might be worth altering its format. Arafat thought otherwise: the existing PLO should actually be made more and more united, to "foil the plots."[12]

Abu Iyyad did not take part in the Tunis discussion, which was mainly Jihadist, but Abu Mazen represented his line. Not only did Arafat not support him, he emphasized the need to strengthen the historical PLO. What he saw as the most important thing was not promoting the meeting in Cairo, but safeguarding the PLO and foiling the "plots."

The disputes between the two PLO wings, then, began to intensify even then, when Arafat took up positions closer to the rejectionist organizations than to the political wing of the Fatah. In Abu Mazen's remarks at that meeting the first shoots can be seen of support for the future Palestinian delegation within the PLO organization itself.

It may be no coincidence that it was actually Abu Mazen who dwelt on the vital need to launch a dialogue with the Israelis, because he had been responsible for contact with Israel. Abu Mazen, who was born in Safed in 1944, was one of the founders of Fatah, but was part not of the military, but of the political wing. He was responsible for contact with Jordan and with the Israeli left. His familiarity with Israel sharpened his awareness that the familiar PLO format would have to be altered to present the Israelis with a more palatable negotiating partner, and on this point he found

himself in dispute with Arafat and also, of course, with the extremists in the classic PLO, the Fatah and the rejectionist organizations.

Palestinian journalist Samir Sa'ad a-Din was later to publish the
PLO's hesitations on the eve of the Madrid Conference. This journalist was involved in everything that occurred in the PLO leadership
at that time, and he testifies that Arafat was frustrated over being
unable to go to Madrid. Sa'ad a-Din asked Abu Mazen whether
Husseini did not represent an alternative leadership of the PLO,
and the answer was: "Why not? After all, it is our task . . . to train
our successors and carry on with our path, generation after generation." According to him, Abu al-Ala and Farouk Qaddumi (!) had
articulated a similar position. In contrast to Abu Mazen, Arafat used
to flourish his pen, saying: here is the Palestinan legitimacy.[13]

*   *   *

The inter-Arab crisis set Saudi Arabia against the PLO leadership
on the one hand and, on the other, inevitably led to frictions
between the Palestinians of the Intifada and the leadership in
Tunis. The leadership feared for its historical status and rights
when the wealthy diaspora, free of pressures, came to the help of the
Palestinians of the Intifada. This complex situation accelerated the
overt appearance of the local leadership, headed by Faisal Husseini,
as a delegation from the territories to the peace talks.

The tripartite Saudi Arabian–United States–delegation connection was neither simple nor easy. It had many facets and internal
contradictions, which were ultimately responsible for its failure. In
order to try to understand them, it is essential to acquire a close
familiarity with the nature of the dialogue conducted over the years
between the United States and the PLO and the Palestinians, and
the stubborn struggle to further the PLO's pro-US orientation.

7

The Command versus Force 17

The genuine dialogue between the United States and the PLO did not begin on 14 December 1988, when President Reagan, at a special news conference, announced the opening of an official dialogue with the Palestinian organization. The genuine dialogue had begun long before that, beginning with the Black September terrorist organization, loathed by Israel and Jordan. This organization committed the massacre of the Israeli sportsmen in Munich and struck down the Jordanian prime minister, Wasfi Tal, in Cairo. It was thanks to the dialogue with the Americans that Black September disappeared, to be replaced by Arafat's bodyguard apparatus: Force 17. Abu Iyyad headed the Black September organization and there were people from the PLO's internal security apparatus, including Force 17, who were close to him.

On 20 July 1990 the United States announced the suspension of the dialogue with the PLO, but the dialogue between it and the successors of the Black September organization never stopped, nor was there any connection between it and the "official" dialogue. Those who thought the United States' links with the Palestinian organization could be summed up by those eighteen months of fruitless talks in Tunis between Ambassador Robert Pelletreau and Yaser Abd a-Rabbo, then still Nayef Hawatma's deputy in the leadership of the Democratic Front for the Liberation of Palestine, were not familiar with the widespread ramifications of the US–PLO relations over many years. The Americans' genuine dialogue with the PLO actually began very much earlier and was never halted. Furthermore, the contacts the Americans maintained with the PLO had implications for several of the Intifada characteristics and the development toward the peace process.

The campaign for the Palestinians' pro-US orientation was filled with severe internal complications, and such Western elements as

France saw fit to compete with the mounting US influence on the Palestinians; this involvement took a surprising form in the Intifada.

Salama and the Americans

On 22 January 1979 a car bomb in Beirut cut short the life of Ali Hasan Salama, Abu Iyyad's deputy in the PLO's internal security apparatus. Many think this was Israel's handiwork, revenge on the perpetrators of the massacre of the Israeli sportsmen in Munich seven years previously.[1] It is also conceivable that Israel might have liquidated Salama not just for his part in planning the murder of the sportsmen in Munich, but also to block an undesirable development between the US intelligence service and one of the PLO's terrorist wings. The liquidation of Salama, the son of Hasan Salama, one of the leaders of the Palestinian fighting force in the 1948 war, laid bare a very interesting development in US–PLO relations.

Salama was born in Jaffa in 1932. He was operations officer in Black September, the organization under Abu Iyyad's command. In 1972 Arafat appointed him to head his bodyguards' unit, Force 17. A year later, Arafat authorized Salama to embark on contacts with the CIA bureau chief in Beirut. It was on that day in 1973 when a CIA man and the young Salama met for the first time that the dialogue between the United States and the PLO began. It was actually Black September, whose attacks had not spared US targets and oil facilities, which was the pioneer in contacts with the United States. The fact that Arafat gave the task of setting up the link with the Americans to the man in charge of his bodyguards is of great significance. It was by way of being a hint to the United States that Arafat did not trust the military wing and wanted US protection and auspices.

While, as far as Israel is concerned, Black September and Force 17 are ghastly reminders of an unbridled terror organization, on anything involving PLO–United States relations, the PLO's transition stage from a military to a political organization actually began with this organization, and it is no coincidence that later on its leader, Abu Iyyad, actually headed the pro-US wing of the PLO.

Force 17, then, was the military force of the Iyyadist wing. This

should not be taken to mean that the military organization abandoned terrorism, throwing all its interests into promoting peace.
Force 17 did indeed become the force protecting the pro-US wing of
the PLO, but it still acted as a revolutionary terror organization, with
all that involved. The force's pro-US positions found expression in
the civil war in Lebanon, to the point of operational cooperation.
During the civil war in Lebanon, Force 17 protected the US citizens
and in 1976 it defended the safe evacuation of US citizens from
Beirut. Salama's terrorist past did not stop him being invited to
the United States. On the contrary, it was actually because of this
past that he was invited twice to the CIA headquarters in Langley,
Virginia, to lecture on the PLO.[2]

From Force 17 to the Popular Army

The fact that Black September pioneered the dialogue with the
United States does not mean that all its actions, or blunders, can be
understood against the backdrop of its ties with the Americans, but
we may say in general that this apparatus was the military force of
those circles in the PLO that supported a tightening of the ties with
Washington and so were more prepared to accept the US terms in
the political process.

The military infrastructure of Black September and Force 17
balanced the military power of Abu Jihad and his attack mechanism
within the PLO. While Abu Jihad's mechanism had connections
with those Arab world forces which were opposed to the United
States, such as Iran and Libya, Arafat's bodyguard apparatus established an infrastructure of cooperation with the CIA. Patrick Seale,
in his book on Abu Nidal, maintains that in the lectures he delivered
to officers of the CIA Salama refuted the US fear that the PLO was a
Soviet satellite and proved the PLO was getting its financial aid from
Saudi Arabia and the Gulf states. It is hard to believe the CIA officers
were unaware of the PLO's sources of funding. This matter should
be understood differently: the Saudis funded this pro-US PLO wing.
They reinforced Force 17 against Abu Jihad's revolutionary, anti-US
and anti-Saudi apparatus. The rift that was to break out in the PLO
in the Gulf crisis – between the pro-Saudi Abu Iyyad and the the
revolutionary wing founded by Abu Jihad – was already beginning
to emerge in these possible distinctions by Salama halfway through
the 1970s.

In Lebanon these conflicts had powerful implications on relations within the Fatah. Force 17 waged a hard military battle against Abu Jihad's group headed by Abd al-Aziz Shahin. Shahin, Abu Jihad's man, was close to Iran and so was helped in the struggle against Force 17 by the pro-Iranian organization, the Hizballah. Genuine battles were waged between the two Fatah streams and in 1978, on the very eve of the Intifada, Rasem al-Ghul, the Force 17 commander in Beirut, was liquidated in the Ein al-Hilwa camp. Shahin was taken to Tunis for trial and sentenced to jail. In order to prevent the fighting cadres staging an open revolt against Arafat, however, he was released from his cell shortly after.

Sari Nusseiba Versus Abu Tayyib's Popular Army

Sari Nusseiba is one of the most moderate figures in the occupied territories, with pragmatic stands, a committed member of the political stream and with excellent ties in Israel. In 1991 he published a joint research in Hebrew with Mark Heller, an Israeli academic from the leftist circles. The two sketched out a possible Israeli–Palestinian agreement for the future.[3] Surprisingly, Nusseiba saw fit to note that the man to whom the Palestinians owed thanks for encouragement of the peace process was Abu Jihad:

> From the beginning of the 1980s . . . the PLO began to encourage a strategy of non-violent civil disobedience. The "father figure" in the PLO, who provided encouragement for the development of this strategy, was none other than Khalil al-Wazir (Abu Jihad); also the man who was gunned down by bullets from the rifles of an assassination squad in 1988. It may be that there is some truth to the claim that he saw this strategy as obligatory, complimenting the continuation of the military struggle against Israel, but it is true to the same extent that he put most of his trust in people from the occupied territories and so, too, in a workable strategy for them.[4]

Nusseiba's need to put these remarks down in writing is noteworthy because it indicates that Nusseiba, despite his Iyyadist views as expressed in his research, belongs, organizationally speaking, to the Jihadist wing. We can discover an important phenomenon here, which is that the traditional organizational affiliation sometimes obscures personal opinions. In any event, despite Sari Nusseiba's extremely pragmatic stands, in the struggle between Abu Jihad's and Abu Iyyad's personnel in the territories, Nusseiba helped the Jihadist wing against Force 17, that is, he worked against a rapprochement with the United States. This is no surprise because afterwards, when the Palestinian delegation was established, Nusseiba opted not to be named among its members.

In Lebanon the fight between Force 17 and Abu Jihad's group claimed many victims. Both these military wings of the Fatah also fought each other in the Intifada. Although it did not come to actual battles in the territories, the fighting between them worsened and afterwards this left its stamp on the fight over the establishment of the Palestinian delegation and determination of the parameters for the peace process. Immediately after the outbreak of the Intifada, Abu Jihad saw to organizing some of his youth bands, known as "Shabiba," into as military a framework as possible. They were called "Abu Jihad's Platoons." These platoons wiped out collaborators, punished anyone who committed a breach of Intifada discipline, held military parades of masked men and published their own leaflets. They established a parallel hierarchy to that the Unified Intifada Command attempted to establish in the territories. "Abu Jihad's Platoons" were not disbanded after his liquidation, but became the "Platoons of the Martyred ("shahid") Abu Jihad."

Force 17 did not wait long before deciding to appear in great strength in the Intifada. The organization Force 17 established in the territories was called the "Popular Army." The Popular Army's first leaflet was distributed in the Gaza Strip in September 1988. Arafat's bodyguard Mahmud a-Natur ("Abu Tayyib"), took responsibility for this army. Basically, these were bands of youths, members of Intifada committees, who organized themselves separately. They, too, held parades of masked men, imposed the Intifada discipline on the Palestinians and published leaflets.

The first to come out against the Popular Army's activity was Nayef Hawatma, the leader of the radical wing in the Democratic front. In an interview in the Kuwaiti *al-Anba* on 19 January 1989, Hawatma claimed the Popular Army was eroding the authority of the Unified Intifada Command. Anyone who did not know the genuine reason for the Popular Army's appearance in the territories must have been surprised, since the Popular Army spoke in terms of the same revolutionary rhetoric that also characterized Hawatma. What is more, the Popular Army boasted of speaking in the name of the Unified Command. What did disturb Hawatma was the appearance of the military force of the pro-American wing in the territories, since Hawatma was an anti-American Jihadist and since the argument over pro-US orientation was at the basis of the rift with Abd a-Rabbo. He realized that the appearance of Force 17 in the territories was designed to take the Unified Command out of the Jihadists' hands. Hawatma's comment was illuminating. Force 17 joined the Intifada to provide military defense for those circles in the territories who wanted to free themselves of Abu Jihad's grip, because Abu Iyyad and his people in Tunis had decided to steer the Intifada toward a peace process. Hawatma understood this; which is why he was alerted.

At that time the Jihadist wing had great power because of Abu Jihad's close, long-established ties with the Palestinians in the occupied territories. The Unified Command at that time expressed the power of the Jihadist "organizations" as against the Iyyadist "Corps of Personalities" who were being crushed under the steamroller of the Jihadist military wing. The original intention may well have been to provide the "corps of personalities" and those Iyyadist forces who were battling for control of the Unified Command with military power. Hawatma himself was no great disciple of the Unified Command, and the Command members from the Democratic Front were Abd a-Rabbo's people. His concern stemmed mainly from the fact that in this Force 17 activity in the territories he identified a desire by the pro-American wing to drive a wedge into the Intifada. This is why he did not find the drawbacks in Abu Jihad's platoons that he found in the Popular Army.

The man who headed the ideological struggle against the Popular Army of Force 17 in the territories was Sari Nusseiba. In the course of 1989 he published a weekly report in English on the situation of the Intifada, called *Monday Report*. It is hard not to be impressed by the report's one-sidedness, for the Abu Jihad platoons and against the Popular Army. In his publications Nusseiba stressed that the Popular Army's activity was unacceptable to the Unified Intifada Command and that the Command was actually ignoring the Popular Army. He claimed that only the "Beating Forces" were entitled to impose Intifada discipline.

Nusseiba's hostile approach to the Popular Army gained him a hard-hitting, hostile leaflet. "Where has the Lord Doctor fled to?" asked a Popular Army leaflet circulated at that time, halfway through 1989 (without noting the exact date of circulation), when Nusseiba once went to London. The leaflet levels grave and unfounded charges at Nusseiba, involving the division of the Intifada funds, to the point of "commerce in the blood of the fallen." Accusing well-known figures in the territories of taking advantage of the Intifada for the purpose of personal enrichment was a common method in use at that time between political rivals, and the leaflet's remarks should not be taken literally. What is noteworthy is that at that period of time the tension between Force 17 and the Abu Jihad wing moved from Lebanon to the territories and very little was needed for there to have been a very real flareup between the two wings.

France's Involvement

At the same time Israel tried several of the Intifada activists who had been charged with membership of the Unified Command. From their interrogations it emerged that Nusseiba was the channel for the transfer of funds from the PLO office in Paris. Halfway through 1993 it turned out that Ibrahim Sus, the PLO representative in Paris, had been granted French citizenship. The funds he sent to the Intifada Command were PLO funds but, as far as can be seen, there was just a suspicion, maybe more, of French directives sticking to them. In the struggle between the "organizations" that were members of the Intifada Command and the "corps of personalities" Force 17 was trying to defend, France opted to support the "organizations."

In view of the campaign that developed at that time between Force 17 and Abu Jihad's mechanism, it is interesting to see that Paris (both the PLO office and the French themselves) harnessed itself to the fight against the Popular Army. The money from France to fund the Jihadist Command did indeed come from the PLO office, not from genuinely French elements, but the policy the PLO's Paris office took against Force 17 fitted in perfectly with the French political trends.

It turns out that France was trying to fill the vacuum the Soviet Union had left behind on its withdrawal from the Middle East; it attempted to establish another force to combat the Palestinian force the United States was trying to build up. This does not mean France was trying to support the "extremists" against the "moderates"; Ibrahim Sus, too, like Nusseiba and other Palestinian representatives, was affiliated to the moderate political streams of thought; but it is the organizational affiliation that counts. In the wider scale of their affiliations they were members of the anti-US,

Jihadist club, but their opposition to the US policy did not take the form of preaching the armed struggle, but of opposition to the US political initiatives, especially in the period prior to the Gulf crisis, at which time Washington claimed exclusive rights to the political initiatives, such as that of the Cairo dialogue. It is no coincidence that at that time the Unified Command of the organizations, which survived on the funds that came from Paris, opposed the delegation of "personalities" from the territories which was supposed to go to Cairo under Egyptian–US auspices. By supporting the "Command" against the "personalities" France thought it would be able to further its own national interests. France's support for the Unified Command was part and parcel of its comprehensive policy in the Middle East: in general it preferred to support Saddam Hussein against Egypt and the pro-American Gulf states and helped Jordan thwart the initiative for the dialogue in Cairo.

With the Gulf crisis this rivalry melted away when, on the one hand, France realized that its genuine interests required maintaining the profound influence of the United States in the Middle East as a deterrent force against extremism, and that undermining Washington's interests was actually lopping off the branch it was sitting on; but on the other hand, Washington also realized that it needed allies and could not further political initiatives that pushed them out. Accordingly, after the war it decided to convert its striving for exclusiveness in the moves for peace to a broad framework in which its allies also participated.

Halfway through March 1991, Presidents Bush and Mitterrand met for a US–French summit on the island of Martinique. Roland Dumas, the French foreign minister, boasted to the journalists, commenting by the way that it had been France that had persuaded the Palestinians in the territories, headed by Faisal Husseini, to come to meet US Secretary of State James Baker for those long rounds of talks held immediately after the end of the war in which the Palestinian delegation was established and the parameters of the peace process determined in Madrid.

The French foreign minister's boasting was apparently well founded, since when one is familiar with the dispute with the Americans over the matter of the Unified Command and the initiative on the dialogue in Cairo, France's agreement to forward the status of the Iyyadists was tantamount to an innovation, which made it easier for Husseini and his colleagues to come and shake Baker's hand. It is very likely that France took advantage of its links with the Jihadist wing to enable Husseini to make the transfer to the Iyyadist wing in relative safety.

The change in the French position originated in its weakness after the war, since it was difficult to withstand the victorious Bush-Baker duo, who had invested such great resources in the war on Saddam Hussein.

To some extent Saddam Hussein's defeat undermined the status of France from another aspect, since on the eve of the war Baghdad was considered a European stronghold and consistently preferred relations with Europe to relations with the United States. After the outbreak of the crisis, however, Saddam prevented them taking an independent stand by rejecting all the French mediation initiatives. France was compelled, then, to swing into orbit around the United States. Before the crisis it had had the strength to back the Jihadist wing against the Iyyadists' attempts to reinforce their power in order to take over the Intifada leadership. After the crisis, the Jihadist wing was greatly weakened, together with its French supporters.

It is against the background of these struggles that that period of eighteen months in which the United States maintained a dialogue with the PLO should be examined. The intention, then, was not to come closer to the PLO, but to bring about an upheaval within it in which the members of the pro-American Iyyadist wing would take over the reins of rule and bring about an internal change in concepts; an upheaval that was later to be expressed in Abu Iyyad's article, "Lowering the Sword."

In the territories the confrontation between the two sections of the PLO was covert and known only to the inner circles. This was not the case in Tunis. The electrifying tension mounted with the outbreak of the Gulf crisis, leading to Abu Iyyad's liquidation.

8

A Fatal Linkage

In the end it was the fight over pro-American orientation, covering the Palestinians and the entire Middle East, which killed Abu Iyyad.

The Iraqi Army's invasion of Kuwait in August 1990 and an entire Arab state's occupation by another Arab state produced an earthquake in the Middle East. The fact that Kuwait was an economic power and dominated a considerable proportion of the oil supplies to the West made the invasion a world crisis. The United States headed the world effort to recruit support for Kuwait and Iraq's expulsion from there, which had led to the mustering of the different forces backing it.

Arafat led the Palestinians to support Saddam Hussein. He did not have a hard job, since the Iraqi president had fired the Palestinians' imagination and they saw him as a new messiah who would liberate them from the Israeli yoke. The spontaneous sympathy for Saddam Hussein was reinforced when, as soon as the invasion of Kuwait was complete, he released his program for a conclusion to the crisis; in it he expressed willingness to withdraw from Kuwait if Israel were to pull out of the territories and the Syrian Army to withdraw from Lebanon. This stipulation was called the "linkage." The Palestinians believed Saddam had also embarked on the conquest of Kuwait to accelerate a solution to the Palestinian problem. It was clear to any experienced observer that Saddam had designed his plan so that the withdrawal from Kuwait would be tied up with a solution to the Palestinian problem, from the desire to gain time in order to consolidate his rule in Kuwait. The ordinary Palestinian saw matters simply: Saddam Hussein had set out to liberate Palestine. Among the Palestinian political circles, however, an argument sprang up over the linkage. The groups who wanted to maintain the ties with the United States, headed by Abu Iyyad, opposed this linkage, but they were all swallowed up in the uproar of the Palestinians' blanket support for the line introduced by Yaser Arafat. At the same time, it is important to delineate the forces opposed to the linkage, since it later turned out that immediately after the fighting died down, it was around those circles that the Palestinian delegation was formulated.

Generally speaking, there was no Palestinian who publicly supported the military callup of non-Arab armies for a war on as important an Arab country as Iraq; not even Abu Iyyad. Some two weeks after the invasion, Abu Iyyad was interviewed by the Arab daily that appears in London, al-Arab.[1] In the interview Abu Iyyad expressed opposition to the worldwide recruitment against Iraq but, at the same time, ruled that the Palestinians had to consider the interests of the Palestinian community in the Gulf, that is, not support Saddam Hussein. He also ruled: "It is inconceivable that we should support an occupation and change of regime in other countries." Two days later the East Jerusalem Palestinian weekly a-Nadwa published an interview in which Abu Iyyad conveyed a similar message. He said he had summoned the Saudi Arabian ambassador to Tunis to explain the "Palestinian stand" to him. That is, his stand, that there could be no support for one Arab state occupying another. He denied that the Palestinians were involved in the occupation in order to preserve their interests in the Gulf.

On the second anniversary of his murder, the Palestinian weekly al-Bayader a-Siyasi[2] quoted remarks Abu Iyyad had made in closed circles two days prior to his death, on the eve of the outbreak of the war, levelling criticism of the Palestinians' positions in the crisis: "The entire world will be affected by the war, but the Palestinians will be unable to escape the severe results it will bring about." The weekly noted that Abu Iyyad was predicting the suffering of the Palestinians who were expelled from Kuwait and the economic blockade on the Palestinians in the occupied territories. In the a-Nadwa interview Abu Iyyad disclosed that he had sent King Fahd of Saudi Arabia a verbal message expressing vigorous reservations about Arafat's support for Saddam Hussein. It is worth noting the main point: in not one of Abu Iyyad's statements at that period of time did he voice support for Saddam Hussein's program to link the solution to the problem of Kuwait with the solution to the Palestinian problem. One day before his assassination he granted the Paris paper La Croix an interview in which he expressed his opposition to the program. He said he did not want his problem linked to the destruction of the Arabs. The interview was published one day after his murder. He predicted a long war which would affect the entire world, but with the main price being paid by the Palestinians. Abu Iyyad reported that the PLO had tried to persuade Iraq to pull out of Kuwait in return for a UN announcement on a link between the Kuwait problem and the problems of the Middle East, that is, the Palestinian and Lebanese problems; but the PLO failed. Abu Iyyad himself had reservations about this policy: "As a Palestinian, it is hard for me to reject the link between the Gulf crisis and my Palestinian problem but, at the same time, I do not want my problem to be linked to the destruction of the Arab region." Abu Iyyad was not the only one. Senior personalities whom we may call the Iyyadist circles, who supported the Palestinian delegation after the war, shared his opposition to Arafat's policy. Furthermore, it was from within this circle that the Iyyadist wing of the delegation was formed, the wing headed by Faisal al-Husseini.

Several focal points can be located in this group: the Palestinian Embassy in Cairo, headed by Ambassador Sa'id Kamal; the Palestinian center in the Gulf, headed by the al-Hasan brothers, Khaled and Hani, and also such PLO financiers as Jawid al-Ghussein and Ahmad Qrei', who were later to conduct the Oslo talks, and with them the leaders of the Palestinians in exile, particularly London representative Afif Safia, and in the United States Professors Edward Said, Ibrahim Abu Lughd and Hisham Sharabi, who had called for an "intifada within the PLO" as far back as the eve of the crisis.

Sa'id Kamal, the ambassador in Cairo, levelled open criticism at the support for Saddam Hussein and was rebuked by Arafat for doing so. The Voice of Palestine from Cairo was a full partner to the Arab coalition's propaganda line against Saddam Hussein. To this group we may also attach the pragmatic personalities who were conspicuous by their links with Husseini's wing: Nabil Sha'ath and Abu Mazen. Mahmud Abbas, that is: Abu Mazen, kept silent about his criticism of Arafat, while Sha'ath found the courage to articulate his thoughts after the war. Thus, for instance, he told Chaim Bar'am, a correspondent for the local Jerusalem paper *Kol Ha'Ir*,[3] that Arafat's kiss for Saddam Hussein was "fatal for the Palestinian cause." He did indeed charge the CNN TV network with having "worked overtime on that kiss, although it is just a common Arab custom," and at the same time his criticism, even though implied, was powerful, all the more as he semi-admitted that "errors were made" and there were "second thoughts."

Bar'am commented that Sha'ath was living in Cairo and there was significance to his place of residence in a country that had already made peace with Israel. He also quoted Sha'ath as having said he supported Husseini's and Ashrawi's meetings with Baker.

In February 1991 Sha'ath made even more forceful remarks in London; in actual fact, he condemned the invasion in retrospect. He admitted the PLO felt solidarity with the peoples of Kuwait and Iraq, but his official stand was support for a withdrawal from Kuwait, and he commented: "We have accepted the contents of Security Council Resolution 660," that is: an unconditional withdrawal from Kuwait.[4] This is a statement of an Iyyadist nature, reflecting the group's position on the internal arguments in the crisis, and it is a continuation of remarks made by Abu Iyyad on the eve of his murder.

In Saudi Arabia and the Gulf there was another focus headed by the al-Hasan brothers, from among the founders of the Fatah organization. Khaled al-Hasan did not often speak at that time, and his silence was thunderous. He distanced himself from Arafat. In the course of the crisis, he and his brother Hani met with King Fahd, and there was a prevalent view that Saudi Arabia had studied a plan to replace Arafat in the PLO leadership with a "troika," to include Abu Iyyad, Khaled al-Hasan and Abu Mazen.

After the war an Arab journalist visited Khaled al-Hasan in his office in Tunis and reported[5] that there were large pictures of Abu Iyyad and Abu al-Hol hanging on the wall; not of Arafat, and certainly not of Abu Jihad. The central Fatah council met in Tunis at that time and, according to the *al-Watan al-Arabi* report, during the crisis in the Gulf there were coordination contacts between Khaled al-Hasan, Abu Iyyad, and Abu al-Hol, with the goal of turning that session into one from where charges would be levelled at Arafat over his positions in the crisis.

The man who was in overt contact with Saudi Arabia was Hani, the younger brother of Khaled al-Hasan. A month after the outbreak of the crisis he sent King Fahd a letter expressing willingness to participate in the defense of Saudi Arabia and its sovereignty. In his letter[6] Hani al-Hasan thanked King Fahd for the support he had given the Palestinian people over many years and expressed his confidence that nothing could give rise to a rift between the Palestinians and Saudi Arabians. Hani al-Hasan promised King Fahd that the soil of Saudi Arabia was no less dear to the Palestinians than that of Jerusalem. In April 1991 – despite the Saudi Arabian anger with the Palestinians – King Fahd agreed to meet with Hani al-Hasan. Hani al-Hasan's letter sparked off resentment in the military wing of the Fatah. Abbas Zaki, the Fatah representative in Amman, a member of the military wing, condemned the letter (which appeared on the pages of the same edition of *a-Nadwa*, reporting that it had been sent to King Fahd without the leadership's approval and expressed the views of the sender alone.

While the Khaled al-Hasan and Hani al-Hasan brothers gained publicity among the Palestinians, their elder brother, Ali, sank into unjustified obscurity, since he was one of the major Hamas string-pullers in the Gulf and Saudi Arabia.

As soon as in August 1990, Afif Safia, the PLO representative in London, said the PLO did not favor taking territories by force. He expressed support for the people of Kuwait and the family of Emirs of the House of Sabah, adding: "We are very concerned by their disaster; more than the US Government." At the same time, he called for a freeze on the recruitment of forces in the Gulf, and for those forces already called up to be placed under the UN flag.[7] Great importance should be attributed to this position by Safia, since immediately after the war he coordinated the London deliberations by the leaders of the Palestinians in exile, who opposed Arafat's moves during the crisis, and it was in these deliberations – which will be discussed in chapter 13 – that the first outlines were drawn up of the Iyyadist wing of the delegation, headed by Husseini. There was hardly a Palestinian of any stature in exile who expressed support for Arafat, and even before the Gulf crisis, one of the most important foundations of the Iyyadist camp was to be found in the Western exile, .

The most decisive position was voiced by Prof. Edward Said, one of the most important of the Palestinian ideologues. Even before the crisis he came out firmly against Arafat on several issues; inter alia, he charged the PLO leadership with being totally ignorant of the special sensitivities of public opinion in the West. After the war, too, in his criticism of the PLO, Said continued to emphasize the lamentable failure to familiarize itself with the Western mentality. He was not satisfied with Palestinian information being entrusted to Hanan Ashrawi, still maintaining that this Palestinian blunder would foil the Palestinians' political effort.

Before Said came out decisively against Arafat, over the years the

ideological formulations bearing his stamp were assimilated into
the different PLO resolutions, and it is hard to imagine the PLO's
ideological stands without the profound mark he impressed upon
them. Accordingly, his firm anti-PLO positions in the crisis were
of special importance. In an article he published in the *al-Majalla*
weekly, at the beginning of September 1990,[8] Said attributed the
main damage to the world of images. He said it would now be
difficult to uproot the deterrent and repulsive image of the Arab,
or of the Muslim, from the Western conceptual world. He went on
to say:

> There is no argument over the fact that the West and the Arab-
> Islamic world in general have economic and strategic interests
> in common, but there are also important differences of opinion
> between them . . . and there is a major bone of contention . . . which
> is connected with the mistaken and distorted image of the Arab-
> Muslim world in the West. The average Westerner's, particularly
> the American's, widespread ignorance and fear of the Arabs and
> Islam, are even more conspicuous now . . . and the way in which
> Israel sees the Arabs and Islam is the dominant way in the West
> . . . we see the attacks on the Arab world and Islam on the part
> of "experts" . . . who basically present the Arabs as suffering from
> a fundamental sickness.

Said ruled that the grave damage caused by the Gulf crisis would
accompany the Arabs for many years to come.

In its edition of 26 October 1990, the Saudi Arabian daily *a-Siyasa*
gives details of the division of forces in the PLO in the aftermath of
Arafat's support for Saddam Hussein. It should indeed be taken into
account that the Saudi organ naturally tended toward exaggeration
when describing Arafat's difficulties, and nevertheless the picture
it showed was quite faithful to the genuine situation in those
days. According to that report, the dissatisfied were headed by
Abu Iyyad, Arafat's second-in-command. He refused to accompany
Arafat on several of his trips and from September he began to shut
himself up in his home, following a vocal quarrel with Iraqi foreign
minister Tariq Aziz in Baghdad. Aziz was angry with Abu Iyyad for
having declared that Iraq would withdraw from Kuwait if guarantees were given that it would not be attacked. Abu Iyyad answered
Aziz that he was not prepared to listen to criticism that did not come
through the PLO hierarchy. Because Arafat had disparaged himself
to the Iraqi minister, Abu Iyyad also attacked Arafat to his face,
charging him with having become a pawn in the Iraqis' hands.

In September Salim a-Za'nun, "Abu Adib," the Fatah representative in the Gulf, who was also deputy head of the Palestine National Council, sent Arafat a letter protesting over the fact that his policy was so harmful to the Palestinians' activities in the Gulf that it would take many years to repair the damage. Za'nun announced that he would not participate in any Palestinian forum as long as the current situation continued. Arafat rebuked Hani al-Hasan for the letter he had sent to King Fahd, but Hani al-Hasan rejected the rebuke. According to the *a-Siyasa* report, it was then that Abu Mazen and Mahmud Darwish embarked on the initiative of bringing pressure to bear on Arafat to alter his policy so as to support a conclusion of Iraq's occupation of Kuwait.

Arafat in the "Same Trench" as Saddam Hussein

The list of those who disagreed with Arafat appears long, but, truth to tell, this was not what decided the Palestinian moods at that time. The Palestinians wholeheartedly supported Saddam Hussein and it was indisputably Arafat's firm support for him that determined the official position of the PLO establishment.

This is why those who disagreed with Arafat were unable to come out openly and decisively against his positions, and the struggle was concealed in codes. Iraq's opponents either rejected the linkage or simply did not mention it. Iraq's supporters, headed by Arafat, set Saddam's initiative – that of linking the Gulf crisis with the other Middle East disputes – as their policy's banner. Furthermore, there are signs to be found that Arafat was aware of the linkage problem even before the crisis. As early as May 1990 he proclaimed to Palestinian students in Baghdad that "There is one campaign and one fate," and that he had come to Baghdad "To continue marching from Baghdad to Jerusalem."

In any event, on 15 November 1990, Arafat told the East Jerusalem Palestinian weekly *al-Usbu' al-Jadid*: "Guaranteeing a comprehensive solution to all the crises in the Middle East will guarantee the security and safety of the Middle East." Even at the peak of the battles to liberate Kuwait, when there was no longer any doubt that the Iraqi occupation's days were numbered, a PLO organ, *Falastin a-Thawra*, published an interview with Arafat in which he declared: "The linkage is a Palestinian demand, which was adopted by Saddam."[9]

A month after the conquest of Kuwait – on 3 September 1991 – Arafat made a speech to Palestinians to mark one thousand days since the outbreak of the Intifada. The Palestinian news agency *WAFA* published his remarks that same day. It was a speech of blood and fire, in the Intifada style of Abu Jihad. He reiterated the jihad slogans and expressed enthusiastic support for a simultaneous solution to all the crises in the Middle East. However, in contrast to Abu Iyyad's remarks in *a-Nadwa*, that the Palestinians were maintaining a neutral position in the dispute, Arafat declared: "We are in the same trench with the man who is fighting imperialism and its allies." In this declaration Arafat went further than Jordanian King Hussein and Saddam Hussein's other allies, such as Yemen and Sudan. These latter gave Saddam Hussein their practical suppport, but without giving this support an ideological dimension, such as a common war on imperialism and its allies. Furthermore, King Hussein explained his policy by the fact that he wanted to formulate internal Arab agreement, without involving the Western powers, and that he was thinking of the genuine good of Kuwait.

The recruitment of Christian armies to defend Saudi Arabia caused the House of Saud great difficulties with the Islamic sages. The PLO's religious establishment exploited these difficulties, and in the internal-Islamic religious argument, the Palestinians contributed "fatwas," religious rulings which caused Saudi Arabia difficulties of principle. Ten days after the invasion, on 12 August 1990, Sheikh Nader Tamimi, the aide to the Mufti of the Palestine Liberation Army in Jordan, handed down a religious ruling that anyone who took the side of the United States and the West in the confrontation with Iraq was considered to be "one who has abandoned the faith of Islam." Ten days later Sheikh Rajab Bayud Tamimi, the Mufti himself, delivered a reasoned religious ruling that conflicts with the religious rulings of the Saudi sheikhs, proving that it was permissible to be accept Christian help.

It was not just the very fact of the support for Saddam Hussein, but also the outspoken style of this support that created a very difficult situation in the Palestinian–Saudi crisis and raised the internal tension inside the PLO – between Arafat and the Jihadist wing on the one side and Abu Iyyad on the other – to dimensions that would turn out to be fatal.

9

The Big Bang

On 19 November 1990, the London Arabic-language weekly *Suraqia* (a play on words combining Syria and Iraq into one name) published a fantastic story describing a worldwide plot by Hamas members to murder Arafat. This book is too short for a description of the plot's details and we can only note that Presidents Bush and Mubarak, as well as Sheikh Sabah, the Emir of Kuwait, were involved. The rationale behind Arafat's murder was to punish both the PLO and Israel's Shamir Government for having foiled Baker's initiative to bring together a Palestinian and an Israeli delegation for a political dialogue in Cairo. The PLO was to be removed violently from the stage in order for a dynamic leadership to be established for the Palestinians in the image of the Hamas, which would compel Israel to seriously confront the Palestinian challenge, which would take the form of the Muslim struggle against the Soviets in Afghanistan. The plot's story was almost certainly a fabrication, but I mention it because it faithfully reflects the electrified atmosphere prevailing in the entire Middle East before the invasion of Kuwait, which was the "big bang" that gave birth to the peace process.

The story, which apparently originated in Iraq, was that Iraqi intelligence came across irregular transfers of funds to banks in Tunis from several financial institutions in the United States with connections to Kuwait. They knew that Usama Hasan Ibrahim Abu Odeh, a Palestinian holding US citizenship, had received 67 million dollars from the New York First National Bank for reasons which were unclear. All the Iraqis knew was that this Palestinian had links with General Brian Lippman, whom the White House's National Security Committee had put in charge of the Islamic groups active in the United States. Abu Odeh, together with Mutwali Hussein Damanhuri, an Islamic sheikh living in the state of Michigan, transferred the funds from the donations to the Intifada's casualties. Sheikh Damanhuri issued a religious ruling permitting the killing of the Palestinian leadership which had recognized Israel. Damanhuri and Odeh prepared six study grants in the United States for six Islamic youths in Gaza. These grants were a cover for their recruitment to Islamic terror. On their way to the United States they were supposed to stop over in Spain for training in an underground Spanish organization. However, the leader of that group, Ahmad Abd al-Halim Habashi, disclosed the program's details to the PLO. These were that the youths were supposed to travel via Tunis, request a meeting with Arafat in order to take a letter from him to the youths of Gaza, and then commit the murder. The weekly does not explain how they were supposed to overcome the close guard surrounding Arafat.

There are serious doubts as to just how genuine this information was, but what is patently obvious is that at that time Arafat was indeed terrified of a plot to murder him and was aware of the dangerous potential for this embodied in the Hamas movement. Arafat also knew something that came to light only after the blowing up of the twin towers in Manhattan three years later: that there was a link between the US intelligence arms and the Hamas, because of their common interests against the Soviets in Afghanistan; but it is hard to believe that the Egyptians or Americans would have had any interest in imposing the Hamas on the Palestinians. What sounds more reasonable is that Arafat feared that after his elimination, he would be replaced by Abu Iyyad. He knew that the strings emanating from Abu Iyyad and the Hamas were leading to the same place: Saudi Arabia and Kuwait.

Throughout this period Arafat attempted to bring the Hamas under his wing, and was wary about any use of threats when talking with it. But shortly before the invasion Arafat's caution slipped. On 5 July 1990, only a month before the Iraqi invasion of Kuwait, the PLO organ Falastin a-Thawra warned the Hamas against playing with fire and charged the Islamic organization with playing into the hands of Israel and the United States. The PLO organ accused the Hamas of having pretensions to being the alternative to the PLO. "It is important that we remind the Hamas that many others have tried to play a similar role in the past, and all have turned to ashes." The Reuter's Agency reported on the article that same day, noting that it had been written under orders from Yaser Arafat.

Did Arafat really decide to use that language of threats because he knew what was going to happen in another month? Was he threatening only the Hamas, or also those who were backing it: Kuwait and Saudi Arabia?

Abu Iyyad's Murder

In December 1992, the *al-Majalla* weekly, which appears in London, published the minutes of the interrogation of Abu Iyyad's assassin, who had been questioned by PLO security personnel in Yemen. The East Jerusalem daily *al-Quds* published *al-Majalla*'s disclosures. There is no certainty that these minutes are complete and that some details of some minutes have not been altered. In any event, the minutes lay bare the murky, contentious world of the different PLO organizations.

The picture that comes to light in the publication is one of a reality in which members of the different organizatons are scattered all over the world, coming and going from centers in East Europe under the vigilant eyes of the East European security services, for whom the presence of the Palestinian terrorists was becoming burdensome. Despite the official rivalry among the different organizations, the fighters associated with each other in their regular meeting places, spying on each other or trying to get each other transferred from their services. Hamza Abu Zeid began his career with Abdallah Abd a-Labib ("Hawari"), the Force 17 representative in Iraq. Hawari, however, quarreled with the Iraqis, and in 1987 Hamza Abu Zeid went to Poland in unclear circumstances. As far as can be seen, it was because of the crisis that broke out in Hawari's Baghdad office that the link between Abu Zeid and his operator was severed and he was open to new offers. Before he was sent to Poland, Abu Zeid had acted as Force 17's bodyguard for Abu al-Hol and was sent to Peshawar in Pakistan against the background of the war in Afghanistan.

In the Teatr coffee house in Warsaw he associated with one of Abu Nidal's people and, after arguing over the state of the organizations and since the Polish security services were pressing him to leave, because he had entered Poland under a forged passport, Abu Zeid agreed to join Abu Nidal's organization. The Poles expelled him to Belgrade and people from Abu Nidal's mechanism sent him to Manilla, to assassinate an Israeli personality who was scheduled to visit the Philippines capital at that time. The explanation for the assassination of the Israeli figure was: to revenge Abu Jihad's death.

That is, the organizations' feelings of solidarity among themselves was more powerful than can be imagined on the basis of the official publications spewing out fire and brimstone at each other. Abu Nidal's organization saw fit to revenge itself on Israel for the blood of Abu Jihad, one the leaders of a different organization.

In Manilla Abu Zeid made friends with someone from another organization, without being able to put a name to the organization, and began helping him to introduce himself as a Palestinian student, since his identity as a sailor on a Greek ship was quite fragile. The assassination of the Israeli personality did not take place, for a simple reason: no such personality arrived. Abu Zeid lifted the surveillance from the Israeli embassy and began spying on the Palestinian students. Primarily, he wanted to find out who had betrayed Abu Nidal's squad to the Philippines security services. In this task, too, he failed, and then he tried to ascertain what chance he had of totally abandoning his terrorist career and emigrating to Australia. His main problem was, of course, the forged papers with which he was furnished, and he was compelled to return to Belgrade.

In May 1989 Abu Zeid was ordered to go to Libya, without knowing what his next mission was to be. He gradually came to realize what this mission was when his hosts, Abu Nidal's people, spelled out to him the crimes of "Arafat's gang, particularly Abu Iyyad."[1] Abu Nidal's people in Tripoli said Abu Iyyad had informed on the "members of the Red Brigades (Italian), the Baader Meinhoff group (German) and part of the 17 November group (Greek), and was behind the liquidation of the five comrades [Abu Nidal's people in the Lebanese valley) during the reciprocal liquidations between Abu Nidal's group and the Fatah in Lebanon at that time, which caused a very serious internal crisis in Abu Nidal's group]." The anti-Abu Iyyad brain-washing was consistent and constant. Abu Nidal's people told Abu Zeid that "Abu Iyyad has caused great harm to the Palestinians and he is the stumbling block to the continuation of the Palestinian struggle." One day he was given a file to read, with press clippings on "Abu Iyyad's irresponsible statements," particularly highlighting his declaration that "The Palestinian revolution did not come out of Beirut and three thousand fighters were left there." The reference was to the PLO's departure from Beirut in 1982. Abu Nidal's people tied the massacre of the Palestinians in Sabra and Shatila to that declaration. Incidentally, on 1 January 1993, David Kimche, who was director of the Israeli Foreign Ministry at the time of the seige on Beirut, granted *Al Hamishmar* an interview marking the publication of his book *The Last Option: the Quest for Peace in the Middle East.* On the affair of Sabra and Shatila, David Kimche said the following:

> Sharon was convinced that there were some two thousand PLO fighters living in Sabra and Shatila who hid in these camps during the PLO's evacuation from Beirut, and he was determined they must be caught and expelled. It was his obsession. At every meeting at that time he would raise this issue, saying there were PLO fighters in the camps and they had to be removed. In my opinion, it was this obsession that led to him thinking there was an opportunity here to enter West Beirut . . . he did not correctly estimate what could break out in both camps. This, in my view, is what happened and it was, of course, a grave error.[2]

Could Abu Iyyad's ill-considered bragging have been understood so misleadingly by Sharon and the Phalangists and been one of the reasons for such tragic results?

Abu Nidal's people also showed Abu Zeid Arab press articles giving details of Abu Iyyad's properties in Kuwait, and articles presenting Abu Iyyad as having, more than anyone else, given away the Palestinian fighters to those who were after their lives.

The clearer his next mission became to Abu Zeid, the more doubtful he felt, and he tried to wriggle out of it. His operators guessed his intention and warned him that they would retaliate on his family if he were to evade the task while, simultaneously, they continued attempting to heighten his motivation by saying: "It is Abu Iyyad, more than anyone else, who bears responsibility for the fatal errors and it is those errors that led the Palestinian people into the current situation. It is Abu Iyyad who is to blame for the fact that it was impossible to deter Hawari and his like." Abu Zeid heard the conversations Abu Nidal's people held among themselves, in which they ruled that Abu Iyyad's liquidation was a "revolutionary act," that is, an act serving the Palestinian revolution against those who were planning to foil it. "It is Abu Iyyad who is responsible for Hawari and Abu Iyyad who is responsible for the errors in the revolution, and it is he who caused the split in Abu Nidal's organization [the reference being to the split in which Atef Abu Bakr, one of the organization's leaders in 1989, resigned after a series of reciprocal liquidations within Abu Nidal's camp] and killed five comrades in the Lebanese valley'."

Abu Zeid was finally convinced. He told his interlocutors: "I was convinced that Abu Iyyad was indeed to blame for all these disasters and that Hawari had to pay the price of his conduct; and this must be done to somebody in the hierarchy above him. Abu Iyyad was the first to advocate violence against Israel and then abandon the violence, and it was he who advocated the armed struggle and then abandoned the armed struggle." Abu Zeid was then taken to meet the "head of the organization" – Abu Nidal's name is not mentioned – who reiterated the charges against Abu Iyyad. The "head of the organization" promised Abu Zeid a good reward for the liquidation, threatening his family if he were to evade it. He was ordered to return to the Fatah or, to be more precise, Force 17, and go back to his former job as Abu al-Hol's bodyguard. He was told to wait for Abu Iyyad to come home and then kill him with the weapon Abu al-Hol had given him in his capacity as bodyguard.

It is noteworthy that Abu Nidal's people made themselves the spokesmen for the entire military wing. Their claims against Abu Iyyad in respect of the damage he had caused them were only part of the comprehensive charge sheet against him. He was accused of having sacrificed the entire military wing and caused damage to international terror in general. As far as can be seen, the emphasis they placed on Hawari, Abu Zeid's former commander in Baghdad, stems from the struggle he waged against Abu Nidal in Baghdad; but this is not certain.

Amazingly, Abu al-Hol accepted Abu Zeid's explanations for his period of absence without making any genuine investigations, and put him back in his group of bodyguards. From October on Abu Zeid waited for Abu Iyyad in Abu al-Hol's villa, and on the 14th of that month he did indeed come; the rest is known.

One day later, on the night between the 15th and 16th of that month, the thunder of the US bombings of Iraq silenced the salvo of bursts that wiped out Abu Iyyad and his Force 17 colleagues. A month later, when the reverberations of the Gulf war also fell silent, the curtain rose on a new era in the Middle East, which opened the window of opportunities for peace arrangements between Israel and the Palestinians and Arab countries.

Part II

Window of Opportunities

10

Moving the PLO to the Territories: FIDA versus the "Organizations"

In the middle of February 1991, the curtain rose on a new Middle East, with Palestinian politics – without Arafat's two deputies, Abu Iyyad and Abu Jihad – at work in a different, but no less contentious and convoluted Middle East. At the end of the process the impossible occurred: Israel and the PLO recognized each other, and in September 1993, PLO Leader Yaser Arafat shook hands with Rabin and Peres, at President Clinton's side, on the White House lawn.

It was a long and winding road from the ringing kiss Arafat planted on Saddam Hussein's cheek in August 1990 to the occasion of the mutual PLO–Israel recognition and historic handshake between Arafat and the Israeli leaders.

The sequel could not have been predicted from the beginning. US Secretary of State James Baker hurried to East Jerusalem and embarked on a series of meetings with Husseini and Ashrawi, to formulate the Palestinian delegation to the peace talks and define the framework of those talks. Baker was then speaking of the window of opportunities, by which he meant the special circumstances that had enabled a genuine peace process to begin. These circumstances were: the defeat of the major power that had whetted the militant spirit, Iraq; the other militant power, Syria, having joined the pro-US camp; the prestige won by the United States as the only superpower; and the desire of such pro-Western Arab countries as Saudi Arabia and Egypt to bring about Middle Eastern stability through resolving the Palestinian problem in talks with Israel.

The window of opportunities was indeed wide open, but the sight it reflected was not especially cheerful. The paved road was filled with potholes. Baker intended to crown Husseini king of the

Palestinians, placing an emphasis on the centrality of the leader-ship in the occupied territories in relation to the leadership in the diaspora; but at the end of a long, intransigent fight, Arafat succeeded in turning the tables. From a situation close to political elimination, Arafat found himself facing a sympathetic world, being hosted on the White House lawn, rubbing elbows with President Clinton and shaking hands with Rabin and Peres.

FIDA Articulates the Positions of the Territories

In order to correctly assess the dimensions of Arafat's achievement, the starting point must be understood. Under the impression of Iraq's defeat, Baker was able to dictate the moves on the Palestinian issue, and he frequently rubbed shoulders with the two original Palestinian delegation leaders, Husseini and Ashrawi. It was obvi-ous to all three that Arafat had fallen, together with Saddam, and the Intifada leadership in the territories would bear the burden of the negotiations. Baker said: "This is your chance to be an internal leadership. If you miss it, either the old PLO or the Arab countries will take over and impose their will on the Palestinians."

Although that at that stage the spotlights were turned on Husseini and Ashrawi, it is actually worth taking a look at the group of Abd a-Rabbo's activists, who were again playing a pioneering role in the formulation of the internal leadership's positions. It should be recalled that this was nevertheless a very small group, whose importance lay not in its objective power, but in the clarity of formulation of the demands for structural reform in the PLO and the reinforcement of its status toward the inside, as against the outside. In this it became the mouthpiece for other broad circles in other organizations, particularly the Fatah.

At the end of 1992 it became apparent that this group leaned toward the establishment of a political party in the occupied ter-ritories. The establishment of a party was important in principle, since this development expressed yet another phase in the transition from military, "revolutionary" consolidation as part of the PLO organizations, to normal political life. The group wanted to call the party FIDA: a reverse acronym for the Democratic Palestinian Association (al-Ittihad a-Dimuqrati al-Filastini). This acronym also has a meaning: dedication to an ideal.

After the deportation of four hundred Hamas activists in December 1992, there was pressure on Israel to make a gesture toward the Palestinians to enable the resumption of the peace talks. One of these gestures was to bring back some thirty senior deportees, and the former Palestinian National Front had a particularly large share in this because they were among most senior of the deportees. They were from among the Communist Party veterans who had worked as part of the Palestinian National Front at the beginning of the 1970s and, of course, members of the Democratic Front for the Liberation of Palestine who, after the great internal split, had naturally followed Yaser Abd a-Rabbo in the pro-American direction. At the end of April 1993 they were brought back and immediately organized themselves into a party.

Following that incident, the new party accumulated impetus, because the most important of the returnees were this group's activists. While still in exile in Amman, they had been in on the secret of FIDA's establishment and when they returned, they no longer concealed the genuine aims of their activity and their undercover positions gradually came to light.

At the beginning of May I spoke with Dr Azmi Shueibi, a returned deportee who had been a member of the al-Bira municipality at the time of the National Guidance Committee. Zahira Kamal, one of the party's prominent female leaders, also took part in the talk. Dr Shueibi was to be elected party secretary in the middle of July 1993, by the temporary secretariat – a body secretly selected, apparently in May 1993, in Amman. Asked about the direction of FIDA's future activity, the two replied:

> After the declaration of the Palestinian state in 1988, a struggle for the organization's democratization began within the Democratic Front. Dr Azmi Shueibi was one of the most important of the figures who led this fight. The FIDA Party was a continuation of the same fight, so Dr Shueibi was naturally in the party. The fight for democratization also included giving major expression to the territories. In the Intifada we saw that the center of gravity was here. The return of Dr Azmi and others to the territories will reinforce the internal front in the territories.[1]

These are specific remarks which, for the first time, openly expressed the genuine moods of that group of veteran activists.

As time went by, the internal differences of opinion between the cadre of political activists and the military cadres began to surface, and it was the FIDA Party that initiated the overt thrashing-out of the argument with the military organizations.

On 23 June 1993, the *a-Nahar* daily published an interview Shueibi had granted the international Arab daily *al-Hayat*, which *al-Hayat* had been deterred from publishing. In the interview, Shueibi detailed the reasons for his vigorous opposition to leaving responsibility for the Palestinians' fate in the hands of the "organizations" (Tanzimat). He explained why, in his opinion, control over the political system in the territories should be taken out of their hands, and why the organizations' Unified Command, which was under the control of the organizations at that time, could not serve as an appropriate framework upon which the new political structure the Palestinians had to erect in the territories could be founded.

According to Shueibi, the main harm involved in the organizations lay in the fact that they had taken over the Intifada, uprooted its popular, public spirit, brought about a severance between the people and its activity and invalidated its broad popular nature. What is more, these organizations were directed in a closely concentrated manner by a leadership from the outside, and so could not head the process of democratic renewal so needed by the Palestinians in the territories. Therefore, national unity could not be achieved by the organizations. Furthermore, because of their nature, each organization dug in behind its ideological barricade, without any connection with the mood of the public in the territories. This being so, links between the inside and outside were very bad, even within the organizations' cadres themselves, to the point where the strikes were decided in Tunis or Damascus, without the organization in the territories participating in setting the date. Shueibi thought the public at large – "jamahir" – should be brought back to activity, but this was impossible, because the decisions were being made in "closed rooms, among the organizations, without the public."

Shueibi charged the organizations with having severely harmed the link between the Palestinian public and the PLO. The organizations' activity was not only putting an end to broad participation in the Intifada, but causing a severance from the PLO itself. This was grave damage, since the PLO could not deploy for the critical period confronting the Palestinians because it was cut off from the people. The organizations were fighting each other and harming the positive connection between the people and the PLO. Shueibi, inspired with fighting spirit, said:

There is no way to put an end to the organizations' fortifying themselves behind barricades. It must be through opening the door to the broadest possible popular basis, in order to create a public opinion capable of confronting [the organizations] with two alternatives: either to resign, or to clash with the people . . . if someone wishes to rule the people, he cannot begin his rule by getting a stranglehold on them.

Shueibi reiterated his known distinction between the organizations, whose activity could lead to the people's severance from the PLO, and the "National Movement." According to him, the forces to amend the situation must come from within the National Movement, not from the organizations, and the Unified Command was unable to play that role because it was no more than a [low level] framework for coordination between the organizations. He also drew a distinction between the PLO as an idea and the existing "PLO institutions," which deserved the criticism levelled against them by the public. Shueibi believed the PLO had to be reborn in the territories, to maintain a living, direct link with the diaspora.

It is hard not to identify the National Movement with the Corps of National Personalities mentioned by the Communist activist, Bassam Salhi. The enmity between it and the "organizations" is the guideline to the fights over the Unified Command, and afterwards for the Palestinian delegation and, after Oslo, over the actualization of the agreements.

Nor did the PLO regard the energetic activists, the brothers Labadi and Zaqut, who had established the Unified Command and rescued the Intifada from the Islamic movements after they had been deported by Israel, with any special esteem, and they were given no genuine role in the PLO, but were shoved aside.

It did not take many days for FIDA to clarify its intentions. In the middle of July 1993, it sent an internal circular around the PLO activists in the territories, calling for the dissolution of the Unified Command and the establishment, in its place, of a new central institution for the territories, to be called: "The Supreme Committee for Follow-up and National Unity." When FIDA described what authorities the new institution was to receive, there was a striking resemblance between it and the former National Guidance Committee. The "Follow-up Committee" was to be responsible for all spheres of life, a sort of internal government for the Palestinians in the territories. The committee was supposed to reinforce the citizens' confidence and fulfill the national missions of concern for the normal functioning of such life systems as health and education.

If we work on the assumption that these ideas were only written down then after having been passed on by word of mouth over the previous years, we can better understand the significance of Abd a-Rabbo's activists' energetic work to found the Unified Command before the organizations took it over; and afterwards, in the establishment of the Palestinian delegation. In the *Hotam* interview, Shueibi described this along the lines of: "Moving the PLO to the territories." The "organizations" had grounds to suspect FIDA of intending to eliminate the PLO altogether. Just as it had advocated the dissolution of the Unified Intifada Command, at a later stage it was able to advocate the disbanding of the PLO's Executive Committee.

The "organizations" did not pass in silence over the challenge FIDA was setting them. At the beginning of July 1993, the Popular Front for the Liberation of Palestine, headed by George Habash, convened its politbureau and, at the end of the deliberations, circulated a leaflet in the territories, summing up its conclusions. The main conclusion was that the PLO had to reinforce the Unified Command and provide it with additional economic resources. The Fatah regarded FIDA's call with pent up fury.

The Command's Activists: a Leadership Vacuum

Azmi Shueibi's ruling that the outside leaderships had also imposed themselves on the "organizations" in the Unified Command was confirmed when those same activists came out openly against their operators in Tunis, charging them with foiling the younger generation of the "organizations'" activists in the territories.

The first to expose the gap created between the activists of the "organizations" in the territories and their operators on the outside was Basem Id, a researcher from Betzelem (a watchdog institution for human rights in the territories). In the first interview of its kind, for the *Hotam* supplement of *Al Hamishmar*, he said: "There are disputes between the commanders abroad and their activists on the ground. These activists – after having done their work faithfully for years – do not have as much as a pack of cigarettes in their pockets. They are trying to get themselves out of the pit into which they have fallen – at any price."[2] His remarks explain why the Popular Front for the Liberation of Palestine saw fit to demand the allocation of financial resources to the Unified Command, since halfway through 1993 this Command was disintegrating.

And indeed, shortly after this (on 17 July 1993) the two great East Jerusalem dailies, *al-Quds* and *a-Nahar*, published interviews with Unified Command activists who did not hesitate to identify themselves by name. They pinned the blame for the "organizations'" failure on Tunis, maintaining that it had occurred because it had stopped the "inside" establishing a leadership, since everything in the territories was directed and ordered by fax from Tunis.

Ihab al-Ashqar from Gaza – who was a candidate for expulsion by Israel because of his membership of the Command – adhered to the basic distinction between the "personalities" and the "organizations," saying: "In my view, as soon as there was reliance on the national political personalities . . . the role of the Unified Command expired, and it only remained for the purpose of signing leaflets published in Jerusalem." This is an important comment, which I will expand on in the next chapter, since it touches on the Command's expropriation, for some space of time, from the "organizations," for the benefit of Husseini's mini-PLO, but al-Ashqar also pointed an accusing finger at Tunis: "There is a historic vacuum [of significance] in the leadership [in the territories], because the occupation has set itself the supreme goal of suppressing it and has flatly rejected the establishment of a young national command that would gain the respect of the street and be capable of guiding the public, but, to our regret, this fits in with the concept of several groups on the outside, who think the leadership in the occupied territories would become an alternative, rather than a complimentary leadership."

Ghazi Abu Jayyab, an activist for the Popular Front for the Liberation of Palestine in Gaza (it is not clear whether he was a Command member) said: "It is no secret that the National Unified Command has no presence, in the meaning of the existence of a body that acts continuously and holds the wheel of the Intifada struggle . . . and without an action plan for the National Command, the leadership is nothing but an insignificant leaflet." He accused Tunis directly of having created the distinction between it and the leadership in the territories, as though Tunis and the territories were two bodies fighting each other. This concept, Abu Jayyab said, could not ultimately serve the objectives of the struggle. "It depends on the PLO's concepts. It does not, even for a minute, accept that a young leadership should arise from within the occupied territories, for they mistakenly think the existence of a strong leadership could have a bad affect on there being only one leadership, the PLO. The territories cannot be treated as though they were satellites of the outside." Abu Jayyab also distinguished between the cadres of the "organizations" and the political "personalities"; but he accused the PLO of having imposed the "personalities" on the "organizations," ruling: "[It is impossible] to seek foundations in order to define them as a 'political leadership' which, when it comes down to it, does not merit this title." In circles close to these personalities the word went round that, in actual fact, the PLO had foiled the Intifada in order to prevent the growth of a leadership in the territories.

In a conversation with me, not for attribution, in July 1993, one of the Unified Command activists at that time confirmed the complaints by Abu Jayyab and Ihab al-Ashqar: "There was no such thing as a Unified Command. What there was, was a disgrace. Some teams lasted for two weeks, with my team being one of the longest-lived: three months. The Shin Bet [Israeli security services] always came out on top, but neither did the PLO have any interest in the Unified Command having permanent members for any length of time." The Command used to meet in Ramallah or Bir Zeit, in the home of Mufid Arqub, a Command member on behalf of the Communist party. "The Shin Bet noticed lights burning in Arqub's home late at night and, since it knew that this was not a brothel – it got on our trail," that activist joked.

The Command member added that relations between members of the organizations were bad and it was hard to text leaflets, because each organization imposed a veto on any text it did not like. Arguments emerged on various issues, for instance, on the number of strike days. Because of the difficulty in finding wordings acceptable to all, a method was institutionalized whereby each organization texted a leaflet in turn, which was faxed to Tunis for Arafat's approval. Arafat apparently did not even read the leaflets, approving them a few hours later. He noted that he did not recall any changes, since Arafat did not want to quarrel with the organizations.

That same Command member explained Abu Jayyab's comment about the imposition of the "personalities" on the Command. In June 1990, an order came in for Husseini to text the leaflets, "And since then it has been impossible to say that the Intifada has a Command in the territories."

It is indeed strange that it was just then, while he was in the process of rapprochement with Saddam Hussein after having marked
out the dangers Abu Iyyad's wing posed to him, that Arafat took
the Command away from the "organizations" and transferred it
to Husseini and the "personalities." Abu Jayyab and al-Ashqar's
conclusion from this was that Arafat had made a political decision to
move toward a US solution, together with Husseini, but the developments that followed do not confirm their thinking. The decision
to transfer the command to Husseini originated partly in Arafat's
desire to please the United States, after Abu al-Abbas' coastal
operation the previous month, but, mainly, Arafat had apparently
begun to fear that the Unified Command of the "organizations" was
beginning to accumulate prestige and power and that such figures
as al-Ashqar and Abu Jayyab could truly push the PLO/Tunis out
and take its place. It was not only the Iyyadist wing that threatened
him, but also the Jihadist wing, and he feared an alliance between
the Unified Command and the military cadres on the outside.
Handing over the Command to Husseini was yet another step in
Arafat's policy of balances.

Husseini did not continue to head the Command for long, and a
year after the Madrid Conference it was given back to the "organizations," but in the meantime they had lost their enthusiasm and
their determination to succeed. Arafat did not regret this – neither,
obviously, did the "commanders" across the border – as Basem Id
phrased it.

Nusseiba: New Thinking about the
Political Committees

The FIDA Party may have set hidden thoughts free, but in principle
its fight on the organizations was only part of the general fighting
between the two PLO wings – the Iyyadist and the Jihadist –
and it encompassed the territories and the diaspora along very
similar lines. Just as Shueibi attacked the military organizations, the
organizations attacked the political echelons in the Fatah. As will be
recalled, it had been Shahin, a man from the Fatah's Abu Jihad wing,
who sharpened his attacks on the smooth politicians surrounding
Arafat, in a letter he sent to the territories during the Intifada.

In his article in *a-Nahar*, Shueibi claimed that it was because of
the organizations' activity that no political infrastructure had been

established in the territories upon which the needs of the "next stage," that is, the establishment of the political entity, could be founded, recalling the fact that the "popular committees" established for the purpose of the Intifada had "melted away as though they had never been" because of their link to the organizations. Sari Nusseiba, who at that time headed the "political committees" which had been established from the nucleus of the Intifada committees, joined in the views expressed by Shueibi, but less vigorously. He published an article in the *Al-Quds* daily whose title indicates its contents: "The Political Activity Committees – Toward New Thinking."[3]

The political committees were established in the territories immediately after the Madrid Conference, from the wing of the Intifada committees. The names of the political committee members were published officially, thus emerging from the underground to overt, official action. On this issue opinions differed with the organizations, who opted to remain in the shade, because they did not believe the time had come to bring the revolution to an end for the benefit of the political work. This wing of Intifada activists may be said to have crossed the lines, from the Jihadist to the Iyyadist camp, and had links with the Palestinian delegation. Sari Nusseiba was one of the leaders of these committees and thus took a step toward ridding himself of the burden of the Jihadists. (At that time Arafat held talks in Khartoum with Hamas representatives and rejected the idea of a transition to political organizing activities.)

After he had rejected the accusations levelled at these committees, that they were trying to serve as an alternative to the armed struggle in order to eliminate it, and emphasized their organizational link with the "Mother Movement" – that is, the Fatah Organization – he articulated his deepest feelings:

> When we go to [talks] in Washington . . . we aspire to reach an agreement that will lead us to the skeleton of an entity which will develop into a state, and we here on the land will have to cover this skeleton with the content we wish, and our challenge is a democratic challenge, one of human rights, and we, *we do not want just a state, but a state that will defend us and our rights as individuals in a civilian society, in which we will find rest and a future for our children after us.* [emphasis added]

Accordingly, Nusseiba found it essential to maintain a free, tolerant and open society which permits varied political activity in equality and democracy. Despite Nusseiba's fear of being cut off from the broad organizations framework, there is more than a hint here that the direction of his thinking was not much, if at all, different from that of Shueibi. This may prove that at that time FIDA was a mouthpiece for Fatah circles, such as Nusseiba, that feared to openly disobey the organization's discipline.

Al-Asifa Warns

In order to understand the fears of Nusseiba and his colleagues, a leaflet published by the Fatah military wing in the occupied territories, on 3 May 1993, should be studied. Under the title of "The Forces of al-Asifa, the Military Wing of the Fatah Movement," Sari Nusseiba was warned by name, along with other members of the Palestinian delegation and Orient House – the Palestinian delegation's home – not to undermine the basic foundations of the armed struggle and the Palestinian revolution. "Al-Asifa Forces" was the Fatah organization's original name in the time of Abu Jihad, and one prevalent story has it that it was the original name of the basic cell in Gaza in the years when Arafat and his comrades were just setting out, before they established the Fatah in Kuwait.

"We will not give up the armed struggle," stated the military wing, "nor the secret activity . . . the lovers of television, offices, the fax and the mobile phone live in peace with the occupation and beautify its ugly face, and the only things they do well are festivals and lectures." The genuine Fatah is not them, but the "Fatah of suffering, the Fatah of the fire on the Zionist enemy." The genuine Fatah is not the Fatah of the functionaries, but the Fatah of the firing line and the revolution. The leaflet reminds them that "politics" is based on the muzzles of guns, not the other way round. The military Fatah called on the other organizations to devise tactics for how to deploy themselves to confront the challenge.

Nusseiba had reasons for special fear of the military wing since, as will be recalled, from the very beginning the Jihadist military wing had regarded him as one of them and during the Intifada it fought the Jihadist wing's war on the Iyyadist Force 17 in his name. The military cadres might treat a known and declared enemy less seriously, but could not forgive the traitor and deserter to the "enemy" ranks. This was the basic dilemma of Nusseiba, a moderate, peace-loving man who was trapped in the Jihadist framework which had been imposed on him.

Whether he meant it or not, the military wing of the Fatah suspected him of intending to turn the political committees of the Intifada into a sort of Fatah FIDA. In those days the pressure on him made him consider abandoning his political preoccupations in the territories and going on a sabbatical in the United States and eventually, right after the signing of the Oslo agreements, he went to the United States, taking his family with him.

*   *   *

The PLO organization had its suspicions about what was occurring in the territories: it suspected both Husseini's mini-PLO group and the cadres of the organizations, which it set against Husseini. On the "outside" the state of affairs was no more simple: the military wing suspected Arafat and from day to day it became more insolent toward him. The bottom line, however, is that it can be stated that all the PLO streams, including the different Fatah groups, were prepared to cooperate against the leadership in the territories, without this cooperation easing the tension between them on the outside. The grounds for the fears of the "outside" originated not just in the US effort to establish a political leadership in the territories, but also in its placing at their disposal a military and economic mechanism and elected parliament.

Along with the argument over the very fact of establishing a delegation, the PLO followed another two trends with concern: Husseini's attempts to establish a Palestinian "police" force, to be recruited entirely from the territories, and to establish an economic mechanism in the territories to take in the international aid, instead of the old PLO. The intention to elect a parliament in the territories to replace the old Palestine National Council also worried the PLO.

Had US diplomacy succeeded in achieving these goals: the consolidation of a leadership in the territories, supported by an internal economic institution and equipped with a police force whose legitimacy originated in an elected parliament; it would have meant the end of the PLO. Arafat could not agree to such a move and so, despite the never-ending disputes with the Jihadist wing, eventually a concealed line connected them – "foiling the US plots," whose main point was to foil the delegation from the territories on whose establishment Baker toiled as soon as the fighting died down in the Gulf.

11

Imposing a Delegation on Arafat: in "Dishonorable Conditions"

The danger reflected to Arafat's leadership from within the occupied territories was, in the end, the direct cause of his decision to accept the agreements prepared between Abu Mazen and Peres in secret in the period in which Arafat was conducting his bitter struggles against the formula imposed on him after the Gulf War.

In a letter sent to Arab American journalists meeting for a conference in Los Angeles in January 1993, Arafat wrote: "We entered the talks in the most complex Arab and international circumstances, and in dishonorable conditions, designed to nullify the Palestinian participation."[1] Arafat attributed his own success in the period after the war mainly to the fact that "We emphasized our presence on the political map, and expanded the areas of world support for the Palestinians' rights . . . the rights to return, self-determination and the establishment of a state with sacred Jerusalem as its capital." Arafat reiterated this motif in contacts he maintained at that time with the Hamas movement and when, a month later, in February 1993, he met in Khartoum with Jordanian journalists, Arafat again ruled: "We went to Madrid against our will, and in dishonorable conditions."[2]

And indeed, in the wake of the Madrid conference Arafat's policy toward the Palestinian delegation was consistent, with one goal: to foil the delegation. Arafat prevented it progressing along the paved road of the letter of invitation to Madrid, that is, the achievement of an agreement for an interim period in general lines of self-rule, as sketched out in the Camp David Agreement, and, parallel with this, sought allies in the Arab world against the Palestinian delegation. On the former, all through the period Arafat pressed for strong foundations of permanent agreements, especially on the Jerusalem issue, to be introduced into the negotiations, and on the second matter he paid court to two major elements: Jordan and the Hamas. He also tried to interest Iraq in his attempts to demolish the foundations of the Palestinian delegation, but post-war Iraq had more pressing matters on its mind.

However, neither Jordan nor the Hamas had any interest in allying themselves with Arafat against the Palestinian delegation. Throughout the period, Hussein continued the line to which he had committed himself to Shamir at their meeting in the Aravah in September 1991: not to support Arafat. Furthermore, Hussein initiated the meeting with Shamir after he had made up his mind to put an end to the longstanding alliance with the PLO leader. The Hamas could not support Arafat, not only because of its opposition in principle to the PLO and its leader, but also because of its sources of support, Saudi Arabia and Iran, which opposed Arafat and strove to overthrow him.

Arafat did not give up. He followed with interest the secret connection worked out between the Israeli Foreign Ministry and Abu Mazen, and as long as this connection bore no fruit, he often visited the two focuses with whom he believed he would be able to create a genuine alliance against the delegation: Amman and Khartoum. In Amman he pressed King Hussein to bring forward the declaration of a confederation between the two Banks, in order to create a political force headed by him and King Hussein, which would have the power to rule the delegation in particular and the leadership of the territories in general. Arafat reminded Hussein that while the PLO and Jordan had a long tradition of cooperation and trust, Faisal Husseini, as a new leader from the territories whose basis of action was in East Jerusalem, was a danger to Hashemite legitimacy in the Holy City, and in the West Bank as a whole, all the more as he was a descendant of the Husseinite family – the Hashemites' ancient enemy. As it happened, Arafat's remarks in Amman did not fall on barren ground. The Jordanians were indeed aware of the anti-Jordanian line Husseini was taking at that time, one that caused them considerable disturbance, but they also knew that the United States was reserving the place of honor for Husseini and his delegation colleagues. Husseini's anti-Jordanian activity disturbed them, but they preferred to contain it in other ways, not by a renewal of the alliance with Arafat.

Arafat's attempts to persuade King Hussein to renew the early confederation recipe began very soon, together with the efforts to compose the Palestinian delegation. Very close to the convening of the Madrid conference in November 1991, Arafat was still trying to persuade King Hussein to cancel the severance of links between the Banks, and according to a report in *a-Sharq al-Awast*, a Saudi Arabian daily that appears in London, from 5 November 1991, Hussein turned Arafat down flat, telling him that his grandfather, King Abdallah, had erred when he annexed the West Bank to Jordan. In the choice between Hussein and Husseini, Arafat opted for the Jordanian king, but Hussein confirmed to him that a resumption of the talks on a confederation was out of the question. "We will not ally ourselves with the Intifada," Hussein explained the obvious to Arafat.

Building a Delegation: the "Inadmissible of the Command" versus the Classic PLO

Against the background of these severe pressures, when Arafat's political status had reached its lowest ebb after Saddam's defeat in war, contacts on the delegation's composition began between the United States and Husseini. The starting point was that the Palestinian delegation headed by Husseini was supposed to represent the positions Abu Iyyad had expressed a year previously, because of which he had been murdered, and the scales of the Palestinian leadership would be tipped from Tunis to the occupied territories.

Had matters gone as US Secretary of State James Baker wanted, Husseini would have headed the delegation and, in the absence of any genuine deterrence by the PLO, which was licking its wounds, defeated Iraq, and Syria, which did not dare to come out sharply against the United States, Husseini would have steered the Palestinians into rapid arrangements with Israel on the basis of self-rule for the Palestinians in the territories. This was the "window of opportunities" Baker talked of in his lightning visits to the Middle East immediately after the Gulf War. But matters did not go well, because Arafat succeeded in neutralizing Husseini by the appointment of the dogmatic Haidar Abd a-Shafi, who was not prepared to discuss anything less than a Palestinian state. Abd a-Shafi was appointed to head the delegation to Washington and Husseini to head all the negotiating teams. But they fought between themselves over who would steer the Washington delegation, and Abd a-Shafi refused to take orders from anyone.

Husseini accompanied the establishment of the Palestinian delegation from its beginning and after the end of the Gulf War he remained almost alone, or with a handful of confidants, particularly Dr Hanan Ashrawi. The two were the hard core which conducted almost intimate talks with James Baker. Abd a-Shafi, on the other hand, found his place only after his speech at the Madrid Conference, following which his status was reinforced at Husseini's expense.

Abd a-Shafi and Husseini came to the delegation from two different sources. As will be recalled, Husseini formed the mini-PLO from the Intifada cadres which, on the one hand, did not fit in the classic PLO's organizations, but neither did they identify with the group of "national personalities" who up to the Intifada had been the mainstay of the public figures in the territories. This group took up an intermediate position between the Command and the "Personalities," opposing both of them. However, after they succeeded in distancing the old group of "personalities," they inherited their name as against the organizations. Husseini's group came from among the Intifada activists, but was the successor of the old group of "personalities" it had pushed out.

The Americans were only too happy to accept the existence of Husseini's group, since they viewed it as the natural successor of Abu Iyyad's group and saw a special advantage in the fact that they came from the territories. They hoped that, with the impetus of the talks, Husseini's group would manage to neutralize the Unified Command and put an end to the Intifada. On the eve of the convening of the Madrid conference, Baker himself declared in Jerusalem that one of the immediate goals of the impending talks was to stop the Intifada.

Abd a-Shafi came to the delegation from the top echelons of the Communist Party. Although he, too, had been a member of the National Guidance Committee, he was not a major member, like the future FIDA members. More than anything else, it was the fact that he had been one of the founding fathers of the PLO organization at the beginning of the 1960s that affected his political consciousness. Despite his Communist Party seniority, he had not acquired any official status in it, nor was he one of the party leaders. The grounds for his selection for the delegation were more that he was an independent man with a leftist background than that he was an institutionalized leader of the Communists. The role of party leader was reserved for Bashir Barghuti from Ramallah, the editor of the party organ *a-Tali'a*.

Husseini represented a group whose members may be described as the "Command rejects." Abd a-Rabbo's group sent the best of its people into the Command, but the Fatah and the Popular Front prevented their seniors from joining the Command. It was difficult for those seniors to stand by and watch less important activists being sent to run the Intifada from inside the Command. Riyad al-Malki, one of the senior people in the Popular Front in the territories, skilled in rhetorics and leadership, could not accept the barrier his own movement had set up between him and the acquisition of leadership status in the territories, by opting to send field activists to the Command instead of him. He found a solution in the framework suggested to him by Faisal Husseini – who had also been distanced from the Command by the Fatah. The framework Husseini formulated developed in an Iyyadist direction because of the very fact of the fight he got into with the combatant organizations: he adopted the future FIDA's basic approach on emphasizing the weight of the inside against the outside, because of the differences of opinion that surfaced with the exterior leadership over the manning of the Unified Command. The Intifada also intensified the internal activists' awareness of their importance as those who would bring about the decisive Palestinian battle for independence.

Yaser Arafat at once grasped the nature of Husseini's group, and when they got down to composing the delegation after the Gulf war, he did all in his power to keep Husseini out; and just as the organizations' representatives had got rid of the "personalities" (the organizations drew no distinction between Husseini and Nusseiba and Ilyas Freij and Siniora; as far as they were concerned, they were all "personalities") from the Unified Command, he wanted to repeat that exercise at the stage of the delegation's establishment. Then, however, after Saddam Hussein's defeat, Arafat was at his lowest ebb and unable to actualize his intention, and it was to this he was referring when, two years later, he ruled that the "Madrid formulation was imposed on us in dishonorable conditions."

On 25 May 1993, Ms Molly Williamson, the US Consul General in Jerusalem, visited the head offices of the FIDA Party in Ramallah and met with three of its leaders: Azmi Shueibi, Ms. Zahira Kamal and Sami Kilani, a delegation member from Nablus. The *a-Nahar* daily published extracts of the talk's minutes that throw some light on the circumstances of the delegation's establishment,

as Azmi Shueibi explained them to the US diplomat.[3] Consulate
members claimed afterwards that these minutes were a forgery by
Hawatmas' people, who wanted to blacken their rivals.

A similar claim was also made by FIDA members. Nevertheless,
it is interesting to look at them, because the forger – if indeed there
was forgery – knew his job, to censure concealed moods among his
opponents, with whom he was very familiar.

Shueibi accused the PLO leadership of treating the Palestinian
delegation like "officials whose role is restricted to following their
orders," and described the circumstances of Abd a-Shafi's appointment as delegation head:

> I was in Tunis when the delegation was composed, and several
> names were put forward and discussed in principle, and Haidar
> Abd a-Shafi's name was not among them; the names put forward
> from Gaza were Fayez Abu Rahma and As'ad Saftawi [who was
> murdered immediately after the signing of the Oslo Agreements]
> and then we were surprised that it was Dr Haidar Abd a-Shafi
> who was the delegation head. When we made up the delegation,
> Arafat intended to write a letter of thanks to Faisal Husseini and
> Hanan Ashrawi for [the fulfillment of] their national task and
> what the letter meant was the end of their roles but, after great
> efforts, some of the more logical, realistic people succeeded in
> convincing Arafat of the error [embodied] in this move. Arafat
> tried with all his might to convince the Popular Front and the
> Democratic Front to join the delegation, knowing the truth of
> their extremist positions. Accordingly, he tried to bring them in
> order to foil the talks right from the beginning.

Whether the minutes were forged or not, a perusal of editions of
the PLO organ, *Falastin a-Thawra*, from the same period, confirms
that at that time Arafat was indeed seeking the proximity of Habash
and Hawatma.[4]

It may be assumed that the "logical, realistic" person Shueibi
was referring to was Akram Haniya, his friend from the National
Palestinian Front. Haniya stood by Husseini and the delegation
from the territories at that period and it is almost certain that,
along with Shueibi, he was taken by surprise by Abd a-Shafi's
appointment as delegation head, and afterwards stopped Arafat
throwing them out.

Akram Haniya, Arafat's adviser on affairs of the territories, was
one of the key figures at that time and was of great help to Husseini
in composing the Palestinian delegation on the basis of his mini-PLO

and keeping the old band of personalities out of the delegation. Needless to say, the organizations willingly kept themselves apart, after Arafat failed to persuade them to take over a major place in the delegation for themselves.

The fact which clarifies Haniya's precise political location is that he was a dominant and initiating member of the National Guidance Committee in the territories in the 1970s and, according to one story, Haniya even held the post of Committee secretary. Accordingly, Haniya may be viewed as one of the connecting links between FIDA's ideas and Husseini.

Haniya was deported in December 1986, after having played two senior roles in the territories: secretary of the journalists' union and editor of the *a-Shaab* daily, which articulated the moods in the Fatah. It is no coincidence that Salhi gives Haniya – and rightly – a place of honor in the internal leadership system in the territories. After his deportation, his status was reinforced and he was considered Arafat's most senior adviser on affairs of the territories during the Intifada. When the contacts over the establishment of the Palestinian delegation were underway, he stood by Husseini, helping him in struggles against the organizations over its manning. Haniya also played a similar role in Tunis; Arafat brought him into the Revolutionary Council of the fighting cadres in order to weaken the strength of the military wing in his constant game of balances.

The Popular Front for the Liberation of Palestine: Arafat is a Traitor

Arafat's endless policy of balances exposed him to accusations by both sides of preferring the other. While, in actual fact, all the signs point to Arafat having set himself the major goal of foiling the delegation from the territories in order to save the PLO, the military wing of the organizations accused Arafat of deceit in favor of the political wing, from the desire to eliminate the PLO! This motif recurs in almost all the leaflets of the rejectionist organizations, especially the Popular Front, and it took an unusual expression in an article Dr Labib Qamhawi, one of the leaders of the Popular Front activists in Amman, wrote at the beginning of September 1992 in the *a-Ra'i* daily in Amman.[5] It turns out that the two delegation heads, Husseini and Abd a-Shafi, had poured their hearts out to him and he quoted from what the two people had told him, or spoken of in

closed circles in the Jordanian capital. Qamhawi's starting point is
that the "Palestinian policy maker," that is, Arafat, was cooperating
with the Americans on the PLO's elimination.

Dr Qamhawi sketched out a scenario agreed by Arafat and
the Americans, according to which the right to self-determination
would be actualized by a confederation with Jordan and the PLO
would gradually expire through the annulment of its institutions,
and be left as a title without content. Instead of the organization's
institutions, the PLO would work through Arafat's "advisers," who
were loyal to him personally, not necessarily to the organization.
Qamhawi was relying on talks he held with Faisal Husseini in
Ramadan (February–March) 1992, in which he confirmed this scenario to him. In July Qamhawi met with the head of the negotiating
team, Dr Haidar Abd a-Shafi, and found that Abd a-Shafi was also
aware of this danger and the major goal facing him as delegation
leader was that of foiling the plot. Abd al-Shafi was not prepared to
conform with the scenario of the PLO's elimination, since "He was
most sensitive to the pulse of the Palestinian man in the street." Abd
a-Shafi told Qamhawi that he had again asked to meet with Habash
and Hawatma, but Arafat stopped him. Abd a-Shafi pressed for a
meeting with the two large organization heads because he wanted
to prevent a move that would lead to the PLO's elimination, since
he was one of the organization's founders. He felt an urgent need to
press Arafat to coordinate his moves with the two rejectionist leaders, in order to constitute a counter-weight to the "advisers'" policy
of bringing about the destruction of the Palestinian organization. In
the division between the "personalities" and the "organizations,"
Abd a-Shafi affiliated himself with the "organizations," because
he identified Husseini as head of the "personalities" wing – the
equivalent of the "advisers" in Tunis, as Qamhawi phrased it. In
times to come, halfway through July 1993, Abd a-Shafi came out
openly against Arafat when he called for the establishment of a
collective PLO leadership. Abd a-Shafi's worldwide publicity gave
the impression that it was he who came up with the original idea,
and this was not so. The demand for Arafat to be surrounded with
a collective leadership was a permanent motif in the rhetorics of
the Popular Front and Democratic Front and something can be
found in remarks Qamhawi published the previous year to explain
Abd a-Shafi's innermost motives. It is surprising that Abd a-Shafi
thought Arafat was plotting with the "personalities" to destroy the
PLO, while Shueibi from the "national personalities" wing (if his

remarks were indeed not forged) was accusing Arafat of appointing Abd a-Shafi, and of the intention to incorporate Hawatma's and Habash' people in the delegation, to block the "personalities"! Indeed, Arafat's policy of balances ultimately set all sections of the PLO against him. If we treat Shueibi's remarks to Williamson as authentic, the chain of circumstances can be described thus: Arafat tried to bring the organizations of Habash and Hawatma into the delegation in order to weaken Husseini. When he failed – he appointed Abd a-Shafi, who was close to them, for the same reason. Abd a-Shafi eventually joined forces with Habash and Hawatma in the desire to foil not just Husseini, but also Arafat. This latter stayed on guard and crushed the various alliances against him with the agreement he made with Israel.

The Four Delegation Wings and the Exterior Wing

Three of the important delegation wings are identified above: Husseini's wing, which was supposed to develop into an alternative leadership to the PLO from inside the territories; Abd a-Shafi's wing, which to a great extent expressed the position of the "organizations," despite the fact that in principle they had turned down Arafat's request to join the delegation. Arafat also appointed Abd a-Shafi from the desire to contain Husseini; the little FIDA Party-to-be had minimal representation: Dr Sami Kilani from Arraba, who was not one of the party's leaders.

Another important group in the delegation was the People's Party headed by Bashir Barghuti. The delegation's representative was Ghassan al-Khatib of the Bir-Zeit University. Al-Khatib was a member of Husseini's group, so his inclusion in the delegation was natural. The party's positions on the peace process move were not unambiguous; it was the direct successor of the Palestinian Communist Party and, as such, rejected the armed struggle and favored the peace process for many years. However, on all the contentious problems it leaned toward support for the positions of the organizations, as presented by Abd a-Shafi. It was the group closest to Abd a-Shafi, a Communist himself by his world view, although he was not a registered party member and so was able to take independent positions.

Bashir Barghuti, the party leader, did not support the overt contacts between Husseini and Baker from their start, viewing

them as a US attempt to establish a PLO leadership from the
territories. He did not conceal his position, voicing it, inter alia,
in an article he published in the party organ *a-Tali'a*:

> There are some [that is, Husseini] who think that the meet-
> ings with Baker are for the purpose of requesting and hearing
> clarifications; yet this is not how Baker sees them. The special
> mechanism and great number of meetings are creating a specific
> Palestinian representation reality, which is developing from the
> request for give and take clarifications and, in the end, into
> negotiations.[6]

Barghuti called for Arafat's declarations to be accepted as the
basis for contacts, with no falling into the trap the Palestinians had
fallen for when the delegation for the Cairo dialogue was being
established. Nevertheless, Ghassan al-Khatib eventually went to
Madrid as the party's representative and participated in several
rounds of talks in Washington. Barghuti, a wise, experienced leader,
realized that the party was too weak to participate in the talks
without the backing of the organizations. In times to come, after
the Oslo agreements, in fact, the People's Party walked out of the
talks, while FIDA stepped up its participation.

When it emerged during the talks that the People's Party was
close to the positions of Abd a-Shafi, not Husseini, Husseini began
encouraging FIDA to join the delegation. FIDA became a counter-
weight to Barghuti's People's Party and in time stepped up its
support for Husseini. The People's Party was a thoroughly Iyyadist
party since, as a Communist party, it had been the first to reject
the armed struggle and recognize the 1967 borders as the realistic
borders of the Palestinian state, but nevertheless, after the political process opened, leaned toward backing the organizations
against Husseini, while FIDA sided with Husseini against the
organizations. The reason for this may have been psychological:
the Communists always felt themselves a minority group which
must not lose its link with the street. Their point of origin was
hesitant from the very beginning. FIDA grew up from the very
heart of the PLO and felt it had the power to change things since,
after all, its origins were in Nayef Hawatma's Democratic Front. It
did not lose the feeling of power because of being the genuine PLO
even after a long series of splits which left it, finally, with special
positions, but not many supporters.

In the end the Palestinian delegation was a coalition of several forces: Husseini, who supported interim arrangements; Abd a-Shafi, who saw them as a recipe for the PLO's destruction; FIDA, which called openly for a transfer of the Palestinians' center of gravity from the outside to the territories; and the People's Party, which was hostile to both FIDA and Husseini and joined Abd a-Shafi, while winking at the organizations, even though it rejected their military path.

Despite the disputes between these four wings, they had a common interest: distancing the "personalities" group which was prominent in the period prior to the Intifada: Freij, a-Natsha, Siniora, Abu Rahma, and others. Freij and a-Natshah had indeed been in groups that preceded the delegation, went to the Madrid Conference and were included in the delegation list for the first Washington talks, but were constantly kept at a distance until finally being thrown out. Also distanced were the "personalities" who were Arafat's supporters, headed by Radwan abu Ayyash and Jamil Tarifi, who headed the move of the dialogue in Cairo on the eve of the outbreak of the Gulf crisis. The old group of "personalities" had to wait for Arafat to overcome Husseini in Oslo to get back its old status.

Sari Nusseiba and the Political Committees

Immediately after Husseini's return from the Madrid Conference, enveloped in a black Palestinian kafiya – surrounded by cheering Palestinians waving olive branches in the celebrations hall of East Jerusalem's Hakawati Theater – he received information that did not please him. "Delegation circles" who had not gone to Madrid, but stayed behind to organize the celebrations, read him lists of Palestinians from all the towns in the territories who had been declared "political committees," headed by Sari Nusseiba. The surprised Husseini's facial expression showed he had not been in on the secret of the political committees' establishment. The committees were comprised of Intifada youths from the local Fatah committees, who had decided to come out of the underground, to overt activity. The word "political" is not used in its usual sense – that these were political figures right from the start – and should be understood against the background of the arguments within the Fatah. These youths had decided to emerge from the military wing to one that could be defined as "political" in comparison with the military cadres who had remained in the underground. This was an internal decision inside the military wing of Abu Jihad's former supporters – to follow Husseini and Nusseiba into the political wing.

In the years that followed, in addition to these "political committees" Nusseiba also established "technical committees" to deal with the preparation of papers to formulate the Palestinian concept of the emergent state. Not much came of these papers, and the importance of the "political committees" and "technical committees" lies in an understanding of the Palestinian political structure in the territories in the period following the Madrid Conference. Sari Nusseiba did not join the Palestinian delegation for the rounds of talks in Washington. This was by order of Arafat, covering up an intention to train a replacement for Husseini, if his position as delegation leader were to provide him with too much power and there should be a need to get rid of him. Nusseiba, who had been the spokesman of Abu Jihad's wing against Force 17 at the beginning of the Intifada, despite his pragmatic personal opinions, kept his distance from the Americans and did not actually join the Iyyadist wing.

The structure created was more or less as follows: the "Black Panthers" in the West Bank and the "Fatah Hawks" in Gaza, the combatant groups of the Fatah, kept faith with Abu Jihad's original line; after them in how much faith they kept with the original Fatah spirit came the Intifada activists who did not bear arms, but worked underground in the Fatah framework. They gave birth to the "political committees," which did indeed concede secrecy and declare themselves members of the "political wing," but did not go as far as joining Husseini's wing, which was defined as "personalities." Between the "political committees" and Husseini was Sari Nusseiba, whom Arafat had appointed to head them, but many of them were not prepared to accept Nusseiba, regarding him as an outsider who had been imposed on them. This was the reason for the many disputes and quarrels between the "political committees" and the brilliant lecturer from Bir Zeit University who was divorced from the mentality in which the Intifada youths had grown up. The very fact of their emergence from the underground took them out of the Jihadist wing and tension mounted in Ramallah, particularly between them and their colleagues who had not emerged from the underground. Those who had not emerged from the underground were identified as an "organization" ("tanzim"). In June 1993, the tension reached its peak when members of Fatah – the "Organization" – attacked members of the "political committees," kidnapping many of them, beating them up and burning their stores. That was a time when violent incidents broke out in Jenin between these two groups, apparently against a similar background, taking a toll in human lives.

The tension in Ramallah paralleled similar tension in Tunis: Jibril Rajub, Arafat's adviser, supported the political committees; the leaders of the Jihadist wing – Muhammad Jihad, Sakhar Habash and others – supported the "tanzim." This division would be of importance after the signing of the Oslo Agreements; Rajub was to continue with the move of severance from the classic Fatah, emerge from the underground and be given the post of "head of pre-emptive security" in the West Bank in a worsening confrontation with his former colleagues who had remained in the underground. But Rajub was not to complete the move, nor would he make the move to the Iyyadist wing, but would remain personally loyal to Arafat. The difficulty in distinguishing between the "political committees" and the "organization" lay in the fact that they both adhered to the name "Fatah," in order to be the legal successors of the old organization.

In general, Nusseiba kept silent; however, from time to time he levelled criticism at the delegation and its way of working and conducting the talks; thus, for instance, just at the time his people in Ramallah were squabbling with the Jihadist wing, Nusseiba said it would be preferable to be annexed to Israel with equality, or choose the option of "no peace and no talks," if what was on the agenda was "those talks and their results."[7]

Nusseiba confronted Husseini, but Abu Jihad's wing did not forgive his people for having abandoned them for Nusseiba's "political committees." In May 1993 the military wing of the "al-Asifa" (the forces of the storm), the original name of the military Fatah organization from the time of Abu Jihad, published a leaflet attacking the entire political wing, including Nusseiba and all those "who have forgotten the secret activity," that is: the "political committees." This warning did indeed move from the realm of written words to that of the reality in the stormy events in Ramallah a month later, which were also an overture to violent incidents between the two wings for a long time yet to come.

12

Who Blew Up the New York Trade Center?

In order to get out of his dire straits, Arafat sought allies against the delegation, especially in the Hamas movement. On 2 February 1993 the Beirut daily *a-Safir* published the minutes of one of the decisive meetings between Arafat and the Hamas, which took place in the Sudanese capital Khartoum at the beginning of that January. It turned out that the central point in Arafat's remarks involved the danger the political process was posing to the PLO's continued existence. He was aggressive in his demand that the Hamas join the PLO in order to stop the United States and Israel from establishing an alternative leadership in the occupied territories. On hearing the Hamas reply, Arafat became extremely irritated and walked out of the room; only to return within seconds. The head of the Hamas politbureau, Dr Musa Abu Marzuq, rejected Arafat's approach out of hand, saying it would be preferable for the Palestinians to have another leadership – the Hamas – to take over from the current one, if it were to collapse because of the political process. Hamas Spokesman Ibrahim Ghoshe voiced another view. He said that although the Hamas–PLO cooperation could be renewed, the PLO would first have to retract its recognition of UN Security Council Resolution 242.

Arafat riposted that if they did not join the PLO, they would be tantamount to foreign agents and should not labor under the delusion that the oil sheikhs would continue to support them for any length of time. He yelled at them that he had more political experience than they and was more familiar with the "Arab bastards." What Arafat and his interlocutors did not realize at that time was that not only did the Kuwait crisis give rise to the peace process, it also created a dramatic mutation in the Muslim

Brotherhood movement. It was actually from the pro-US wing, which had cooperated with the United States in the Afghanistan war, that an extremely dangerous terror movement emerged, which commenced operations in the crowded urban centers of the Western, Christian powers.

The Linkage is Revived

The "Big Bang" of January 1991 seemed to have blown away the old argument over the "linkage" which had split the PLO leadership in the Kuwait crisis, but on 1 May 1995, that is, four years after this argument in the PLO had died down, the linkage surfaced from a totally unexpected direction: on the first of that month Yusef al-Azem, one of the leaders of the Muslim Brotherhood in Jordan, published an article in the East Jerusalem daily *a-Nahar*, praising Iraq for the link it had established between Arabism and Islam and lauding the Iraqi Ba'ath Party's stand on Islam – "Arabism is the body and Islam is the soul" – and was unable to conceal his excitement over the new life that was enlightening the religious institutions in Iraq.

Yusef al-Azem, as known, is not just an Islamic theoretician, but a central figure in the world Muslim Brotherhood Movement, and it was with him that Sheikh Yassin worked out the first plot they put into practice when the Hamas had just been established.

Support for Iraq by a man of this type makes us wonder whether the Kuwait crisis gave birth not just to the peace process, but also to the blowing up of the World Trade Center in New York on 26 February 1993. Just as the argument over the linkage was tantamount to a code signifying support for or opposition to Saddam Hussein, so Yusef al-Azem's article should make us ask whether one of the Muslim Brotherhood wings had moved over to support for Iraq. The article should not be seen as linking al-Azem himself to terrorism, it could be considered a milestone marking a possible Iraqi infiltration into the Muslim Brotherhood leadership.

It was Yusef al-Azem who represented the Jordanian Muslim Brotherhood on the movement's Supreme Guidance Committee in Cairo. Since the movement did not recognize the borders between Jordan and the occupied territories, the Muslim Brotherhood in Jordan also represented the Palestinians. Not much is known about this Guidance Committee, which was supposed to be the Muslim

Brotherhood's umbrella organization, other than that it contains thirteen members, most of them Egyptian, but it also has representatives to the movement's branches all over the Muslim world. It was headed by Sheikh Muhammad Abu Nasr.[1]

The existence of a Muslim Brotherhood Movement umbrella committee does not necessarily mean there is complete unanimity among all sections of this enormous movement. The internal arguments in the movement were also reflected among its members, and it is doubtful that all the movement's factions, wherever they were, could have had representation on this committee. Sheikh Yassin, for instance, was not represented on the committee, since the conservative sheikhs had not yet accustomed themselves to a situation in which the Islamic Palestinians had different interests and desires from their colleagues from the eastern side of Jordan and, as they saw it, al-Azem represented both Jordan and Palestine. There is something in al-Azem's article to indicate that the Islamic robe Saddam Hussein donned in the Kuwait crisis gave Iraq a foothold in the Muslim Brotherhood leadership which met in Cairo, and concealed threads may have stretched from Baghdad, via the Muslim Brotherhood in Jordan, to the terror squad which blew up the twin towers in New York. It was not just the desire to take revenge on the United States for the disgrace of the defeat which may have moved Iraq to want to operate terror squads in New York, but an interest in getting the superpower to invest all its energies in its own domestic affairs, to reinforce its isolationist trends so as to create another opportunity for Saddam Hussein to take over the oil reserves of his neighbors to the south. Sheikh Abu Nasr was arrested for "instigation" during the festival of Id al-Adha, in March 1994; but the genuine reason goes far deeper, and was not publicized in Cairo. It was no small matter for the Egyptian Government to arrest such an important Islamic sheikh, with whom it had hoped to establish relations of an alliance, and there is considerably more concealed than disclosed of what goes on in the inner sancta of the Muslim Brotherhood leadership in Cairo.

Responsibility for this act of terror was taken by an Islamic group which had gotten organized in the New Jersey mosque headed by the blind Islamic leader from Egypt, Sheikh Umar Abd a-Rahman, who after a nomadic existence all over the world, had settled down in New York with the generous aid of the US intelligence arms, who wanted to use this type of Muslim Brotherhood movement preacher's help in the war on the Soviets in

Afghanistan. It turns out that the group's pretensions were expanding to many places in the Arab world, but it devoted special attention to the Palestinian problem. It embarked on its terrorist activity at the peak of the Kuwait crisis, with the murder of Rabbi Meir Kahane, the leader of the Israeli Kakh Movement, which was later to be outlawed in Israel because of its terrorist, racist nature. It is interesting to note that New York was one of the arenas of confrontation between Jewish and Islamic extremists, and the intersect struggles in New York also had projections on the territories, and were projected back, from the territories to New York.

Iran, too, could be said to have had an interest in perpetrating the act of terror in New York. Its terror arms are the Hizballah Movement and the Islamic Jihad. No possibility can be entirely dismissed until all the motives are confirmed and out in the open, but the blind sheikh in New York, Umar Abd a-Rahman, clearly belonged to Muslim Brotherhood circles who, with US aid, were active in Afghanistan, not to the various pro-Iranian, anti-US groups. We already know that the pro-Iranian Hizballah definitely did not participate in that war, and judging by the litmus test of the linkage, the Islamic Jihad–Palestine movement headed by Fathi Shqaqi rejected the linkage right from the start, taking clear positions against Saddam Hussein's stands in the Kuwait crisis. In contrast to Sheikh al-Azem and his like, Shqaqi's Islamic Jihad regarded Saddam Hussein as an apostate, dismissing his religious pretensions. A leaflet it published in the territories determined: "The invasion of Kuwait served only . . . to wear out the Arab masses in imaginary battles, far from the Palestinian problem, which is the primary one."[2] This being so, it is only natural that the Hizballah and Islamic Jihad people were not tempted to go to the Islamic conferences Saddam Hussein called in Baghdad to steer Islam against the United States. Iran rejected Saddam Hussein's appeasement attempts, restricting its opposition to the mustering of the Christian armies in the Gulf to verbal statements, nor did it aid the Shi'ite rebellion in southern Iraq immediately after the collapse of Saddam's army, because it believed the United States had an interest in maintaining Iraq's integrity. It was Yusef al-Azem and his like who went to Saddam Hussein's conferences in Baghdad, and it was from among them that the Iraqi intelligence could have recruited terror squads to go to the United States – had it wanted.

Ramzi Yusef and the Islamic Liberation Army

It had not yet become clear whether or not it did want to recruit terror squads, but the CIA, for some time, at least, did indeed think Iraq was interested in recruiting agents from among the Muslim Brotherhood Movement members who had supported it in the crisis. This emerges from an interview the dangerous terrorist, Abd al-Baset Balushi, better known by his undercover name Ramzi Yusef, granted the Arab daily *al-Hayat* from his New York jail in April 1995, after he had been extradited from Pakistan to the United States on suspicion of having prepared the explosive material that blew up the twin towers in the World Trade Center in Manhattan.[3] He confirmed that the Americans suspected him of being an Iraqi agent and wanted to prove that Iraq was supporting him in order to have another pretext for stepping up the pressure on Iraq, but he denied these suspicions: "I have no connection with Iraq, or with any other governmental bodies. I am just one of the supporters of the Liberation Army, which has taken upon itself responsibility for blowing up the World Trade Center building." It was not only the Americans, but also the Pakistanis who interrogated him on his links with Iraq. Judging by what he said, the gist of the main interrogation was his links with Iraq, and the Pakistanis questioned him about bombs that had been planted in Iran. And this is what he said: "The charges by the Pakistani authorities, that I took part in activity against the Irani Government, are also quite incorrect. They are trying to exploit the matter for their own good: by proving that I am funded by Iraq, they are hinting to the Iranian Government that Iraq organized the operations attributed to me inside Iran in order to bring Irani–Iraqi relations to a crisis point." If this was the case, not only did the security authorities of the United States and Pakistan not suspect Iran of backing this terrorist operation, they were investigating a possibility that the Liberation Army had been acting against Iran itself – on a mission for Iraq.

What is this "Liberation Army" Ramzi Yusef was speaking about? He himself replied: "It is a world movement that takes an interest in the problems of the world's armed Islamic movements . . . there is a special way of communicating among them, and the movement has groups and units which take an interest in affairs of the Islamic movements in the different countries . . . Sometimes they take military actions without taking responsibility upon themselves." Ramzi Yusef detailed the Islamic terror movements helped by the Liberation Army: "The Islamic bands (gama'at) and jihad groups in Egypt, the Hamas movement and Islamic Jihad in Palestine, the Liberation Front, and the armed Islamic movements in Algeria, and it almost carried out retaliatory operations in Saudi Arabia, after the series of arrests of Islamic opposition figures made there at the end of 1994 and beginning of 1995." Particularly interesting is his comment on how the different groups communicated among themselves. As will be recalled, when Sheikh Yassin decided in 1983 to set up a link with Yusef al-Azem, he sent him an envoy, with a password identifying him as coming from the Muslim Brotherhood. Were Ramzi Yusef's remarks about the methods used by the different groups for communications among themselves based on the Muslim Brotherhood's passwords?

In any event, the Palestinian problem was Ramzi Yusef's main motive for blowing up the twin towers. Altogether, even though he was born in Kuwait (1968) and was a Palestinian only on his mother's side – his father was Pakistani – he clearly defines his nationality as Palestinian. He has relatives in Haifa, Israel, in Kuwait and in Pakistan. Although he was born and brought up in Kuwait, he categorically denies any connection with Kuwaiti nationalism; he is a Pakistani only from the aspect of his citizenship. He completed his high school studies in Kuwait, and studied electrical engineering at the Swansea University, Wales. He is married, with two daughters. He arrived in the United States on 1 September 1992, leaving there the day of the explosion and becoming the US legal authorities' most important wanted man. The United States offered a reward of two million dollars to anyone informing on him. In January 1995, Pakistan extradited him to the legal authorities in the United States. Ramzi Yusef was not the only Palestinian in the gang. Among the first detainees was Muhammad Salame, born in 1967 in Kafr Bidya in the northwest West Bank, near the towns Tulkarm and Qalqilya, which had always been a center of Islamic Fundamentalist activity. The entire area, and Kafr Bidya in particular, suffered greatly from the Israeli Likud government's "land theft" perpetrated in order to establish large settlements, such as Ariel, all around it. In that region there was a particularly radical Islamic party called the "Islamic Liberation Party"; is the Liberation Army an offspring of that Palestinian party in that region of the West Bank, as its name indicates? It was Salame who packed the explosive materials Ramzi Yusef had prepared into the car and planted it under the twin towers. It was, then, two Palestinians who did the main work. Ramzi explained his motives in these words: "Israel is an illegal state and, morally and legally, its existence is negated, as determined by the resolutions of the [General Assembly of the] United Nations and Security Council . . . and the Palestinian people may take reprisals on them. Any foreign intervention on Israel's behalf is considered a violation of international law and participation in a crime against the Palestinian people. Just as the Palestinians may attack Israel's targets, so they may attack all the targets of those who have intervened on Israel's behalf . . . if the law does not support this, what does [the law] say about my grandmother's house in Haifa and the homes of my relatives in the territories occupied in 1948?" In his opinion, the Palestinians are entitled to attack US targets, because the United States "Is a partner to what is happening in Palestine, because it is funding [Israel] and equipping it with arms from the US tax-payer's money . . . a man like me sees the material aid and weapons pouring in to those who are doing this against his family and homeland. What will he do to stop this aid?"

The avowed motive, of bringing about a stop to the aid to Israel, actually means causing a situation in which the United States will contemplate pulling out of the Middle East. This is in keeping with a possible Iraqi interest: in the wake of the Soviet Union's collapse, to make the United States move toward isolationism, leaving the way clear for the construction of an Islamic Arab power with its center in Baghdad. His positions on the peace process are firm: the territories for peace formulation supported by the PLO is unacceptable, since a situation of normal peace with Israel is unattainable, a cessation of hostilities being the most that can be hoped for. A solution to the Palestinian problem, however, can only be achieved after all the Zionists are evacuated from Palestine, their leaders tried as war criminals, and the Palestinians paid war compensation.

Usama Ibn Ladun: The Saudi Arabian Millionaire Who Crossed the Lines

Despite the CIA's suspicions of Iraq, Ramzi Yusef may have been telling the truth and the Islamic Liberation Army had no link with Iraq. If this was so, who was behind it? Hamas Movement sources in the West Bank point to the Saudi Arabian millionaire Usama Ibn Ladun as backing Ramzi Yusef and his gang. If this is so, the background to the act of terror in New York is linked to the war in Afghanistan, and Sheikh Umar Abd a-Rahman did, after all, go to New York against the backdrop of that war. At that time Pakistan was a meeting place for all sorts of extremist Islamic elements, and Ibn Ladun, with his government's blessing, also went there to help in the war on Communism. When the war ended, Ibn Ladun did not obey his government's orders to disarm and return home, but went to Sudan, from where he used his enormous wealth to support the underground Islamic movements, including the New York group he had got to know in the war in Afghanistan. Ibn Ladun's activity also had a Palestinian connection. Hamas sources in the territories have told the author that he was close to Sheikh Abdallah Azzam, a Palestinian fighter, one of the leaders of the Mujahidin, who fell to an assassin in the Afghan war. The irate Saudi Arabian government removed his citizenship, but he did not appear to be overly upset about this.

Ibn Ladun, Umar Abd a-Rahman, and another member of the New Jersey group, Ahmad Muhammad Ajjaj, had been among Sheikh Azzam's admirers from the time they had worked together in Pakistan and Afghanistan during the war. According to Hamas sources in the territories, it was Ajjaj who brought Ibn Ladun's funds to the New Jersey group.

The Muslim Brotherhood Movement, then, fostered two models of fighting sheikhs with connections to the Palestinian problem: Az a-Din al-Qassam, a Syrian sheikh who had fallen in Palestine and was adopted by the Islamic Jihad and the pro-Syrian, pro-Iranian wings of the Hamas, and Sheikh Abdallah Azzam, a Palestinian sheikh who fell in mysterious circumstances far from his homeland, in distant Afghanistan.

The Muslim Brotherhood Movement is a complex labyrinth, where the unexpected is to be expected. It was actually the wing which had always been considered pro-American which struck a blow at the heart of New York and actually the pro-Syrian, pro-Iranian wing which developed a stream favoring negotiations with the United States.

Abu Marzuq: Founder of "Az a-Din al-Qassam"

It is noteworthy that Ramzi Yusef did not claim he was a representative of the Hamas movement, but was helping it, as he did with all the armed Islamic movements. The Hamas movement lost no time in announcing that it had no connection with the act of terror in the heart of New York, and credence should be placed in this statement. The US security arms, too, were capable of distinguishing between the "Liberation Army" of Ramzi Yusef and the Hamas, and while they pursued Ramzi Yusef to the ends of the world, they built up complex, not necessarily negative, relations with the Hamas. The complexity of the US attitude toward the fundamentalist Palestinian movement originated in the complex developments this movement had undergone and the nature of the internal struggles within it.

In order to understand what happened to the movement in the territories, we must again go back to the Kuwait crisis and the developments in the Islamic movement in the United States. While Ramzi Yusef's "Liberation Army" is suspected of pro-Iraqi trends, another branch of militant Islam based in the United States developed pro-Iranian–Syrian tendencies. Since at that time Syria was a respectable member of the anti-Saddam Hussein coalition and later entered the peace process, the potential emerged for a positive link between this wing and the United States. While all eyes were on the Gulf, in December 1990 the Hamas Movement convened a congress in Kansas City. It was attended by Hamas and Islamic Jihad circles close to Iran. Sheikh Ahmad Yassin, the founder of the Hamas, had no representatives at that congress. The fact that the annual Hamas congress was actually convened in the United States, not the territories, was of importance that went far beyond logistical convenience, that is, the inability to convene such a meeting in the territories under the Israeli conquest. Its genuine importance lay in the transfer of leadership from the inside to the outside – from the founders, Sheikh Yassin and his colleagues, to Abu Marzuq and his colleagues – members of the organization's politbureau, located in Damascus, Tehran, and Amman.

There were many reasons for this transfer, one of the most important being: it was with apprehension and suspicion that the external Muslim Brotherhood leadership followed the development of a sweeping, charismatic movement leadership in the territories, adorning itself in the Intifada's glory. No leader of the Imam Khomeini type ever emerged from within the Muslim Brotherhood Movement, which was actually a collection of colorless functionaries. It had no interest in encouraging the growth of a competing leadership from within the Intifada in Gaza.

This move by the external Muslim Brotherhood leadership had not begun at the Kansas City congress, but some four months previously, in September 1989, when Dr Musa Abu Marzuq arrived in the territories and re-established the Hamas movement; this time not subordinate to Sheikh Yassin, but to he himself, and his politbureau. Abu Marzuq was born in Khan Yunis, in the Gaza Strip. After nomadism in several countries in the world,[4] he settled in the United States, near the capital, Washington. It was Israel that unknowingly enabled him to establish the militant wing of Az a-Din al-Qassam, not just because it was unaware of the importance of his visit to the territories, but by a massive wave of arrests among the activists of Sheikh Yassin's "Majd," such organization commanders as Salah Shada and Ibrahim Abu Samra, and others. Later Sheikh Yassin himself was also arrested. But Israel had no choice, because Sheikh Yassin's militant wing had begun to kidnap and kill Israeli soldiers waiting on the highways for lifts. The man who helped Abu Marzuq to establish the Az a-Din al-Qassam brigades was the young, dynamic Sheikh Jamil Hamami, a key figure in the Hamas activity in the Intifida period in the West Bank. Along with Abu Marzuq, he attended the Hamas congress in Kansas City which, in many senses, was where activists of combatant Islam in the Arab world and Palestine got to know each other. Abu Marzuq also set up links with other Hamas activists in the territories, who afterwards represented his positions: Imad Faluji and Sayyed Abu Musameh, both from Gaza. During his visit to the territories Abu Marzuq did not ally himself with the absolute supporters of Sheikh Yassin, nor did he invite them to the Kansas City congress, and in actual fact he negated Sheikh Yassin's ability to command the militant wing. A Palestinian political activist who participated in the Kansas City congress later told me that its importance actually lay not in what was said there, but in the extensive familiarizations that took place among Islamic activists from not just the Islamic world, but all over, even from Greece and Russia. Outside the speeches hall there were "secondary congresses" in nearby hotels, at which infrastructures may have been worked out for terror organizations of the Az a-Din al-Qassam variety. Abu Marzuq's guests from the territories participated in this extensive series of familiarizations. The congress was given by the Muslim MAYA (Muslim Arab Youth Association), which is attached to the Islamic organizations in the United States. The organization's secretary is Yaser Bushnaq. Abu Marzuq himself was not conspicuous at the official meetings site, and may have spent quite some time keeping an eye on the "secondary sites" in the nearby hotels.

The Three Hamas Wings: Yassin, Ghoshe Abn, Marzuq – and What was Between Them

The establishment of an external politbureau, however, to confront Sheikh Yassin's original Hamas, still did not signify that it spoke with one voice. The politbureau spoke in two voices: that of Abu Marzuq himself and his supporters, such as the representative in Iran, Imad Alami. The other voice was that of Ibrahim Ghoshe, who took a stand in the middle, between the internal leadership and Abu Marzuq.

Abu Marzuq wanted to overthrow Arafat and take his place; the internal leadership, headed by Sheikh Yassin, wanted to exploit the deployment of the first Palestinian administration to reinforce its status. It found an interest in actually reinforcing Arafat in order to grab chunks of the administration. In contrast to him, Abu Marzuq opened offices in Damascus and Tehran and joined the ten rejectionist front organizations under the auspices of Syria and Iran. He also used the Az a-Din al-Qassam to complicate relations between Israel and Arafat. Because of the Az a-Din al-Qassam wing's great power in Gaza, it was difficult for Yassin's people to materialize their intentions of incorporation into Arafat's administration, but their counterparts in the West Bank, headed by Sheikh Hamed Bitawi from Nablus, were incorporated in the religious administration of the Palestinian authority in the West Bank. Sheikh Bitawi himself was appointed head of the Shari'a religious courts in the West Bank. Sheikh Bitawi also headed the "League of Palestinian Sages," which brought together all the veteran Muslim Brotherhood people from before the establishment of the Hamas. The difference between it and Az a-Din al-Qassam is that Bitawi and his people have no connections at all with Syria; on the contrary, they are opposed to any connection with it, in contrast to Abu Marzuq, who is settled in Damascus. Bitawi's people have no militant wing, so they are not involved in terror, but their political position on Israel is uncompromising: in a "fatwa" issued on 19 September 1994 they rejected any agreement with the "conquering infidels" and determined that the agreements with the "Zionists" were a great sin.

In contrast to this, Abu Marzuq's approach is quite the reverse: on the one hand, he operates a militant wing and, on the other, he has a pragmatic approach toward Israel. In an interview one of his people in Gaza, Sheikh Ahmad Bahr, granted the pro-Syrian weekly published in East Jerusalem, *al-Umma*, he said (13 January 1995) that the terror would escalate, but he also ruled that, from the religious aspect, there was nothing against talking to the "Israeli Government"; that is: he does not speak in the old linguistic coinage, containing lack of recognition of Israel. He recalled that Abu Marzuq had issued a political program and ruled that "There is no alternative to a dialogue [with the Israeli government] if it gives the Palestinian people its rights." As opposed to the uncompromising "fatwa" of those clerics who decided to join the Palestinian administration on anything involving recognition of Israel, Az a-Din al-Qassam's leaflets, including those taking responsibility for the kidnapping and killing of IDF soldiers, addressed Israel as an existing fact, appealed to the "Israeli Government," and put forward all sorts of demands that may also be regarded as the beginning of a presentation of positions for future negotiations, such as the October 1994 leaflet explaining the kidnapping of the soldier Nachshon Wachsman as a means to fulfil demands against the "Judaization of Jerusalem." That is: through this violent path, Az a-Din al-Qassam was trying to compel the "Israeli Government" to conduct some sort of negotiations over Jerusalem with it.

Nonetheless, the internal division is not so clearcut. Sheikh Bitawi's fatwa also mentions the possibility of a "hudna," that is, a cease-fire with Israel. Non-recognition of Israel does not mean eternal war, a state of a cessation of hostilities also comes into account, but without recognition of Israel. In December 1992, that is, more than a year before the publication of the Oslo agreements, Dr Mahmud Zahhar, known to be one of Sheikh Yassin's people in Gaza, issued a similar program calling for a disengagement between the Israeli Army and the Palestinians in Gaza. He said: "The Intifada is tied up with the occupation, and if the occupation distances itself from the occupied lands, the severity of the confrontation between the Palestinians and the occupation's soldiers will automatically be eased. But if the occupation and its soldiers remain, and with them the settlers, nothing in the world will be able to stop the people from upholding the precept of the jihad."[5]

If this is the case, the wing relying on Damascus is prepared to speak with Israel, but is escalating the terror in order to achieve a strong position against it. Anyone who is prepared to speak with Israel obviously want to overthrow Arafat and take over his place. In its June 1994 edition the movement's organ, the *Falastin al-Muslim*, a monthly, published an article by one of the Hamas leaders in Washington, Dr Ahmad Yusef, on the Hamas' options, which are: political activity; the "Jihadist opposition"; or a combination of "opposition" and political activity.

As for the option of dedication to political activity, Dr Yusef hinted at internal differences of opinion. He reported that the Hamas was faced with the option of joining the self-rule institutions in order to participate in elections, but: "this option . . . second rank cadres and the Az a-Din al-Qassam brigades reject it. This is a burden which the Hamas Movement's decision-makers are incapable of overcoming." From these remarks it may be understood that the "first rank" level, that is, the veteran generation of clerics, the original pre-Intifada Muslim Brotherhood people, want to join the PLO's autonomy, but their way is blocked by the militant echelons and the younger generation of activists who grew up in the Intifada.

Dr Yusef's attitude toward the jihad issue is noteworthy. He rejects the option of a continuation of the "pure" jihad, saying it would set all those participating in the peace process against the Hamas. Moreover, he cast doubts on the Hamas' ability to withstand this coalition: "At this stage the risks involved in this option are grave, it will cost more than the movement can pay and exist. All the more as America and many Arab countries are being caught up in this arrangement, and want to implement it by force. These are extremely hard conditions, and use of the jihad alone will make the movement a target for all the official forces in the area and bring about an alliance against it between the Israeli rule and the Palestinians . . . " This leads Dr Yusef to the main option, a combination of the jihad and political activity.

Abu Marzuq and the Americans

On 25 July 1995, one day after a terror operation in Ramat Gan, one of the suburbs of Israel's Tel Aviv, Abu Marzuq was arrested in the United States. His arrest, however, should not mislead us. The US Administration was in constant touch with the Hamas politbureau, including with Abu Marzuq himself, and this process peaked when, in January–February 1995, Abu Marzuq met in Washington with US officials.

The United States had never followed a policy of confrontation with Islam and after it was actually from the wing of its former friends, the admirers of Sheikh Azzam, that Ramzi Yusef's underground emerged, it was only natural for Washington to try its luck with the pro-Syrian, pro-Iranian wing of those who revered al-Qassam's memory.

The blowing up of the twin towers in New York cut short, officially, too, an important move by the Western countries, including the United States, toward the beginnings of political contacts with the Hamas; in point of fact, with Abu Marzuq's politbureau. Diplomats from several Western countries, including Spain and Denmark, Britain and Italy, met with Hamas representatives in Jordan, Cairo and Khartoum. On 3 March 1993, the Hamas Movement in Amman issued a statement of regret about the previous day's US announcement on a stop to the contacts with the Hamas. State Department Spokesman Richard Boucher confirmed that his country was conducting talks with people affiliated to the Hamas, but the State Department ordered the talks stopped. A Hamas representative in Amman, Muhammad Nazzal, said the contacts with the Western countries were not just for the "purpose of minutes," but were practical, and the Hamas had used them to make its positions clear on a series of issues, including terror. He reported that there had been two contacts with the "political counsellor" in the US Embassy in Amman, but when the movement demanded a meeting with Ambassador Roger Harrison, it encountered a refusal. Nazzal said the movement had prepared a document on its positions and had already submitted it to the ambassadors of Germany, Italy and Britain at meetings with them in the Jordanian capital, and it also intended to meet with representatives of Russia, Japan, France, Canada and China.

The very fact of the Hamas' striving for official contact with the United States arouses interest, since it conflicts sharply with the approach by Ramzi Yusef, the Islamic terrorist from New York. The Hamas did not publish the salient points it had brought to the Western powers' attention, and Hamas sources in Hebron have told us the Hamas world-view was that its militant struggle was anchored in international law and the UN Charter, covering people fighting for liberation from occupation. What this implies is that the Hamas is not striving for Israel's destruction, but for the fulfilment of the Palestinian rights in a state whose regime is to be based on the Islamic Shari'a. The Islamic movement cannot afford Israel de jure recognition, but if Israel agrees to restore the Palestinians' rights, a version of a "hudna" – a cease-fire of the type known in the Middle Ages between the Islamic caliphates and the Christian countries – could be found. The Hamas is committed to waging a jihad on Israel, because Israel has not willingly granted the Palestinians their rights. The Hamas has undertaken not to harm civilians, but only the soldiers of the occupation, as bound by the rules of war. And indeed, for a certain period of time the Hamas concentrated its militant activity against soldiers, as though to abide by its commitments to the West, but not for long. In the course of 1994 there were several attacks by Az a-Din al-Qassam brigades on Israeli civilians at bus stops and in the heart of Tel Aviv. The strings led not to Ghoshe in Amman, but straight to Abu Marzuq in Damascus. This terror was designed to signal to the West that it was Abu Marzuq, not Ghoshe, who held the strings. This signal was important for Abu Marzuq, not just because Western diplomacy had opted to ignore him, but because he had genuine differences of opinion with his colleagues in the politbureau in Amman, as was revealed at a meeting with Arafat in Khartoum: while Ghoshe was prepared to renew the link with Arafat in the format of the common struggles in Gaza against the pro-Syrian left, Abu Marzuq was determined to push Arafat until he fell. His locating himself in Damascus and Tehran was no coincidence.

Ultimately, Western interest in Ghoshe did indeed die down, and despite the US decision to sever the link with the Hamas – it was never stopped. US diplomatic sources have told us the connection with elements in Gaza were continued in devious ways.

Despite all the reversals, the basic fact must be noted that the Hamas did show an interest in talking with the United States. It is no less important, however, to follow the developments in the PLO's pro-US wing, that of Abu Iyyad's successors.

13

Who is to Succeed Abu Iyyad?

The London Forum

While Abd a-Shafi was working for an alliance with the organizations, particularly those on the left, Husseini was trying to tighten his links with the powerful Iyyadist wing in the diaspora. London was one of the important focal points for the formulation of the Palestinian delegation, under the auspices of PLO representative Afif Safia. As will be recalled, over the years Safia had been one of the critics of the PLO's policy, and he summoned Palestinian intellectuals from the most important of the Western universities, who also had harsh criticism of the PLO.

Many of these professors, such as Kamil Mansur from Paris and the Khaldis – Walid, Rashid and Ahmad – from London, later held positions in the PLO delegations in the multinational track, or in the advisory committees of the bilateral talks. Edward Said and Ibrahim Abu Lughd from the United States decided to waive their membership of the Palestine National Council (September 1992), both as a sign of protest over the PLO policy in the crisis, but also, and primarily, so that they could go to the territories and maintain regular contacts with the Iyyadist wing of the Palestinian delegation. The focal points of the Iyyadist wing's power can be delineated by following these London meetings: as well as the leaders of the diaspora Palestinians, Husseini and Ashrawi from the territories also went to the deliberations in London, and were later joined by people from the FIDA party-to-be, such as Zahira Kamal; the Cairo group was represented by Nabil Sha'ath. The deliberators were later also joined by several genuine PLO people, such as Naser al-Qudwa, the organization's UN representative. In any event, the PLO people's joining the discussions only reinforced the legitimacy of the London forum, whose members were all "personalities" or "advisers," without any arms-bearers or representatives of the "organizations." Needless to say, Abd a-Shafi shook the dust of that forum off his feet.

Safia's gatherings took place halfway through 1991 and from September on the "Arab Club," the official name of the London forum, issued official statements giving the impression that it was a new organizational framework. For instance, at the beginning of September 1991, this forum sent the Israeli Government a letter via the United States, containing a list of the twenty-eight gestures required for confidence-building with the Palestinians. This list followed on from the famous fourteen demands the "national personalities" put to Rabin on the outbreak of the Intifada, and was the basis for the deliberations of the subcommittee on human rights affairs. These were issues afflicting the Palestinians in the Intifada, such as the Israelis' trigger-happiness, the return of the deportees, a stop to the demolition of houses, granting freedom of political organization, freedom of speech and expression, non-interference with regular school studies, etc. The letter to the United States also enumerated demands in respect of the guarantees to be given to the Palestinians.

The fact that Safia described these demands as coming from the PLO only reinforced the inner feelings of those organization members who had not participated in the gatherings, that the reference was to the establishment of a new PLO, with an Iyyadist nature.[1]

In these deliberations the decision was made, inter alia, to appoint Ashrawi as spokeswoman of the Palestinian delegation-to-be. This could be learned from Ashrawi's statement in London that the Arab Club had decided to establish a "Palestinian information institution, to appeal to world public opinion in modern terms."[2]

Yaser Abd a-Rabbo, the head of the PLO's information department, was not happy with this statement. Nor was Professor Said pleased that this position was given to Ashrawi, since he thought she did not have the skills required to cope with the main task: that of changing the Arab's repellent image in Western public opinion. As will be recalled, these were the grounds for his criticism of Arafat's support for Saddam Hussein. He thought Hanan Ashrawi was incapable of shouldering this burden. On one of his visits to the territories, Professor Said granted an interview to the *al-Fajr* daily[3] in which he ruled that over the previous two years Ashrawi had proved she had absolutely no understanding of US affairs.

In another statement Nabil Sha'ath made on behalf of the London forum, he confirmed that the participants had discussed the Palestinian representation at the peace conference and that these deliberations had been held behind closed doors.[4] He cited an official release, reporting that the deliberations had revolved around three issues: Palestinian information in the United States, the realization of the national goals as formulated by the PLO, and how the distress of the Palestinians in the territories could be demonstrated to the world. The deliberations focused on the question of how to build a new political and informational tool for the Palestinians, which would be more efficient than the old PLO in its appeal to Western public opinion. No less important was the fact that the new framework had begun issuing official statements in the PLO's name, and the Jihadist wing viewed this as evidence of the intention to establish a new PLO, without it.

Remarks made by Ashrawi when she went to Amman from London the following June also testify that the London deliberators dealt with internal Palestinian affairs, too. She called for elections to be held in the territories: to a Palestinian parliament.[5] At that time the Palestinian delegation was indeed preoccupied with attempts to persuade the Israeli delegation of the need for elections to be held in the territories to a council with legislative rights, but nobody disputed the fact of the Palestine National Council being the authorized Palestinian parliament. The need to determine the Palestinian leadership through elections was dominant in the London Club's closed discussions, and no wonder the deliberations were held behind closed doors.

These views were also shared by Nabil Sha'ath. It was generally hard to catch out Sha'ath, who was cautious about what he said, saying anything that deviated from what had also been agreed by the organizations. Moreover, many of his statements in the Arab press certainly could befit the weapons-bearers. He kept his genuine views very much to himself, in order to disclose them when the time was right, but from time to time he let dissident statements slip through. In September 1992 the *al-Aalam al-Yom* weekly[6] wrote of the risks to the PLO involved in autonomy. It said that, despite the PLO's control over the delegation members, it was aware that autonomy would come at its expense. PLO members were quoted as saying they were not prepared to agree to elections in the territories, because there would be a clash between the two parliaments: the PLO's, and the parliament in the territories.

It is important to address Nabil Sha'ath's remarks on this issue. In contrast to these unnamed members, he actually supported elections in the territories and thought the elected council in the territories could be incorporated in the National Council; and it was no coincidence that the Palestinians were demanding 180 members for the legislative council in the territories, since this was the number set for the PLO council. These positions are still acceptable to extensive circles in the PLO, despite the fear that elections in the territories would topple the PLO institution's superiority. But Sha'ath kept the sting in his remarks for the end. He said that immediately after the proclamation of the Palestinian state, the PLO would disappear, all Palestinians would be citizens of the state, the Palestinians outside and inside would be combined, and if Arafat wished to continue as leader, he would have to compete for the position in elections.

Sha'ath did, of course, cover himself, sketching out an apocalyptic scenario, but in the immediate sense his remarks signified that Arafat was not an elected leader, and this was a blot on the legitimacy of his leadership. The blot would be rectified when the Palestinian state chose its leadership through elections. Nor did Sha'ath conceal the genuine aims of the peace process: to put an end to the uprising and get the Palestinians to move over to patterns of democratic political behavior befitting Western criteria. It is extremely doubtful whether this was also the vision of Habash and Hawatma, or even of Shahin, from among the leaders of the Fatah militant wing.

FIDA also shared this concept. When I met in Tunis with one of its leaders, Mamduh Nawfal, he reiterated his fears that Arafat would prefer a police state to a one founded on elections.[7] "Rabin and Arafat have one thing in common: neither of them wants elections. The Palestinian opposition is helping Arafat in this. They are creating an emergency situation, to enable Rabin and Arafat to evade elections and establish a police state in the area to be evacuated. FIDA will insist on elections being held, and we will not give up."

In April 1990, that is, before the Gulf crisis, Sha'ath visited Holland and made remarks that went beyond what was acceptable to the militant wing: the Camp David agreements could be a "limited basis" for far-reaching arrangements between Israel and the Palestinians.[8] He did, it is true, add that there could also be other bases, but in the final analysis, his remarks were an important crack in the Palestinian refusal to accept the Camp David agreements as a basis for discussions.

Dr Hisham Sharabi of Georgetown University, Washington DC, disclosed further details of the genuine mood among these circles in an interview he granted the *a-Nahar* daily.[9] Sharabi disagreed with the view that had become accepted by the public, that the Palestinian delegation did not have the people's support, claiming it was Israel's tough policy that was creating this feeling. He strongly defended the Palestinian delegation, revealing that the Center of Palestinian Studies in Washington, headed by him, was supplying the Palestinian delegation with the material it needed for its work. He said he was convinced that they had to persist in working to achieve peace with Israel at any price, because the Palestinians had been "defeated in their hundred years' war on the Israelis," and now they had to save what they could, "even if it involves concessions on what we consider to be basic national and human rights." Sharabi went on: "We entered into talks and became absorbed in the current political activity in order to maintain Palestinian existence on Palestinian soil. If we succeed in reaching a solution with the Labor Government . . . we will be able to say we succeeded at the last minute, despite our historic fragility as Arabs and Palestinians against Israel, to rescue a foothold, which will guarantee the Palestinians sections of their land and remove the nightmare of annihilation and maintain the Palestinian identity and Palestinian right."

An important comment by Sharabi should be noted in this interview. He reported that Dr Muhammad Hallaj, the head of the Palestinian teams to the multinational track, was on the staff of his research institute in Washington, and it was he who was his contact – that is, not the PLO – in the multinational talks. Hallaj also headed the Palestinian delegation on refugee affairs; the delegation that dealt with the most sensitive issue, as far as the Palestinians were concerned. Hallaj did not continue for long with his work, and Ahmad Qrei', Abu al-Ala, also from the Iyyadist wing, replaced him. It is no coincidence that the Palestinians took moderate stands in the discussions on the refugees, in the spirit of Abu Iyyad's legacy. In retrospect, these replacements were to be of decisive importance, since Abu al-Ala was conducting contacts with the Israeli Foreign Ministry on the agreement signed by Abu Mazen, Abu al-Ala's superior. With time it was to emerge that Abu Mazen was the leader of the Iyyadist wing, Abu Iyyad's direct successor and executor of his will.

When Sharabi was asked about his institute's connection with the Palestinian delegation and the PLO's link with it, he said this delegation had proved that it was capable of overcoming the "bureaucracy," the usual term of censure for the PLO, and was acting in a way that, for the first time, was making US public opinion treat the Palestinians as a nation of human beings. In other words, Sharabi and Said were unanimous on the image damage the PLO had inflicted on the Palestinians.

Faisal Husseini, the delegation head, was very close to this approach, but did not often speak of it. At the same time, there was a hint of his genuine mood in remarks he made to Palestinian teachers in East Jerusalem in September 1992: "Nobody conceded Andalus [the Arab name for Spain], nevertheless Arab Andalus is now Christian Spain."[10]

The Cairo Bureau – Cradle of the Oslo Agreement

It would be a mistake to view the Iyyadist wing as being one complete block. Over the years there were internal struggles within it which gave rise to severe tensions between the two camps which, logically, should have helped each other; we are talking of Husseini's camp in Jerusalem and Abu Mazen's camp, which had one of its most important centers in Cairo.

Abu Mazen viewed Husseini not as an Iyyadist right from the start, but a new recruit – after the Gulf war. He hoped that after the war the Americans would continue the dialogue they had begun with Abu Iyyad with him, recognizing him as his successor. Abu Mazen accepted the verdict and at first he helped Husseini, but when he realized he was inacapable of overcoming the obstacles Arafat was setting in his path, he decided to get rid of him and take his place.

In the two years following the Gulf War, Abu Mazen and Nabil Sha'ath supported the Palestinian delegation headed by Husseini. Immediately after the war, there was a seminar in the Stanford University in the United States, where leftist groups from Israel attained a joint paper with the PLO. The figures from Israel formed the impression that Nabil Sha'ath, the head of the Palestinian delegation, was in regular touch with Husseini and took orders from him. In the following two years, when Husseini and Abu Mazen visited the Gulf states to muster funds for the Palestinians, Husseini was the official spokesman and Abu Mazen, the escort. Back then, when Abu Mazen and Hakam Bal'awi had managed to force a chink in the oil states' rejectionist wall for aid for the Palestinians, they had to call on Hanan Ashrawi to join them because of the Gulf States' insistence that the seniority be given to Palestinians in the territories.

Both Nabil Sha'ath and Abu Mazen were involved in the Iyyadist center in Cairo, and two years after the end of the war, policy lines began to develop which did not fit in with those of Husseini, and it began to demand the Iyyadist seniority for itself.

Egypt did not support Husseini's camp, keeping faith with Abu Mazen and his people. Unlike Husseini's camp, Egypt opted for the "Gaza first" formula, and worked hard for the talks with Israel on this formula to be conducted by Abu Mazen, not the Husseini camp. Husseini preferred the "West Bank first" formula, which gave preference to resolving the problems of the West Bank, not Gaza, because of its proximity to Egypt and the mutual influences between Islamic fanaticism in Gaza and Egypt. Egypt also hoped Abu Mazen's camp would make the Palestinians accept the Camp David agreements line. As stated, Nabil Sha'ath was prepared to accept the Camp David agreements, but Husseini's delegation continued to reject them. It was very important to the Egyptians for the Palestinians to grant legitimacy in retrospect to the agreements signed by Egypt and Israel.

It is, then, no coincidence that Egypt backed the Oslo agreements and gave Abu Mazen's people their legal adviser, Taher Shash, whom Husseini had rejected for the delegation to Washington at his meeting with Mubarak immediately after the Washington talks began. It was the different centers of the group which supported Husseini's wing in the delegation when it was just starting out that actually set its goals: the territories center articulated the desire to transfer the center of the Palestinians' political activity from the exterior to the interior; the Cairo center voiced support for the Camp David agreements as the basis for the peace talks in the Palestinian track, too; the Western diaspora center expressed the exiled Palestinian leaders' desire for Palestinian nationalism to be formulated in accordance with norms of Western democracy, and an enlightened society established in Palestine, to bring about an upheaval in the Arab's image in the West. All these goals were in conflict with the mentality of the classic PLO, which felt hostility toward the West, took an active anti-US policy, retained a nationalist-Marxist or Islamic fundamentalist ideology, and whose democracy was a gun democracy, as Arafat phrased it.

The al-Hasan Brothers and the Focal Point in the Gulf

Another of the Iyyadist wing's focal points was the leadership of the al-Hasan brothers, mainly that of Khaled and Hani. This camp did not integrate with others, but followed its own policy; its base was in Saudi Arabia and the Gulf. Bilal, their youngest brother, had his political roots in Hawatma's Democratic Front. He had indeed abandoned Hawatma some considerable time before this, but found it difficult to actually come out against Arafat, like his two brothers. Before the crisis he had edited a Palestinian weekly issued in Paris, *al-Yom a-Sabe'* (The Seventh Day) in which he took an acutely anti-American line. At the same time, he did not support the linkage idea in the Gulf crisis; in actual fact, he never became involved in that argument. After the war, the weekly was cut down in scale and later closed down because of budgetary difficulties. The eldest brother, Ali, was their liaison with the Hamas.

When the anti-Saddam coalition was giving some thought to the postwar period, Khaled al-Hasan was its candidate to participate in the "troika" which was to replace Arafat, together with Abu Iyyad and Abu Mazen. On the eve of the eruption of the fighting, Khaled al-Hasan, together with Abu Iyyad and his people, was toiling over the preparations for the Fatah's central council meeting, at which they were going to demand some accounting from Arafat. Abu Iyyad's liquidation silenced Khaled al-Hasan. After the war his health deteriorated, too, and he never recovered. His main contribution to the Palestinians' post-war political effort was the publication of his program for a Swiss-style tripartite confederation between Israel, the Palestinians, and Jordan. Jordanian King Hussein rejected the model, but his brother, Crown Prince Hasan, accepted it. Khaled al-Hasan supported a renewal of the joint Jordanian-Palestinian delegation, thus actually expressing non-confidence in the Palestinian delegation headed by Husseini.

Hani al-Hasan was more active than his brothers but, surprisingly, his activity was among the combatant cadres, and he put pressure on Arafat from within the Fatah's military wing. In contrast to all the opponents of Saddam Hussein's linkage initiative, Hani al-Hasan's political development was unusual. On several occasions he added his signature to petitions by the arms-bearers, coming very close to the rejectionist organizations in Damascus. In the wake of his meeting with King Fahd, he spoke of his loyalty to him, sending him a letter of support. As the war came closer, however, his position changed, and he predicted that the United States would lose the long war of attrition Saddam Hussein was going to impose on it. He accompanied Arafat on his visits to Baghdad even after Abu Iyyad had ceased these visits. In so doing, not only did he avoid assassinate attempts against him, he put down roots in the military wing, almost certainly with Saudi Arabia's approval, in order to strike out at Arafat from within that wing. The change that occurred in Hani al-Hasan was, then, tactical, not genuine. In actual fact, from within the military wing he complimented the pressure Arafat was exerting from within Abu Mazen's political wing.

At the Fatah revolutionary council session that met in June 1992, Hani al-Hasan submitted a position paper proposing an alternative to Arafat's policy. Hani al-Hasan attacked Arafat on three main points: (1) for the fact that his policy was not taking into account the possibilities embodied in an appeasement with Saudi Arabia; (2) for the fact that Arafat's policy was producing a clash with the Palestinian opposition, particularly with the Hamas, instead of adopting these movements into the peace process framework; (3) for the fact that the Palestinian delegation was ignoring the "Arab–Palestinian" dimension and concentrating solely on the "Palestinian dimension," that is, on the special issues of the Palestinians in the territories, and rejecting a link with the outside.[11]

In July 1993, Hani al-Hasan and other Fatah seniors, such as Abbas Zaki, met with Arafat in Tunis, daring to speak their minds to him. Arafat told them they were acting like Abu Musa, who had rebelled against him in the Lebanon war, so they would have to resign. Their response to him was that they were the genuine Fatah, and it was he who would have to resign.

Khaled al-Hasan, his elder brother, was also the senior of the brothers in the political sense. In May 1991, Faruq Qaddumi, the head of the PLO's political department, reported that Khaled al-Hasan and Hakam Bal'awi, his colleague in the "Central Surveillance" mechanism, "a-Rasd al-Markazi," one of the mainstays of Force 17 and the PLO ambassador in Tunis, had put themselves forward as candidates to succeed Abu Iyyad and Abu al-Hol.

Arafat's stand on this is not known. As for Khaled al-Hasan – he was not given any such position, and remained head only of the Palestine National Council's foreign affairs committee. Hakam Bal'awi succeeded in entering the Fatah Central Committee. Arafat had no interest in the rapid promotion of such absolute representatives of the Iyyadist wing.

Despite his absolute affiliation to the Iyyadist wing, Khaled was not far from Hani's positions on reservations about the Palestinian delegation. This issue was the main bone of contention between the Saudi center of the Iyyadist wing and the diaspora in the West. Another important bone of contention was Khaled al-Hasan's reservations about Abu Iyyad's interpretation of the actualization of the right to return.

In April 1992, Khaled al-Hasan granted an interview to the London daily *al-Hayat*.[12] In the interview, he described his world view at length, focusing primarily on the familiar idea of the tripartite confederation.

According to him, the main drawback in conducting the peace talks – as his brother Hani had maintained to the members of the Fatah Revolutionary Council – was that it ignored the pan-Arab issue, focusing on purely Palestinian affairs. He announced that he could not accept any concession on the right to return and that, immediately after the actualization of the "current stage" of the peace talks, that is, autonomy, he would establish a political party to represent the 1948 refugees, since it was inconceivable to him that the right to return should be conceded. At the same time, he expressed his Iyyadist position by rejecting the organizations and ruling that, with the actualization of the interim stage, the PLO would have to disband, and also in his concept of Palestinian security. He said: "I know that several organizations have put the democratic reform issue on the agenda, and I hope they will do this in the right way . . . not in order to gain some achievements for the organizations, so that the leadership will come from the people, not from the organizations." His concepts were identical with those of the future FIDA. His statement that he would establish a party, not an organization, also carried an Iyyadist message. When Arafat met with Hamas people in Khartoum, he warned them not to establish a party, but to join the PLO as an organization.

On this issue, it is important to note his positions on the future of the PLO. When asked why he would not act within the PLO framework, only from the outside, he replied: "As for the PLO, its role will come to an end immediately after the return of the territories conquered in 1967, for the organizations within it will become a party within the Palestinian entity." This, in his view, gave rise to the need to establish a party to represent the 1948 refugees and see to it that the right to return was not taken away.

Despite his disagreement with Abu Iyyad over the right to return, Khaled al-Hasan certainly was Iyyadist on the major issue of Palestinian security. He did not believe the Palestinians were capable of defending themelves through the combatant organizations. He anticipated that sooner or later they would disintegrate. In any event, "There is no place in modern history for small states, and total independence has no standing in the new world economy." In his view, "the solution is regional" and Palestinian security would also be "regional security." This is a variation of Abu Iyyad's concept of a demilitarized Palestinian state. Abu Iyyad spoke of demilitarization and protection by international forces. Khaled al-Hasan, too, did not base Palestinian security on a Palestinian army, but on regional security arrangements. (Incidentally, Faisal Husseini voiced similar positions on various occasions.)

Another aspect of the al-Hasan brothers' basically Iyyadist approach was their positive attitude toward the contacts with the Israelis. The leftist Matityahu Peled, one of the first to seek a way to approach the PLO, later testified that it had been Khaled al-Hasan who, to the best of his ability, had helped to actualize these contacts in the earliest days.[13] As far as is known, Hani al-Hasan also participated in the contacts with the Israelis prior to the outbreak of the Gulf War, meeting, among others, in Paris with Yossi Ginosar, one of the Israeli security service seniors.

Khaled al-Hasan's "regional" concept also creates an opening to a "regional" solution to the refugee problem; that is, the problem did not actually have to be resolved in Palestine, but in the Arab world, since the al-Hasan brothers were speaking of the problem's "Arab depth," after all. At the same time, they did not want the problem resolved in accordance with this framework. This was a knotty problem to which there was no answer. If every difficulty, including Palestinian security, were to be resolved regionally, why should the right to return not be realized regionally, that is, they would be settled where they were living and nevertheless be considered Palestinian citizens.

In other camps of the Iyyadist wing, including that of Abu al-Ala, who conducted the talks with Israel on refugee affairs, the approach was clearly that it was not essential for the refugee problem to actually be resolved in the territories, they could be settled wherever they were living in the Arab world.

What did the al-Hasan brothers mean by attacking the delegation for a lack of "Arab depth"? Hani al-Hasan meant that there was no close link with Saudi Arabia. His brother Khaled was referring mainly to the absence of a healthy link with Jordan. When he was in Amman in the August of 1991, Khaled supported the joint Jordanian–Palestinian delegation format, because the "establishment of an independent Palestinian delegation meant the rejection of any chance that the delegation would succeed . . . Israel would not give the delegation a single sentence of agreement."[14] In that interview the Iyyadists' main goal – the elimination of the PLO – was expressed in his proposal for the establishment of a temporary Palestinian government.

Hani and Khaled were Kuwaiti citizens, and Khaled's pronouncements on the desired link with Jordan raised the tension with the Kuwaiti government, which took away his citizenship. This did not particularly bother him, and he upped roots, to Jedda. The Saudi Arabians realized that the tripartite confederation model was to Jordan's disadvantage, because with a tripartite model Jerusalem, the meeting point between Israel and the Palestinians, might develop into the principal quasi-capital of the tripartite confederation, pushing Amman out to the fringes, and they may have supported it secretly. In any event, Khaled al-Hasan, like his brother, naturally favored the desired link with Saudi Arabia and, like Hani, favored the Hamas' inclusion within the PLO, and certainly within the Palestine National Council. In an interview he granted the BBC on 1 May 1991, Khaled al-Hasan levelled criticism at US Secretary of State James Baker's meetings with Husseini and Ashrawi, maintaining that they would not get the PLO out of its isolation. The solution, according to him, was Arab: a joint delegation with Jordan and a temporary Palestinian government, that is, the organizations' elimination. The Palestinians had to rely on Saudi Arabia and Egypt. In an interview he granted in Jedda, he added the importance of reliance on Syria, expressing his confidence that the United States was serious this time in its attempts to found peace in the Middle East.[15] Khaled al-Hasan's firm views on the matter of non-conceding the right to return was unusual in this wing of the PLO. Abu Iyyad had also not given up the right to return, it is true, but he was prepared to hedge it about with reservations that do not exist in Khaled al-Hasan's approach. In principle, the Palestinians' pragmatic approach in the deliberations of the committee on refugee affairs in the multinational track originated in the fact that it was headed by people affiliated to the Iyyadist wing, from Hisham Sharabi's pragmatic school of thought. The al-Hasan brothers' reservations about Husseini's delegation were to be of great importance in the course of time. Saudi Arabia's attitude toward Husseini cooled the more it came to realize that he was not capable of, or not interested in, rising to the status of Arafat's replacement.

The "Arab" versus the "Palestinian" approach was a genuine bone of contention between Khaled al-Hasan and Faisal Husseini. At the end of March 1992, Khaled al-Hasan issued a statement that led, a year later, to the breakdown between the Cairo center and the Abu Iyyad's successors' East Jerusalem center. Khaled al-Hasan called for Egypt to be enabled to demand the return of the Gaza Strip, on the basis of Resolution 242, and supported the immediate foundation of a confederation with Jordan, to enable Jordan to demand the West Bank. Al-Hasan made these remarks in Tunis, on the fringes of the Fatah senior echelons' deliberations on the confederation issue.

There was more unanimity between the centers in Cairo and the Gulf than with the group around Husseini, and although they were supposed to help each other, there was only partial cooperation between them. When the Palestinian delegation was still just setting out, Abu Mazen and Nabil Sha'ath did indeed back it, but the more time passed and the different political approaches became more accentuated, a crisis also emerged within the Iyyadist wing. It was from this crisis between Abu Mazen and Husseini that the Israeli–Palestinian agreement grew later, in September 1993.

$$* \qquad * \qquad *$$

When reviewing the structure of the Iyyadist forces which conducted the political process in that window of opportunities which opened up after the Gulf War, Husseini's group can be seen on the one hand, and Abu Mazen's group on the other. Husseini's group wanted to achieve an interim solution for all the territories, giving the West Bank and East Jerusalem preference over Gaza. With the encouragement of the United States, this group improved its relations with Jordan, after there had been difficulties between them at the beginning of the process. Arafat regarded this group as the main threat to his status. After Arafat's failure to establish an alliance against it with Hussein or the Hamas, he pinned his hopes on the agreement that was being worked out between Israel and the Iyyadist group's opposing bloc which had its center in Cairo, headed by Abu Mazen.

There were basic differences of opinion between the two wings: in principle, they both accepted Abu Iyyad's framework as formulated in "Lowering the Sword." While Husseini, however, failed to establish any significant relations with Saudi Arabia, moving closer and closer to Jordan, Abu Mazen's group based itself in Cairo, Jordan's rival from the time of the Gulf crisis, and when Husseini failed to promote the talks in Washington and let the Saudi Arabians down by his lack of ability, or will, to sever himself from Arafat, at the last minute Abu Mazen's group did succeed in defeating Husseini and his people, thanks to the links the Oslo agreement had created with Israel.

Abu Iyyad's successors' wing took over all the negotiating tracks in the multinational talks, and the delegation heads appointed were all figures who had had connections, in one way or another, with Abu Iyyad in his lifetime. One of the principal reasons for this was that the other wings in the PLO and the Fatah Organization did not want to participate in the peace talks.

The original Iyyadist wing, of Abu Mazen and his colleagues in Tunis, had a conspicuous edge in the multinational track. While the composition of the Palestinian delegations to the multinational track was quite homogeneous – most of the figures were among Abu Mazen's people – it was difficult for Husseini to control how things were going in the bilateral track in Washington, since the delegation had a construction made up of a complex bunch of parties and groups which did not accept Husseini's discipline, and Arafat had appointed Haidar Abd a-Shafi, a tough, uncompromising man, over them all.

The diaspora in the United States continued to support Husseini, and did not look kindly on Arafat's success in wriggling out of the pincers in which he found himself after the war. Professor Said turned down Clinton's invitation to participate in the mutual PLO–Israel recognition ceremony, even though he himself had texted the ideological platform for that mutual recognition. Six months later, Professor Said called for Arafat's dismissal. His reason for so doing was that Said's group regarded the delegation from the territories not as a delegation whose goal was to hold negotiations, but a tool to change the PLO's face and exhibit a positive image of the new Palestinian, acceptable to Western public opinion. They were very disappointed when they saw Arafat's unacceptable figure on the White House lawn. They constituted a tough opposition to the Tunis leadership, and it was not easy for them to digest their defeat. Arafat did not invite Husseini to the ceremony in the White House, and Husseini had not intended to go, but the Americans persuaded him to trample on his honor. He went to the ceremony, but his gloomy countenance in the back rows of the guests gave away his dissatisfaction.

Along with the rivalry that developed between Abu Mazen's wing and Husseini's delegation, an enigmatic Saudi Arabian wing, of the two Khaled and Hani al-Hasan brothers, who were among the Fatah's founders, was active, exerting pressure on Arafat from within the military cadres. Like Abu Mazen, they were disappointed by Baker's decision to carry on the link that had begun with Abu Iyyad with Husseini, rather than with the wing in Tunis, but they expressed this differently. While Abu Mazen was putting all his energies into political activities, Hani al-Hasan was actuallly deepening his links with the military wing, and it was from that wing that he demanded that Arafat rely on Saudi Arabia.

14

Ashrawi or Qaddumi? Washington or Paris?

After Abu Iyyad's liquidation, the Americans had to defend the Iyyadist wing against the threats of the militant wing. In the wake of the Gulf War the security of the Iyyadist wing figures was in serious jeopardy; Arafat naturally had no confidence in his bodyguards under the command of Abu Tayyib, the Force 17 commander. A dispute, the nature of which is unclear, broke out between Arafat and Abu Tayyib, and when it was over, Force 17 was disbanded and Abu Tayyib distanced from Tunis. But even after Force 17 was formally disbanded it actually continued to exist, since its mechanisms were incorporated into Abu Iyyad's internal security system, "a-Rasd al-Markazi," "The Central Surveillance," under the command of Hakam Bal'awi, Abu Mazen's right-hand man.

Once the delegation was established, it had to be protected from the pressures of the PLO's militant wing. Even before it was disbanded by Arafat, Force 17 had not managed to get a foothold in the territories. The United States based the delegation's defense on various diplomatic measures.

The peace talks began in Madrid, but immediately after the ceremony the practical talks were moved to Washington. The Israeli government of the time feared US pressures, and wanted the talks transferred to the Middle East, or as close as possible.

In May 1991 a first round of talks in the Mediterranean basin on the bilateral track was scheduled to be held in Rome, but US Secretary of State James Baker initiated its cancellation, and the talks continued in Washington. To understand the reason for this, it is necessary to go back to the events at the end of the Madrid conference. Despite the great excitement and high spirits, the historic event was not without its dissonances. One of these events was of great concern to the Americans: the delegation heads were summoned urgently to Morocco, where an irate Arafat was awaiting them. It turned out that the speech Haidar Abd al-Shafi had delivered was not the one he had been handed by PLO people in Amman. Nor was Arafat pleased about Husseini and Ashrawi's having diverged from the format of the joint delegation with Jordan. Convening a press conference on the steps of the press hall aroused Arafat's ire. But, primarily, he wanted to show them "who is the boss," after the very discouraging beginning, from his viewpoint. Arafat had no interest in the success of the conference, which had been "imposed on him in dishonorable conditions."

The Americans learned a clear lesson from this affair. They realized that they would not fulfil their objectives unless they distanced the Palestinian negotiator from the PLO's pressures. In conflict with the views of the Israeli government, the Americans thought the talks should be distanced from, not brought closer, to the Middle East. The US policy of bringing these talks closer to the United States, rather than to the Middle East, had been formulated at the peak of the Gulf crisis, when the United States distinguished between the different Palestinian leadership groups and the US entry visa became a sort of sieve used to pick the Iyyadists out from all the rest. Those who stood up to these criteria were enabled to enter the United States; what was more, various US elements even invited them. Those who did not stand up to these criteria were rejected. Thus, for instance, as early as in November 1990, at the peak of the Gulf crisis, such people as Afif Safia, who organized the "London Forum" immediately after the fighting ended, Sari Nusseiba from the territories, and Professor Muhammad Hallaj, a US citizen who was chairman of the Palestinian delegation to the refugee conference deliberations in the multinational track, were called to Washington. The fact of these three figures having been brought together under one roof was an indication of what was to come; the Americans wanted to tie up all the ends of the Iyyadist camp: the territories, the European diaspora, the US diaspora, and members of this wing of the PLO, such as Nabil Sha'ath, who visited Washington many times during this period. Khaled al-Hasan also visited Washington, for some time also receiving medical treatment in the United States. Arafat's application for an entry visa was turned down, as were those by other figures, such as Bassam Abu Sharif, on the grounds of their being terrorists.

It was on the basis of these criteria that the United States summoned the Washington talks. The PLO did not want to lose its influence on the delegation, and established a supreme inspection committee for the talks. There are various stories about just who headed this committee. Some claim it was Arafat himself who headed the committee, others say it was Abu Mazen. One way or another, since Arafat knew who did and who did not stand up to the US criteria for entering the United States, he had to appoint the supervisory committee's members in accordance with US requisites. The inspection committee contained some people, such as Faruq Qaddumi, who could never have dreamed of receiving an entrance visa to the United States. This being so, their "inspection" was in any event somewhat less than perfect. In contrast to this, those Washington identified as Iyyadists, such as Nabil Sha'ath and Akram Haniya, were permitted to enter. When they were in Washington, these latter described themselves as the "leadership committee"; a term unacceptable to Haidar Abd a-Shafi, the head of the negotiating team. To some extent, the US goal – to surround the Palestinian delegation with a defensive Iyyadist wall against the militant wing, or historical PLO – succeeded.

The "US sieve" was in operation all through that period of time. Thus, for example, in January 1993 the PLO tried to insinu- ate figures unacceptable to the Americans into Washington, and in addition to the visa application for Nabil Sha'ath, PLO Spokesman Ahmad Abd a-Rahman also submitted an application. The Americans approved Sha'ath's application and rejected that of Abd a-Rahman.

An Executive Bureau in the Territories as Opposed to an Executive Committee in Tunis

The PLO was indeed distanced from the delegation in Washington, but it did not give up its hold on it, impeding its development toward an alternative leadership. When Baker embarked on his contacts with Husseini, the latter's home on the slopes of the Mount of Olives in the Sawana quarter was a hotbed of political activity by the delegation. Husseini wanted the activity moved to an impressive office block which would express the delegation's standing, as he saw it. He also issued his official letters under the logo: the "Executive Bureau," as opposed to "Executive Committee" or,

in Arabic: Husseini's "al-Maktab a-Tanfizi" as compared with the
PLO's "a-Lajna a-Tunfiziya." The PLO objected to these logos and
Husseini altered them to read: "Faisal Husseini's Office." It was
only in 1993 that the PLO approved the final wording: "The Head
of the Palestinian Teams to the Peace Conference." The PLO piled
up difficulties for Husseini in his searches for a suitable office block,
and even after he found Orient House, the PLO did not approve of
his calling the building "Palestinian Delegation House" or "Peace
House," but wanted just: "Orient House."

Who is Foreign Minister: Qaddumi or Ashrawi?

In the Intifada, France followed a policy that conflicted with that of
the Americans; Paris supported the classic PLO, in contrast to the
alternative leadership with the Iyyadist trends which the Americans
were trying to install in the territories, and its position influenced
other European capitals, such as Rome and Brussels, whose stands
were closer to Paris than Washington. Baker's decision to move
the talks to Washington was designed, inter alia, to distance the
Palestinians from the pressures of the Europeans, who opted to
support the classic PLO.

Toward the end of 1992 the classic PLO's apprehensions about the
trends that had begun to emerge around the delegation in the political process were mounting. On 1 October 1991, the *a-Nahar* daily
quoted Nayef Hawatma, the leader of the Democratic Front, who
had said in the Yemeni capital San'a that the PLO would disband as
soon as the negotiating parties in the Middle East reached an agreement on self-rule on the basis of Israel's proposals. Several countries
had already informed the PLO that when self-rule was established
in the occupied territories, they would retract their recognition of it
and close down the Palestinian embassies. The tasks of the PLO and
the Palestinian delegations would be over, because these countries
would establish direct contacts with the self-rule authorities.

Hawatma's remarks made a great impression on Faruq Qaddumi,
the head of the PLO's political department. In the middle of November 1992, he visited Damascus, where he proclaimed: "The PLO has
deleted the term self-rule from its lexicon." He devoted his time in
the Syrian capital not only to talks with the heads of the Syrian rule,
but also to talks with the dangerous rejectionist organizations, and
what they said can only be guessed.

Qaddumi had a special cause for concern. By virtue of his position he was tantamount to the Palestinian foreign minister, and here he was, not involved in running the peace talks. He had been identified as close to Syria, and was unacceptable to the Americans. Hanan Ashrawi had taken the post designated for him, and when Hawatma spoke of the PLO's disbanding and the transfer of its duties to the Palestinians in the territories, Qaddumi was only too well aware of what this would mean whenever he thought of the post Ashrawi was holding at his expense.

The internal pressure mounted when Abu Mazen, the head of the supervisory committee, instructed the Palestinian delegation to concede the implementation of Resolution 242 in the interim arrangements, and postpone the implementation of the permanent arrangements. Arafat was furious over having been bypassed in this way, and sent a fax to Washington expressing amazement at Abu Mazen's decision.

This was not the first time relations between Abu Mazen and Arafat had run aground. The previous time involved the argument over whether the Palestinian delegation should enter the deliberations hall when the multilateral track opened in Moscow. After Abu Mazen had promised the Russians the Palestinian delegation would not give way to Syria's pressures for the conference to be boycotted, Arafat ordered the delegation to remain outside. Abu Mazen severed his relations with Arafat for some considerable length of time.

In order to pile up difficulties for the creation of relations between the delegation and the Palestinians in the territories, the PLO initiated an information campaign, claiming the delegation had made no achievements in the exhaustive talks in Washington. At that time Arafat was reiterating his determination that the "results of the talks are nil, or less than nil." Against the backdrop of this tension, in November 1992 Ashrawi went to Tunis, to persuade Arafat to alter his information line and issue one of achievements. On Qaddumi's advice, Arafat's response to her was brutally rude. From Tunis Ashrawi was scheduled to go to Paris for a meeting with Foreign Minister Dumas. While she was packing her bags, Qaddumi sent the Quai d'Orsay a cable announcing that Ashrawi would not be coming. Qaddumi stated that it was the PLO/Tunis, not the Palestinian delegation, which would decide who was to meet with foreign ministers and foreign diplomats. Qaddumi declared himself the Palestinians' foreign minister, replacing Ashrawi.

This was a painful act of reprisal by the PLO, because since the Gulf crisis it had been Faisal Husseini who planned the timetable of the Palestinian delegation's meetings. In November 1992, the PLO/Tunis removed him from this position. At the end of November the Japanese Ambassador to Israel went to Husseini's East Jerusalem office to finalize the details for ten Palestinians to be sent to Tokyo for administration courses there. Husseini told him that, to his regret, Japan would have to finalize the itinerary details with Tunis. A trip to Tokyo planned by Sa'eb Areiqat, Abd a-Shafi's deputy, was also cancelled.

Following this, the PLO bound the delegation members, including all the public figures from the territories, to meet with foreign elements only when accompanied by someone from the PLO. Up to June 1993, Husseini resigned himself to the unfortunate ban. In June he went to Amman and held a confidential meeting with Jordanian Prime Minister Abd a-Salam al-Majali, shortly after he had received his appointment to the post. The visit to Jordan was tantamount to a signal that there had been a thorough Palestinian change, which had its first expression in the crisis in the Palestinian embassy in Paris.

Husseini Closes the Circle with Majali

Husseini's meeting with Majali closed yet another circle. As will be recalled, the main bone of contention between Abu Iyyad and the United States involved the Palestinians' relations with Jordan. Abu Iyyad found it hard to forget the trauma of "Black September," 1970, but his successors listened attentively to the US advice to forget the past. Khaled al-Hasan favored a tripartite Jordanian–Palestinian–Israeli confederation; Abu Mazen and Abu al-Ala, the Force 17 commanders, and Hanan Ashrawi also established special relations with the Hashemites. Husseini was the last to be convinced, because of the historical enmity between the Husseini family from Jerusalem and the Hashemites. After Jordan proved to Husseini that it was serious in its decision to detach itself from the West Bank and Husseini himself became aware of the limitations to his power, he, too, reached the conclusion that he needed the alliance with the Jordanians against Arafat. Up to the visit to Majali, Husseini had worked against Jordan's economic interests in the West Bank. Following the visit he joined Abu al-Ala in following a policy of cooperation with Jordan, including texting common stands on Jerusalem, whose salient points were that the sacred sites were tantamount to a pledge deposited with Jordan until the permanent arrangement, a stand Arafat rejected.

Who Will Replace Ibrahim Sus?

It is no coincidence that the process of restrictions imposed on the Palestinian delegation actually began in Paris, and no coincidence that it was in Paris that there was also an attempt to get out of the strangler's noose. As will be recalled, in the struggle that raged over the control of the Unified Command in the territories at the beginning of the Intifada, the money funding the opposition to the Iyyadist Force 17's disposition came from Paris. From many aspects, the Palestinian embassy in the French capital was the logistic rear guard of the anti-US forces. The most important Palestinian embassy, which was in Faruq Qaddumi's hands, was that in Paris, headed by Palestinian Ambassador Ibrahim Sus.

From June 1993 on rumors were leaked that Ibrahim Sus was about to resign and there was a great deal of speculation about who was to replace him. In July there was an official announcement that Laila Shahid, the ambassador to UNESCO, would come to Paris, and her appointment was received with surprise by the diplomatic staff in Paris and with excitement by the French foreign ministry. The Paris Arabic-language weekly *al-Muharer* reported[1] that the approval for Shahid's expected appointment had been transferred from the Foreign Ministry to the presidential palace and prime minister's office. This was because Laila Shahid was one of Faisal Husseini's maternal relatives, and considered to be closer to this delegation wing than any of the other ambassadors who came under consideration for the appointment. "Is Israeli–Palestinian normalization beginning in Paris?" asked a French diplomat in *al-Muharer*. Arab diplomats commented to the weekly that Shahid was Bahai by faith, and wondered how she could defend Jerusalem. The previous (dismissed?) ambassador, Ibrahim Sus, attacked his replacement in a most undiplomatic manner. He told *al-Manar*[2] that the appointment of a Palestinian ambassador to Paris required precise, stringent selection, expressing dissatisfaction with the "Palestinian situation" that made such a choice possible. To illustrate his meaning, he aggressively stated that the peace talks should be stopped because of the moves Israel was making in the territories.

The circle that had opened in Paris in November 1992 with the insulting door slammed in Hanan Ashrawi's face, closed in July 1993 with Sus being driven away. But it was not only the Palestinian, but also the French and European circles that closed, when France joined the anti-Saddam Hussein pact at the time of the great 1990 crisis. It had begun with aid to the Americans to neutralize the Jihadist opposition to Husseini in 1991, and ended with Sus' removal.

15

The Documents Crisis: Husseini and Arafat on the Brink of a Rift

"In the name of your father, the martyr (shahid), Abd al-Qader, in the name of the shuhada, those who gave up their lives – I beseech you, do not disgrace me," Arafat pleaded to Husseini in a phone call from Tunis at the beginning of August 1993, adding the request: "Submit the document we prepared to Christopher." This was the peak moment in Husseini's status and it led to the great fall.

The document was the text Abu Mazen prepared in response to the draft US paper of principles, as formulated in the Washington talks, in the May round. But Husseini was not appeased. He declined to submit the paper. An eye-witness to this conversation later reported that when Arafat put the receiver down, he cursed Husseini and the delegation, swearing to get his own back on them. This may have been the ebb point in that year's relations between Husseini and Arafat, and the PLO leader's cutting the East Jerusalem delegation head on the White House lawn was only the first instalment in the repayment of the debt.

It was hard for Husseini to conceal his frustration over the publication of the agreement between the PLO and Israel. In the post-Madrid period he himself, with a slender budget, was responsible for carrying the delegation on his own shoulders, making financial improvisations, trying to establish an economic infrastructure in the territories, further the talks to the best of his ability, and protect the peace process against its detractors, with Arafat ceaselessly summing up the delegation's achievements as "nil," at best. And it was just when he plucked up his courage and decided to come out overtly against Arafat – that the PLO leader put him in his place. Husseini had had several previous opportunities to come out against Arafat, but hesitated, enabling Abu Mazen to reap the fruits of his toil.

Six months previously, at the end of April 1993, Israel had decided to bring back a group of veteran deportees in order to encourage the Palestinian delegation to return to the deliberations table in Washington. Husseini was in Washington, and he decided to go to Jericho, to meet them on the Jordan bridges. Arafat ordered him to come to Tunis and Husseini declined, informing Arafat that "he was sending him" delegation members Areiqat and Kilani. Arafat was enraged. Once more the delegation hesitated, and caved in.

One week earlier Faruq Qaddumi, the head of the political department, had attended the Islamic Conference in Karachi, Pakistan. Saudi Arabian Foreign Minister Sa'ud al-Faisal did not condescend to meet with him. Qaddumi nevertheless found a way to make it indirectly clear to him that if the Saudi money was not given to the Palestinians via the PLO – it would simply not reach them. Moreover, he explained that without a resumption of the Saudi aid through the PLO, the Palestinian organization would order the delegation to walk out of the talks. And indeed, it was to no small extent because of this struggle over the Saudi aid funds that the recurrent crises broke out around the deliberations table in Washington. As the Oslo agreements had proved, it was not the practical disputes that caused the permanent crisis atmosphere in Washington, but the PLO's mounting economic difficulties. At that time the PLO's budgetary balances were close to going into the red, and Palestinian sources reported they amounted to no more than $200 million. The PLO was unable to bear the thought that while they were being forced to close down offices and cut expenses, the Palestinians in the territories were about to enjoy the horn of plenty.

All that year, under the impression of Qaddumi's threats, there were contacts over the Saudi aid between Saudi Arabia and Husseini and Abu Mazen. In the April and May of 1993 there were several decisive meetings between Husseini and Christopher, and between him and the Saudis: the ambassador in Washington, Prince Bandar, Saudi Foreign Minister al-Faisal and King Fahd. At his meeting with Fahd in May he was also accompanied by Abu Mazen. The meetings with the Saudis did not go well. They were prepared to aid the alternative leadership in the West Bank, but were unfavorably impressed by Husseini's reluctance to come out openly against Arafat. Bandar made it plain to Husseini that he would do well not to cherish any expectations of the Americans' ability to impose on Saudi Arabia a Palestinian policy it did not want. Husseini met with Saud al-Faisal in Cairo. The Saudi foreign minister was unfavorably impressed by Husseini's inability to itemize and reason his economic demands, and made it plain that Saudi Arabia would not throw its money into a bottomless pit. He claimed their previous experience of aid to the Palestinians had not been good. He explained that the Saudis were prepared to give money to institutions, but not to people, and that Husseini would have to deal with Orient House's debts by himself. Al-Faisal told the Americans that Husseini had not made a good impression on him. He also criticized the fact that Husseini had mentioned certain sums of money in his talks with the Americans, and different sums in his talks with the Saudis on the needs of the Palestinians in the occupied territories. A month later the Saudi demands intensified: they made the resumption of the aid to the Palestinians in the territories provisional on acceptance of the civil administration authorities.

The meeting with King Fahd was decisive, and could be considered a turning point. Husseini made it clear that Arafat had authorized him only to mediate between Saudi Arabia and the PLO, not to transfer the Saudi funds directly to the territories, and that the Saudi Arabian funds were to be sent via the PLO. Abu Mazen sat beside him, keeping his mouth shut. King Fahd asked Husseini angrily whether he did not know their attitude to the PLO, and did not realize that they would not give the PLO so much as a brass cent.

Husseini emerged dejected from the meeting with Fahd. He realized that if he did not come out overtly against Arafat, he would be utterly lost. Abu Mazen, too, noted the opportunity that had fallen into his hands: to transfer the Iyyadist camp leadership's seniority to Abu Iyyad's original successors. A month later, in June, Abu Mazen renewed his overt criticism of Arafat, reserving special criticism for his policy in the Gulf crisis. Parallel with this, the secret Oslo talks with Peres' people began to acquire impetus.

That same month, Hussein appointed Abd a-Salam al-Majali, the head of the Jordanian delegation to the Washington talks, as his prime minister. Husseini decided to disobey Qaddumi's order, and went to meet the new prime minister on his own. By so doing, he was trying to signal his independence. He also began to speak of "moving the PLO to the territories" – in the spirit of the FIDA ideas. The suppressed tension erupted in August. Husseini still did not know he had missed the boat, since Abu al-Ala's and Abu Mazen's envoys had almost completed the agreement with Uri Savir, the director general of the Israeli Foreign Ministry. Arafat supported Abu Mazen, because he still viewed Husseini as his main threat, and also wanted to exacerbate the differences of opinion between the two mainstays of the Iyyadist camp.

Gaza First; the West Bank First

In the first week of August 1993, the differences of opinion between Arafat and the Palestinian delegation were shown up to the world, when three of the delegation's seniors – Faisal Husseini, Sa'eb Areiqat, Abd a-Shafi's deputy in the team negotiating with Israel, and Hanan Ashrawi, the delegation's spokeswoman – threatened to resign. The crisis broke out after the Palestinian delegation had refused to give US Secretary of State Warren Christopher the document prepared by the PLO office in Cairo, containing the Palestinian position on the paper the Americans had prepared to bridge the Israelis' and Palestinians' positions. For the most part, the PLO delegation wings tried to either conceal or downplay the differences of opinion between them, but fluctuations of the sort that shocked the Palestinians in the documents crisis threw the continuing differences of opinion into sharp relief.

The dramatic atmosphere in which the documents crisis broke out was preceded by two other great crises, which rocked the entire Middle East: the expulsion of some four hundred Hamas activists from the territories, in the wake of the increase in acts of Islamic terror in Israel and the territories at the beginning of the year, and the Southern Lebanon crisis at the end of July 1993. In response to the Hizballah's provocations against the IDF forces in the security strip, the IDF launched a heavy bombardment on Southern Lebanon, which led to hundreds of thousands of villagers fleeing northward. The United States intervened, and arranged an understanding for a cease-fire in Southern Lebanon between Israel, Syria and Lebanon. When the first overt crisis erupted between Husseini and Arafat, the general atmosphere was already highly charged. Since Arafat was supporting Abu Mazen at the time, their positions can be seen as being all of a piece. Nevertheless, it was easy to distinguish between the delegation's positions on the one hand, as opposed to the positions of the PLO/Tunis on the other, with the fault line running between East Jerusalem and Tunis.

The dispute between Husseini and Arafat and Abu Mazen focused on three interconnected issues. Tunis wanted the arrangement with Israel to concentrate on Gaza and Jericho, while the delegation wanted it to focus on the West Bank; Tunis wanted the violence against Israel stopped only in Gaza and Jericho, and continued in the West Bank. Husseini and his colleagues were demanding the reverse: that life throughout the territories be restored to its normal track in the West Bank and Gaza and, following this, the violence stopped altogether; the PLO demand insisted on an immediate leap to the permanent stage in Gaza and Jericho, leaving the situation in the West Bank pending. Husseini's demand for a total stop to the violence originated in the fear that the Fatah "Beating" Committees would not only act against Israel, but also continue to threaten the fledgling Palestinian administration – if it were to deviate from the reservations with which Arafat had hedged it about.

From this it may be understood that Husseini was demanding to receive the civil administration authority in the West Bank and Gaza Strip from Israel, as proposed to the Palestinians in the Washington talks, with a warm US "recommendation" and Saudi stipulations with regard to the resumption of the economic aid. Arafat rejected the delegation's acceptance of the West Bank authority, opting for the infrastructure of the Palestinian state to be built only in Gaza and Jericho – and by the PLO. Arafat's repeated demand for international forces or armed auspices in the territories is closely connected with this. As against the delegation's demand for life to be restored to normal, with acceptance of ruling authority in all the territories, Arafat wanted to maintain the revolutionary moods among the Palestinians. This would prevent the leadership in the territories being reinforced by the reception of international aid, and the transferral of this aid to the international organizations, primarily to UNRWA, the United Nations Relief and Work Agency for Palestine Refugees in the Middle East. Hanan Ashrawi shared Husseini's views on this issue, something which emerges from a memo Ashrawi wrote to Arafat at about that time, in which she totally dismissed the Gaza and Jericho first idea. *A-Nahar* published the memo on 6 September 1993, but it was written before details of the secret contacts in Oslo became known. Ashrawi reviewed the difficulties that had emerged in the talks with Israel, and recommended altering the Madrid format in order to introduce ingredients of permanent arrangements, in accordance with a "combined model." What is important for our subject, however, is that when Ashrawi got down to analyzing the Gaza and Jericho first idea, she had difficulty in finding terms to recommend this model. One by one, she detailed all the grave defects embodied in it, ruling: "Judging by the bitter experience we have gained, there is no Arab or international desire or intention to grant the PLO financial and economic aid, and without Arab and international contributions and financial aid, the Gaza/Jericho option can be considered an economic disaster and will end in a resounding failure, something which will have many negative results."

In addition to this basic drawback, Ashrawi put forward other defects: Palestine's division into two separate authorities, Israel's liberation from the burden of Gaza – something which was later to reinforce her position in the negotiations on Jerusalem and the West Bank – and giving an opening to Israel's claim that with the withdrawal from Gaza and Jericho, it had fulfilled its commitments under Resolution 242, which would enable it to step up the pace of constructing the settlements around Jerusalem.

The main bones of contention between the PLO and the delegation can be learned from Ashrawi's memo. The PLO did indeed fear the aid funds being granted exclusively to the delegation if there was an early transfer of authority, and wanted to create a situation in which the aid would be given to Gaza under its rule. It wanted to leave the situation in the West Bank unclear, in order to weaken the Palestinian leadership there, while the PLO was reinforcing its standing in Gaza and Jericho.

Who Will Stop the Intifada?

Arafat was also consistent in his objections to putting a stop to the Intifada, or armed struggle, before the permanent arrangements entered into force. Right at the peak of the first talks in Madrid, Arafat appeared before a Palestinian congress in Rabat, Morocco, and ceremoniously undertook that the "jihad will not end."[1] In December 1991 Arafat entered into a direct confrontation with Iranian President Hashemi Rafsanjani, at a meeting of the Islamic Conference in the Senegalese capital Dakar. That conference, for the first time, approved a concluding resolution which did not mention the precept of the jihad against Israel. Arafat attacked

Rafsanjani directly for having given his agreement to such a resolution. Arafat's stand was received with astonishment by the Egyptian
delegation.

Toward the end of 1992, Israel entered into a severe confrontation
with the US Administration over the question of the assurances
for immigrant absorption. President Bush had promised to grant
Israel these assurances, but made them provisional on a stop to
the settlements in the territories. Parallel with this, the Palestinians
were supposed to announce a stop to the Intifada. There are signs to
indicate that Husseini supported the deal and Arafat opposed it.[2]

Stopping the Intifada was among the central issues discussed
between Baker and the Palestinians in their talks in Jerusalem in
the course of 1991. The Palestinians told Baker they could not just
declare a stop to the Intifada through a leaflet or other proclamation, and that a dynamics of mutual confidence-building gestures
between Israel and the Arabs should be developed. Meanwhile,
the Palestinians said, Israel was following a policy of "badwill
gestures," and they gave Christopher a long list of "confidence-
destroying" moves Israel was making in the territories.

The Americans realized that Husseini and his colleagues did not
have the power to stop the Intifada simply through a political
announcement. Accordingly, one of the important issues discussed
in Washington was agreement on mutual confidence-building gestures between Israel and the Palestinians. The goal was to create a
comfortable atmosphere between the sides, to lead to a weakening
of the Palestinian motivation to continue with the Intifada. The
Palestinian delegation went into deliberations on these gestures
seriously, to arrive at a cease-fire, or a stop to the Intifada, but
the organizations acted to step up the security tension in order to
stop the confidence-building gestures being made.

Faqahani in Gaza

Halfway through August, the Paris-based *al-Muharer* weekly
reported Arafat's considerations on "Gaza first." Arafat had said:
"I ruled Lebanon from Faqahani – and Gaza is several times larger
than Faqahani." What he meant was that he had ruled all of Lebanon
from the Beiruti quarter where the PLO command was sited, and
that from the much larger Gaza he would also be able to rule the
West Bank. The weekly reported that it was clear to the PLO people

to whom he had made the remarks that the West Bank was fated to be split up into cantons, and this was the reason for the dispute within the delegation.

Arafat's position was not new, and Husseini was unable to disclose his opposition to it in public, but the differences of opinion between them did have an indirect expression. Throughout this period of time Husseini expressed an Iyyadist stand, of support for the United States and confidence in its policy. Arafat spouted fire and brimstone at the United States, expressing utter non-confidence in its intentions and policy. Thus, for instance, Husseini told students of the Bir Zeit University: "Washington has begun to come closer to us."[2] He explained the need to meet with Baker by the fact that the PLO was at its lowest ebb and had negotiations not been conducted with Baker, the Americans would have turned to Syria in order to arrange matters in the Palestinian arena with it. Arafat, in contrast to this, said: "We do not put any trust in US promises."

It is interesting to see how profound these differences of opinion were. Back in 1988, when there was an internal struggle in the PLO over the nature of the Intifada, on 25 December Arafat said: "The Palestinian state will have the right to maintain armed forces as long as Israel has an army." As will be recalled, one year later Abu Iyyad informed the Americans that the Palestinian state would be demilitarized. The day following Arafat's statement, Abu Iyyad declared that the "Unified Command" had decided not to use firearms, because the rock had been more successful in the fight on the enemy.

The timing of these two statements is of great importance, because they were made only a week after President Reagan announced the opening of a dialogue with the PLO (14 December 1988).

Not Forsaking Husseini

It was not easy for the Americans to forsake Husseini, because of the original Iyyadist wing's opposition to him, and they did, to the best of their ability, keep faith with him. Because of the background of their contacts with the Iyyadists in Tunis, it was not hard for them to work with Abu Mazen, but they found it difficult to put any trust in Arafat. Accordingly, when the documents crisis broke out, the United States actually supported Husseini. Husseini would not have embarked on the entire resignations process had he not been sure of the US position, and he almost certainly examined this move's chances in a *tête-à-tête* talk he held with Christopher in the King David Hotel in Jerusalem that same day.

Despite his difficulties with the Saudis, Saudi Arabia also supported him. Foreign Minister Saud al-Faisal phoned his Egyptian counterpart, Amr Musa, and informed him: "Husseini is the red line. If Husseini's status is harmed, Arafat can forget any Saudi Arabian aid in the future." If Arafat had any ideas about taking advantage of the resignations to rid himself of the delegation, the Egyptians – on behalf of the Saudis – made him drop them.

On 12 August 1993, Bilal al-Hasan, the younger brother of Khaled and Hani, published an article in the *al-Quds* daily, warning that the differences of opinion between the delegation and the Tunis leadership could give rise to a split. He mentioned that Christopher had seen fit to come to the Middle East immediately after the great crisis in southern Lebanon, in the course of which hundreds of thousands of Lebanese fled their homes and tens of thousands of buildings were destroyed. He noted that this also embodied a threat to the Palestinians in the territories, if the peace talks were to fail.

It should be recalled that in the previous round of talks in Washington, the Americans submitted a paper of principles similar to Abu Mazen's document, in that it put off such thorny problems as Jerusalem, the sphere of jurisdiction, etc., to the next stage. The main difference between the US document and that prepared by Abu Mazen and his colleagues lay in the fact that the Americans demanded that the delegation be given the initial authority in the territories, while the PLO wanted to be given Gaza and Jericho and postpone acceptance of the authority.

Bilal al-Hasan reported that Christopher had, with some difficulty, convinced Husseini to accept the US paper, but warned him – under the impression of the southern Lebanese events – of the dangerous results to the Palestinians if the peace process were to collapse because of the rejection of the US document. The truth is that no great efforts were needed to persuade Husseini, since shortly before this he himself had spoken of the loss of Andalus. On this matter, Bilal al-Hasan recalled that on the eve of the convening of the Madrid Conference, too, similar threats were used on the Palestinians. When the PLO still had no inclination to agree to a conference, the phone in Faruq Qaddumi's home rang after midnight. On the other end of the line was the British Ambassador to Tunisia, who demanded an immediate meeting with Qaddumi. The ambassador declined to postpone the meeting to the morning, maintaining the matter could not be put off. Qaddumi agreed to meet with the ambassador, who handed him an official letter from Britain demanding that the Palestinians accept the Madrid talks framework and enable the delegation to participate under the terms set. This was actually a US warning, since after the suspension of the dialogue with the PLO, Britain was representing the United States with the PLO. The threat that the failure of the peace process would enable Israel to implement a transfer of Palestinians was the background to the pressures on the Palestinians and the PLO to accept the peace process parameters.

Nevertheless, the PLO ordered the delegation to reject the US document and, after Ashrawi had given them good reasons for this, the Palestinian delegation members found that the PLO itself had, via Egypt, met with the United States for negotiations on the document and submitted comments on Christopher's wording to the Americans. The argument was whether to take a position of rejection or one of negotiations. On instructions from the PLO, the delegation took up a rejectionist stand. The PLO itself entered a position of negotiations.

A dispute arose between the delegation and the PLO, in the wake of which a delegation member, Ghassan al-Khatib, a representative of the People's Party, again decided to suspend his membership and the delegation head, Haidar abd a-Shafi, raised the need for a collective leadership to be established around Arafat. The delegation refused to be left in the status of officials who did what they were told. Hanan Ashrawi did indeed issue a public demand that the PLO give the delegation official standing, as decision-makers.

Incorporating – and Undermining – the PLO

Parallel with this, another process was under way, one which aroused the PLO's suspicions. Bilal al-Hasan said that from the very start of the Madrid process the PLO had demanded that it be recognized and the negotiations conducted with it, and now the new Israeli government headed by Rabin was ostensibly moving toward this demand on a series of issues. One after the other, Palestinians from the diaspora who had status in the PLO were incorporated into the negotiations on the multinational tracks, and Husseini, who represented the Jerusalem problem, was also permitted to enter the official negotiating hall in Washington. Israel seemed to have abandoned its ultimative demand that only Palestinians from the territories should participate in the talks.

The PLO, however, saw matters otherwise, reported Bilal al-Hasan. Israel had given its agreement to the incorporation of PLO figures in the circle of official negotiators, but without accepting the political significance of negotiations with the PLO. This was conspicuous in the willingness for Husseini to be incorporated in the Washington talks. This was done without acceptance of the Palestinian demand that the status of Jerusalem be discussed. Israel and the United States were willing for Nabil Sha'ath, too, to be incorporated into the official Palestinian team, but this in return for the Palestinians' agreement to the US paper of principles, that is, recognition of the PLO as a body, with rejection of the PLO from the aspect of its contents.

One of Bilal's conclusions in his article was that Arafat and Rabin must be brought together, and soon, for a meeting. It is not known whether the younger al-Hasan knew of the secret channel which was then working out its conclusions in Oslo, or whether it was just a guess.

In any event, the delegation–PLO crisis ended with a big surprise. Arafat, on the ropes, clung to the lifebelt Abu Mazen extended to him in the form of the agreements texted with the Israeli Foreign Ministry and the delegation crisis concluded in a way nobody could have imagined: in a handshake between Arafat and Rabin and Peres, at Clinton's side on the White House lawn.

16

The Secret Channels: Guns, Flags and the Economy

Not Recognizing the PLO, but Talking With It

While the Israeli and Palestinian delegations were bickering in Washington and Arafat was putting all his inventive skills to work to stop the establishment of an alternative leadership from within the occupied territories, it emerged that the Washington talks were nothing but a cover-up for several other channels for talking between Israel and the PLO. The Washington talks may have been the principal route in Yitzhak Shamir's time, but his successor, Yitzhak Rabin, quickly altered its destination and it became a cover-up for the other channels of conversation between Israel and the PLO. In Israel it was Rabin who held all the strings that led to the talks and, in the PLO – Abu Mazen. It was also Abu Mazen who headed the supervisory committee on the overt talks in Washington, which turned into diversionary talks.

Of all the channels, there was one which acquired impetus: the talks held in Oslo under the baton of the PLO's financier, Abu al-Ala. This was not, however, the only channel: in addition, talks between Knesset Member Ephraim Sneh and Nabil Sha'ath were held in London, and the most important talks, which thrashed out the security problems involved in the implementation of the interim arrangements in the territories, took place in picturesque villages in Britain and Italy. From the Israeli side these talks were coordinated by Yossi Alpher, the director of Tel Aviv University's Jaffe Strategic Studies Center, and from the Palestinian side, by Brigadier General Nizar Ammar, a Force 17 man, one of the leaders of the Abu Mazen's group's security apparatus. Nizar Ammar is the underground name of Nazih Hilmi al-Mubasher, who had already taken part in the Tunis talks with Murphy in March 1990, along with Abu Iyyad. After he entered Gaza in 1995 he became the close adviser to Palestinian Police Commander General Naser Yusef.

A secondary channel to that of Oslo opened between Israel and the PLO, conducted directly between Jerusalem and Tunis, which was run by Health Minister Chaim Ramon and his friend Dr Ahmad Tibi, an Israeli-Arab gynaecologist from the village of Taibe who had been deeply involved in the various contacts between Israel and the PLO in previous years.

Harvard University gave its auspices to the economic talks channel, in which senior economic figures from Israel, the occupied territories, the PLO and Jordan took part. The Tibi–Ramon channel helped to clear up several problems that had held up progress in Oslo, and enabled the move from the non-official to the official contacts. At the same time, there were several important gaps between the understandings achieved in the security channel and those in the Oslo channel, especially on anything connected with Jordan's status; the security channel attached special importance to consolidating Jordan's strategic depth, while the Oslo channel did not see any special importance in Jordan's political status in the future arrangements, and emphasized the bilateral relations between Israel and the Palestinians. In addition, the United States kept a close watch on the deliberations in the security channel. In contrast to this, it showed no interest in the Oslo channel. In the days that followed the exposure of the contacts, these differences were to be of importance. Generally speaking, the substantive differences between the economic and security channels, on the one hand, and the Oslo channel, on the other, lay in the central concept: while the two former wanted to institutionalize tripartite Israeli–Palestinian–Jordanian cooperation, the Oslo channel focused on Israeli–PLO relations and pushed Jordan aside.

Nabil Sha'ath felt he had been cheated. His talks with Sneh had borne no fruit. What is more, he had his suspicions that Rabin had asked for talks with him only to sound him out on Abu Mazen's credibility as far as keeping the secret of the covert contacts was concerned, and to ensure that he was also keeping his own people in the dark on the Oslo channel.

These negotiating channels were preceded by continuous non-official or semi-official efforts in the previous years. Thus, for example, on the eve of the Intifada a Likud channel of negotiations opened, involving Moshe Amirav and his colleagues who, through

Faisal Husseini and his people, set up a link with Arafat. This channel almost led to an agreement between the PLO and Israel, but Prime Minister Yitzhak Shamir decided to shut it down, although he had been in on the secret of these contacts right from the start. There had also been indirect contacts between Abu Mazen and Sharon and they, too, did not go well. There is no need to detail the different contacts by leftist parties with the different groups in the PLO's central stream. The talks between Alpher and Nizar Ammar had been preceded by contacts of a security nature. For instance, Yossi Ginnosar, a senior Shin Bet man, had in the past met in Paris with Hani al-Hasan from the Iyyadist wing. The secret talks were accompanied by overt contacts such as, for example, Minister Yossi Sarid's meetings with Nabil Sha'ath in Cairo.

The Nablus Channel

In most cases these contacts came to nothing. The channel of contacts that opened between the PLO and the Labor Party on the eve of the 1992 elections, however, lasted for that year and was the background to the Oslo talks, possibly without the negotiators in Oslo even being aware of their existence.

There were several interests, not directly interconnected, that were common to the Labor Party and circles in the PLO and the territories, and it was these interests that led to this channel's creation. The Labor Party's elections campaign managers were aware of the need to establish a "blocking bloc" with the Arab lists, to stop the Likud bloc establishing a government. They were aware of the PLO's ability to influence the heads of the Arab lists to rise above the rivalries between them so as not to lose surplus votes.

Parallel with this, Abu Mazen's group and the public leaders in Nablus and Hebron found a common interest in preventing Husseini and the wing that supported him in the Palestinian delegation from gaining a lead in the struggle for Abu Iyyad's succession. It turned out that at some stage Hanan Ashrawi also encouraged the transfer of seniority from East Jerusalem to Abu Mazen's group, but later regretted it when she realized its possible future implications.

Arafat, too, found great interest in thwarting Husseini; not to reinforce Abu Mazen's status by so doing, but to foil the entire Iyyadist wing. The difference between Arafat and Abu Mazen was that, while Abu Mazen wanted to restore the seniority in the struggle within the Iyyadist wing to Abu Iyyad's original successors, Arafat wanted to foil this entire wing – including both Husseini and Abu Mazen.

The man who kept this channel going was Sa'id Kan'an, a Palestinian public figure from Nablus, one of the leaders of the central stream of PLO supporters. Halfway through 1992, shortly before the elections in July, he was summoned urgently to Cairo to meet with Arafat, Abu Mazen and Sa'id Kamal, the Palestinian ambassador in Cairo, one of his relatives. Kan'an himself refuses to elaborate on this affair, but when I was in Tunis in October 1993, PLO sources told me the PLO leaders had asked Kan'an to use his connections with the Labor Party to promote common PLO–Labor Party interests. Kan'an unhesitatingly agreed. In days to come, after I had learned of these contacts, I asked Kan'an for some details, but he remained silent. All he said was that he had agreed to the PLO appeal because the "Palestinians feared the alternative leadership that was forming in Jerusalem, headed by Husseini, which threatened to split the Palestinians between the people in the occupied territories and the people in the diaspora. We wanted to maintain the PLO's integrity, because only it would faithfully represent the people in the territories and those abroad to the same degree. I am convinced that Husseini did not intend to split the people, but we believed that, even against his will, this might be the unavoidable outcome."

At the same time, the common interests between Nablus and Tunis took Kan'an to the Labor Party with the PLO's proposal to help in establishing a blocking bloc with the Arab parties. Since Kan'an did not give any further details, the main "suspect" in the contacts with him was Ephraim Sneh, who had moved over to Rabin's camp shortly before that and who knew Kan'an from when he was head of the Civilian Administration in Judaea and Samaria. Nor was Sneh prepared to talk about these contacts, and dismissed their importance. In any event, the importance of the channel opened with Sa'id Kan'an lay not in the elections campaign, but in the very fact of the setting up of a channel of negotiations which Rabin could have used immediately afterwards. One of the requests the Labor Party made of the PLO was for the Palestinian organization not to declare its support for the party. The Labor Party set Sa'id Kan'an terms for the talks to be conducted: the maintenance of absolute secrecy. If the contacts were to be discovered, the Labor

Party would wash its hands of them at once. The Labor Party's response, then, was positive, but reserved. Arafat and Abu Mazen were pleased with the Labor Party's reaction and decided to open five liaison offices with Israel in Europe; the head office was in Paris. The nature of the Paris office is unclear; it may well have been used as an Israeli-PLO meeting place for direct, covert clarifications.

After the elections, Sa'id Kan'an renewed the communications channel. He made a shuttle trip between Cairo and Tunis as the main liaison between Rabin and the PLO. The difficulties in the Washington talks moved Rabin to seek replacements for the Palestinian delegation and the exhausted talks channel, and it was speedily decided to arrange a meeting in Paris between Rabin and Abu Mazen.

As far as this period – the beginning of 1993 – may be reconstructed, the Foreign Ministry did not know of the talks route Kan'an was running, and opened another communications channel in Oslo. The Oslo channel took Abu Mazen by surprise. When the contacts between the two Israeli academics, Yair Hirschfeld and Ron Pundak, and the PLO began, Abu Mazen was conducting the contacts designed for a meeting with the Israeli prime minister, possibly in the Paris liaison office, and it was then that he was told of the Israeli professors who were trying to mediate between him and Peres. At first Abu Mazen voiced dissatisfaction with these contacts. He thought the contacts with the professors would divert him from the main point – the meeting with Rabin. However, he rapidly changed his stance. Rabin set very hard terms for a meeting. Nor did Rabin give the impression that he was wholehearted, but radiated hesitations and doubts. The reports from Oslo were more encouraging. When Abu Mazen compared the reports on the contacts with Peres with those on the contacts with Rabin, he decided to abandon the contacts with Rabin in favor of the contacts with Peres, in the hope that at some stage the channels would join up – as did indeed occur.

Putting Abu Mazen to the Test

Rabin, too, studied the contacts conducted in the Kan'an and Oslo channels. Although it seemed to him that Peres was progressing too fast, it was actually the Oslo channel that he decided to promote. Before making a final decision, however, he put Abu Mazen and

Arafat through a series of tests. The first was in November 1992. The PLO sent Muhammad Hallaj, a member of the PLO's National Council, to the refugee conference in Ottawa. Hallaj was one of Abu Mazen's people, from Hisham Sharabi's group in Washington. He did not take offence when Abu Mazen asked him to vacate his place for Iliya Zuriq, a Palestinian academic from Canada.

The exchanges were made with Egyptian mediation. As soon as it transpired that it was someone from the Palestine National Council who was being sent to the Ottowa talks, Foreign Minister Shimon Peres phoned his Egyptian counterpart, Amr Musa, and asked him to intervene. Musa responded at once since, for several reasons, Egypt had an interest in furthering this channel: the Washington talks channel had removed it from the center of political activity, after Husseini had declined to accept its aid in counselling the Palestinian delegation. Since Egypt did not have a delegation in Washington, because it had already concluded its peace talks with Israel, Syria took over the center of the stage, threatening Egypt's hegemony over the Arab world. It is no coincidence that the former legal adviser to the Egyptian foreign ministry, Taher Shash, stood by Abu al-Ala in the formulation of the Oslo agreements. Prior to this President Mubarak had offered Husseini the services of Taher Shash, because of the experience he had accumulated in the Camp David talks, but he courteously turned the offer down. Eventually Shash paid him back for the aid he had given Abu Mazen in getting rid of Husseini's delegation. In addition, Egypt was pushed out of the secret talks channels on security and economic issues and the United States opted to incorporate Jordan instead.

The circumstances of Hallaj's dismissal put Abu Mazen right in the middle of the second test of the PLO. He had previously also headed the Palestinian teams to the multinational channel, and in May 1993 he went to Oslo to head the Palestinian delegation at the multinational channel's conference on the refugee problem. Officially, Ilya Zuriq replaced Hallaj, but in practical terms, Abu al-Ala headed the Palestinian delegation. He was the head of all the Palestinian teams in the multinational channel on behalf of the PLO, parallel to Husseini, who bore a similar, but meaningless title. At the refugee conference in Oslo he was accommodated next to the deliberations room and steered the Palestinian delegation. He achieved a joint formulation speaking of the need to rehabilitate the refugee camps in Arab countries, too. This was how the Abu Mazen group passed another test of credibility, as Israel saw it. The Palestinians did, indeed, maintain that the reference was not to giving up the right of return, but to providing refugees with the chance of a decent life until a political solution was found for their problem, but Israel was able to interpret this as a first step toward the actualization of the unwritten understanding with Abu Iyyad's wing, under which the 1948 refugees would not be brought back to their homes in Israel. Rabin was favorably impressed both by the fact that Hallaj had been dismissed in favor of Zuriq, and also that it was Abu al-Ala, the Foreign Ministry staff's interlocutor, who steered the talks at the refugee conference and succeeded in attaining a first understanding with Israel on the most sensitive issue. He might have compared the attainment of this understanding with the endless difficulties in Washington over issues of much less importance. Rabin was also impressed by the fact that Abu al-Ala was able to make his own decisions. He had grounds to believe that Abu al-Ala had authorized the Oslo announcement on the refugees without asking Arafat for his approval. In times to come Dr Ron Pundak, who participated in the preparation of the Oslo agreements and took part in all the contacts, was to testify to the extent of Abu al-Ala's independence; he said: "The most important actor on the Palestinian side was Abu al-Ala. Not only did he head the PLO team to the talks, he also took unusual responsibility upon himself, as well as a considerable amount of independence and maneuvering on the ground, which was not always free of restrictions."[1]

Rabin, then was favorably impressed by Abu Mazen's people's independence in decision-making, but wanted to cover himself from another aspect: the talks' secrecy. One of the major conditions he set the PLO was the maintenance of secrecy, which he viewed as a test of the channel's credibility, both as concerned people who, in principle, were close to Abu Mazen, but also in respect of those who had not shared the secret of the Oslo contacts. One of the men who was close to Abu Mazen and had not been in on the secret of the contacts in Oslo was Nabil Sha'ath. This was because Sha'ath, on Abu Mazen's behalf, headed the committee appointed over the Palestinian delegation in Washington. Abu Mazen supervised the delegation from Tunis, Nabil Sha'ath from Washington. In addition to this, there were his special relations with Hanan Ashrawi. The two used to go to many of the world's capitals as a team. Since it was essential that all information be kept from the delegation in

Washington, in any way possible, there was no choice but to keep Sha'ath away.

Rabin knew this, and wanted to find out how successful Abu Mazen had indeed been in keeping the information on the Oslo talks from the delegation in Washington. Rabin sent Ephraim Sneh to a series of meetings in London with Nabil Sha'ath, parallel with the talks that were already underway in Oslo. From Sneh's briefings Rabin knew that Nabil Sha'ath did indeed know nothing of the Oslo channel. Abu Mazen won yet another credit point, but Arafat passed the main test, in the Hamas deportees crisis. At that time – December 1992 and January–February 1993 – the Palestinian delegation was at the center of a public storm in the territories. Palestinian public opinion was outraged over the expulsion of some four hundred Hamas and Islamic Jihad activists to Lebanon, in reaction to the killing of a Border policeman. In these conditions, the Palestinian delegation refused to participate in the Washington talks. Arafat convened the delegation members in Amman and compelled them to go to Washington. They went, but did not conceal their dissatisfaction with the decision.

Rabin was impressed by Arafat's ability to impose his will and the results were not long in coming. Few noticed an interview published by the fringe weekly, *Ha'Olam Hazeh*, on 5 May 1993. In the interview Rabin said: "Arafat was and still is the boss. Back in Madrid it was clear to all sides that the decisions would be made in Tunis. The split between the Palestinian delegation and the focal points of decision gives the PLO-Tunis a status of significance. I find this formula acceptable." Parallel with this, the first signs reached Oslo that Rabin was authorizing the foreign minister's talks. From what Rabin said in the interview, it was already clear where he was going: even if an agreement could be attained with the Palestinian delegation, its approval and realization would only be possible after the setting up of a direct link with the PLO; all the more so after Arafat succeeded in paralyzing Husseini and his colleagues.

However, Rabin's final decision to set up the link with Arafat was apparently made after a series of meetings in Britain and Italy between Yossi Alpher, the director of the Strategic Studies Center of the Tel Aviv University, and members of Force 17, headed by Nizar Ammar. These latter shared Hisham Sharabi's basic concept that whatever could be obtained from Israel should be obtained in order to gain the Palestinians a foothold in Palestine before the

Israeli right succeeded in carrying out a transfer.

The Oslo Channel

From the day Israel's rule changed it could have been guessed that the new government, in which the prime minister was also the defense minister, would find the Washington talks of less interest, for one simple reason: Rabin had a particular interest in the security aspects of the talks with the Palestinians, and he may have had doubts about Husseini's ability to handle the Hamas and Islamic Jihad, militarily. Husseini was well aware of this limitation and strove to recruit thirty thousand Palestinian youths from the territories, to be called the "Palestinian Police," in order to gain Rabin's confidence. Arafat, too, immediately realized what was happening and foiled Husseini's efforts, in order to give Rabin the option of the Palestine Liberation Army, a force already recruited from Palestinians outside the occupied territories and under the PLO's command. The dispute between Husseini and Arafat over the Palestine Police was: whether to recruit its personnel from within the territories, as Husseini maintained, or move the PLO army from the diaspora to the territories, as Arafat wanted; the dispute between them was basic and profound. Obviously whoever succeeded in recruiting the Palestinian security force for the interim period would win the lead in Israel's recognition; and Husseini lost.

The argument between Husseini and Arafat over the nature of the Palestinian security force also involved the first attempts to formulate subchannels to bypass the obstacle of the Washington talks. The time: halfway through 1992. It was then that Peres met with Faisal Husseini to examine the possibility of arranging a meeting between him and Rabin, for practical talks in which matters could be concluded directly – with Arafat's approval, naturally. Husseini took the proposal to Arafat, but the PLO leader ruled unambiguously that he should be the one to meet with Rabin. This was the background to Arafat's proclamations at that time – June–July 1992 – of the "meeting of the courageous" with Rabin, a meeting at which the leaders of Israel and the PLO, face to face, would resolve the problems holding up the breakthrough in the Washington talks.

Israelis tried to encourage Hanan Ashrawi, the delegation spokeswoman, to support the opening of a subchannel and it was against this background that she met with Professor Yair Hirschfeld. He told her that what was under discussion was the formulation of a channel to accompany the multinational track, so she recommended that a link be set up with Abu al-Ala, who was in charge of the multilateral talks. That was the end of Ashrawi's share in the affair, and she did not share in the talks. Various signs in her conduct point to it having been only toward the middle of 1993 that she began to suspect there was something going on behind the delegation's back.

The Foreign Ministry had no regrets over Arafat's success in blocking Husseini. Shimon Peres had had several contacts with Husseini, and did not have the impression that he would be able to block the Hamas and Palestinian extremism. The die was cast by Peres and his people, who felt Husseini had failed the test of leadership in the territories. This being so, the process of Arafat's weakening worried them, since they believed it was not Husseini who would profit from it, but the Hamas and the Islamic Jihad. They came to the conclusion that the ally in the common fight on fundamentalism was the PLO, not the weak leadership in the territories.

Peres had had several opportunities to establish contact with the PLO, but he was spared this effort in the wake of what was quite a chance meeting that took place at the end of January 1993, at a seminar given by the FaFo (Institute for Applied Social Science) Research Institute in Norway. The Institute was then researching the state of the economy and society in the territories. These researches were used, inter alia, by the participants in the deliberations of the multinational track at the various conferences. During the deliberations two Israeli researchers, Professor Yair Hirschfeld and Dr Ron Pundak, met with Abu al-Ala after Ashrawi had recommended such a meeting. Through them the PLO man wanted to send a message from Abu Mazen and Arafat, that they were interested in talking with Israel, not through the Palestinian delegation, on an issue which, as will be recalled, was unacceptable to the delegation: the implementation of the Gaza first idea. Peres immediately saw the importance of this channel, and it was actually because of the Palestinian economist Abu al-Ala. It fitted in with Peres' belief in the importance of fostering economic welfare in the Middle East as a basic component of the peace agreements and the subjection of the political agreements to mustering economic resources to stabilize the agreements, get the Middle Eastern peoples' latent energy moved from the track of confrontation and war to that of economic construction and regional cooperation, and thus defeat the Islamic fundamentalism. Peres told his circle of confidants that the agreements with the Palestinians should be based "not on a lot of flags – but on a credible economy."

Yossi Beilin was the man who had set up the link between the two Israeli researchers and the FaFo Research Institute, this being back at the time when the Labor Party was in the opposition. Beilin introduced the Institute director, Terje Roed Larsen, to his friend Prof. Hirschfeld, a member of the Labor Party's Mashov Group headed by Beilin. This was at the period following the failure of Peres' attempts to establish a government headed by himself. The Labor Party had walked out of the National Unity Government headed by Shamir and was in the opposition. The FaFo Institute carried out several socioeconomic researches in the territories. It is indeed a non-governmental research institute, but is rooted deep in the Norwegian Foreign Ministry. Roed Larsen's wife was the head of the foreign minister's office in Oslo and the foreign minister's wife held a senior post in the institute.

After several non-binding meetings in London between Abu al-Ala and the two Israeli researchers on the fringes of the Steering Committee for the multilateral talks, the sides decided to move the talks to Norway in order to keep them secret. In February 1993 there was a meeting in Sarpsborg, where a first formulation of the draft for the joint statement of principles was drawn up and, of course, the text of the appendix for economic cooperation. Abu al-Ala shared Peres' view that the arrangement's strength would be based on its economic credibility, not on how many flags the Palestinians would be able to wave. The unanimity on economic matters convinced Peres to establish a team for these negotiations, whose members would be Peres himself, his deputy, Yossi Beilin, the head of his office, Avi Gil, and Beilin's aide, Shlomo Gur. The ministry's legal adviser, Yoel Zinger, was brought into this team later. Hirschfeld and Pundak were, of course, unofficial members of this team. The Foreign Ministry team stayed in Jerusalem and did not establish any direct contact with the Palestinians.

In May the Israeli team reached the conclusion that the time was ripe for official figures to join the secret talks, this being after a series of tests Israel set Abu Mazen's team. After the series of tests the PLO people insisted that official figures join the meetings. Peres' team decided to incorporate the director general, Uri Savir, in the talks. As opposite number to the Palestinians' legal adviser

Hasan Asfur, the Foreign Ministry's legal adviser, Yoel Zinger, was scheduled to join in. He took the papers that had been texted by Abu al-Ala, Hirschfeld and Pundak, and gave them a legal wording. Zinger's wordings were the basis of the constant disputation that developed afterwards. Peres, Beilin and Zinger kept Rabin briefed on the developments. In June Rabin decided to intervene and texted some sixty questions to which he asked the Palestinians for answers. These questions caused considerable excitement among Abu al-Ala and his aides, since they noticed Rabin's fingerprints on them.

Questionnaires to the PLO: Tibi and Ramon's Channel

These sixty questions did indeed give rise to PLO satisfaction, but they also made things very difficult for the Palestinian negotiators because of the answers they had to come up with on extremely substantive issues. The difficulties lay not only in such important questions as the status of state lands, the field of jurisdiction and the status of East Jerusalem, but, in addition, in the security area the Palestinians had to state their position on a stop to the armed struggle and the Intifada and the amendment of the Palestinian Covenant.

In July 1993 Arafat summoned Dr Ahmad Tibi to Tunis. The young Arab-Israeli physician found Arafat in a state of unease. He briefed Tibi on the Oslo talks channel and the fact that they were in a crisis over the Israeli "questionnaire." Arafat also wanted to ascertain that Rabin knew what was going on and supported his foreign minister's moves.

Tibi went back to Israel and called his friend, Health Minister Chaim Ramon. He went to his Ramat Hasharon home, and then began an intensive series of secret contacts and telephone calls, whose main purpose was: the maintenance of a channel of communications between Rabin and Arafat, through Tibi and Ramon. At that time Arafat was supporting Abu Mazen, and there were important telephone conversations between Ramon and Abu Mazen from their homes in Israel and Tunis.

As soon as at the first meeting, Dr Tibi asked Ramon the principal question that was preoccupying Arafat and Abu Mazen: would Rabin be prepared to conduct official negotiations with the PLO?

Since the PLO had difficulties in answering the long question-naire, at some stage Ramon handed Tibi a short questionnaire comprising the four questions which appeared to Rabin to be the most important: the status of East Jerusalem, the principle of the two stages, one interim stage and one permanent; "comprehensive security" (the term Israel used to present its position at that time); and the settlements. Arafat had instructed the Palestinian delegation in Washington to take tough stands on all these problems. Rabin wanted to know whether he would demonstrate flexible stands in direct talks with him. Messages were sent to Rabin through the secret channel of communications on security affairs, that if he were to meet with him, Arafat would be willing not to let Rabin down. Ramon told Tibi that if the answers were to prove satisfactory, the prime minister would show willingness to open negotiations with the PLO.

Tibi's decisive visit to Tunis took place on the 21st of that month. That same day two Israeli Knesset Members also arrived in Tunis: the Labor Party's Yael Dayan and Abd al-Wahhab Darawsha from the Arab Democratic List. Arafat could not make himself free to receive his visitors, because he had to meet with Tibi in Tunis, together with Abu Mazen. When the Knesset Members were told that Arafat had taken off for Cairo, the chairman was already absorbed in those talks. Tibi's report sounded encouraging, and Arafat had hurried to Cairo to brief the Egyptians. Arafat had another program of visits in Yemen on his schedule, but saw fit to wait at the Cairo airport in order to brief Usama al-Baz, President Mubarak's close aide.

After Arafat's departure from Tunis, Tibi and Abu Mazen con-tinued to thrash out the details of the talks. Abu Mazen seemed tense. At first he hesitated over whether to give Rabin positive answers. It is hard to know what he was thinking. He may, even then, have feared that Arafat's promotion to the negotiations front would eventually undermine it. He was finally placated, but intro-duced several terminological changes. Instead of "comprehensive security," he decided on the phrasing that afterwards accompanied the basic principle of the security concept: external security to be Israel's responsibility; internal security for the Palestinians. He gave positive answers to the rest of the questions, but added an unambiguous condition: everything depended on the maintenance of direct negotiations with the PLO. He also said that all these answers were an integral whole that could be neither added to nor detracted from. If these negotiations were to fail, Abu Mazen would resign from his post, and that would mean the collapse of all the secret channels of communications and, in actual fact, the disintegration of the entire peace process.

Tibi hurried to Israel and, as soon as he arrived, shut himself up at midnight in Minister Ramon's office. Ramon was pleased. He thought no problems were to be expected from Rabin. Two days later Ramon phoned Tibi and informed him that Rabin was pleased, but had his fears of the unpolished text on the field of jurisdiction. Rabin feared that through this chink the PLO could undermine the principle of the two stages and the status of Jerusalem, and actually empty the four answers of their contents. Tibi did not share Rabin's fears. In any event, Tibi went to Ramon's house and from there they phoned Abu Mazen in Tunis. Abu Mazen soothed Ramon's fears. The three discussed the texting of the definition of the field of jurisdiction and agreed to adopt a formulation that had already been studied in Washington: "The West Bank and Gaza Strip will be one geographical unit, and the field of jurisdiction will apply to all areas of the West Bank and Gaza." Israel accepted this formulation because, on the one hand, the Palestinians could live with it and, on the other, there was a specific determination that the discussion on the status of Jerusalem would be postponed, so it was not tantamount to being the "West Bank and Gaza."

Ramon went off to brief Rabin and Tibi rushed back to Arafat. The sixty questions crisis in Oslo was, then, resolved through Ramon and Tibi's channel of the four questions. The Palestinians actually agreed to postpone the discussion on the knotty questions of Jerusalem, the settlements, etc. Israel postponed the PLO's clarifications on the armed struggle and an end to the Intifada. By chance or not, at roughly the same time an unclear European source of funding streamed amounts of money into the coffers of the PLO in Tunis that it needed like the breath of life.

Back to Oslo

In August the Foreign Ministry staff were able to brief the prime minister that the agreements with the PLO were coming to fruition. Peres went on a trip to the Scandinavian countries, to complete the documents. Peres and his aides, Zinger and Gil, were hosted in the official guest house in Stockholm, and the talks with Tunis went on throughout the night, with the mediation of the Norwegian foreign minister, Johan Jorgen Holst, his ministry staff and people from the FaFo Research Institute. On the other side were Arafat and Abu al-Ala. At the end of a marathon night of talks they were able to raise glasses in a toast to a good job well done. Peres had to carry on to Norway and Uri Savir, the Foreign Ministry director general, was summoned to Oslo for an initialling ceremony. The Palestinian side was represented by Abu al-Ala and Hasan Asfur. Peres had to conduct his political talks in Oslo while concealing the genuine objective of the visit, and it was only after nightfall that the Palestinians gathered for the signing ceremony in the guest house in the Norwegian capital. The agreements were initialled by Uri Savir and Abu al-Ala. As a mark of esteem for the activities of the two Israeli academics, Prof. Hirschfeld was invited to put his signature to them. The signators could hear the beating of history's wings, but there was a very speedy fall from the heights of euphoria to the hard ground of reality, and the history-makers already took their first pounding in Washington, toward the impressive signing ceremony on the White House lawn on 13 September. Before the signing ceremony Israel and the PLO took another, unplanned step, which was to exchange documents of mutual recognition. Israel must have noticed, without being able to do anything about it, that the role played by Abu Mazen's group ended with the Oslo toasting ceremony, and Arafat changed horses immediately after that. The further contacts with the PLO were with different people, with different concerns on their minds.

It is Hard to Say Goodbye to an Old Love

Despite the talks with the PLO, it was not easy for Israel to sever itself from the old notion of support for the leadership of the occupied territories. At that stage Israel was thinking in terms of a Palestinian delegation which would be given the go-ahead by the PLO which, in turn, would wait for recognition after the interim period. But the PLO was impatient and demanded immediate recognition and it was hard for Israel to refuse, all the more as this was made clear to Abu Mazen in the bypass channel with Ramon and Tibi.

The testimony of Mamduh Nawfal, one of the FIDA leaders, who was a member of the Supervisory Committee for the Washington negotiations, was especially important. In his memoirs he testified[2] that Abu Mazen did not consider the Oslo channel a substitute for the Washington negotiations. In his view, the Oslo channel was intended solely for the formulation of a comprehensive "paper of intentions," after which the negotiations would go back to Washington. Accordingly, Abu Mazen told Husseini and Ashrawi of the paper texted in Oslo so that they could study it and bring it to the knowledge of the Americans, without telling them that it was a document worked out in the secret channel. At that time, March–April 1993, Arafat supported Abd al-Shafi's tough stands in order to prevent the delegation making any progress in the Washington negotiations. In contrast to him, Abu Mazen expressed regret at the hesitations of Husseini and Ashrawi and their fears of opening a secret channel with Israel. Nawfal reported that Rabin had given Minister Sneh the task of persuading Husseini and Ashrawi to open a secret channel. Was it hard for Rabin to swallow the Oslo developments? Was Rabin apprehensive about the implications for US–Israeli relations? One way or another, Arafat frequently fulminated against the link between the two and the Americans. "This is a delegation which is too weak to face up to the Americans," he told Yaser Abd a-Rabbo on one occasion, "They believe whatever the Americans tell them." At the end of July 1993 Christopher held a *tête-à-tête* meeting with Husseini in his Jerusalem hotel room. That was the last time that Christopher pleaded with Husseini to take responsibility for running the talks, without subservience to the PLO. In Tunis, however, in talks with his close circle, Arafat voiced his confidence that Husseini, as a true Fatah stalwart, would not fulfill the Americans' and Rabin's aspirations to split the Palestinians between the inside and outside. Arafat used to tell his confidants: "Oh, my comrades, we have entered into the practical stage of the PLO's erasure and the erasure of this leadership, and a split between the inside and outside." He promised that "If Faisal becomes the alternative, I will overturn the negotiating table with Israel, and to hell with the Americans and Rabin." Arafat ruled that he would not permit "The members of the little families [a dig at Husseini, the aristocrat whose family had known better days] to decide the nation's fate." He called Husseini and Ashrawi "Trojan horses." Back then, halfway through 1993, Arafat was considering convening the PNC to put a stop to the peace talks.

Abu Mazen, who had come to realize Husseini's weakness, began to toe Arafat's line, lost interest in the Washington talks, and went back to talking of the PLO's importance. His depression undoubtedly originated in his realization that Husseini would be unable to stand up to Arafat. Abu Mazen's alliance with Arafat was tactical and he never gave up his original intention of exploiting the Oslo channel just as a means of giving the delegation in Washington another chance. So much for Nawfal's remarks.

When Abu Mazen realized that in the end Arafat had foiled the "plot," it was with a very heavy heart that he flew to Washington for the White House ceremony. It is against this backdrop that his odd comment in the first pages of his memoirs "The Road to Oslo," that he was going to sign an agreement in which he had no share,[3] should be understood.

Mutual Recognition: Changing Horses in Midstream

Peres was later to let slip something that laid bare one of Israel's strategic secrets in the talks with the Palestinians. He said the process with the PLO began with a "happy end." That is, that Israel did not intend to recognize the PLO immediately after the signing of the Oslo agreements, but meant to announce its recognition of the PLO as a prize for the manner in which they honored the agreements afterwards. Israel did not abide by this policy line, because the natural pace of the developments preceded Israel's meticulous strategic timetable.

In any event, Israel demanded that Arafat make an unequivocal statement that he was abandoning terrorism, condemning it and punishing those occupied in it, and that he would call on the Palestinians to stop the Intifada. Israel also prepared a detailed list of any clause in the Palestinian Covenant containing any form of non-recognition of Israel and the aspiration to destroy it. Arafat demanded that Israel regard the PLO as the sole legitimate representative of the Palestinians. In the end, Arafat was content with Israel's recognition that the PLO was the representative of the Palestinian people, but he did not agree to declare an end to either the Intifada or the armed struggle.

The accelerated talks on mutual recognition began back in Oslo, immediately after the initialling ceremony. The Palestinians pressed and the Israelis wriggled. The result was: the paper of principles was texted without Israel's recognition of the PLO. The Israeli team wanted to reach a situation in which the joint paper of principles would "stand on its own feet," as the Israelis put it, that is, it would have no substantive connection with the PLO. At the same time, Israel immediately briefed Christopher that the PLO was interested in official recognition: and to this the United States, ostensibly, had no objections, but nevertheless found it difficult to accept the old PLO. The mutual recognition talks with the PLO were held in two rounds: the first back in Oslo, the second in Paris, immediately after the meeting between Peres and Christopher at the secretary of state's vacation site in California. The talks on the mutual recognition issue were already conducted by phone from Tunis between Uri Savir and the PLO's top echelons, headed by Arafat. Abu Mazen's people no longer played a major role in these contacts.

The Israelis failed to notice that, while in the secret talks channels they had spoken with a very specific wing of the PLO, as soon as word of these talks got out, the negotiators were replaced, and the new PLO interlocutors were interested in other issues. They were riddled with the old fears and suspicions of Abu Mazen's Iyyadist band. At that stage it was the negotiators, not what was written in the documents, that was of special interest to them. They insisted that the PLO be mentioned specifically as negotiator. The joint agreement of principles expressed a formulation agreed between Israel and Abu Mazen. The mutual recognition agreement was a new one, with new people who were interested in other issues. It turned out that changing horses produced immediate frictions, because of which the signing ceremony in the White House was almost cancelled.

Without Suha

The major problem involved in the implementation of the agreement of principles between Israel and the PLO lay in the fact that Israel had made the agreement with a group of Abu Iyyad's successors in Tunis, headed by Abu Mazen, while the implementation had to be with the entire PLO, or at least with the agreement of the Jihadist wing and/or the leadership in the occupied territories. If this was not done, the agreement would have signified an internal explosion and split in the PLO. The differences of interests between Arafat and Abu Mazen found immediate expression: Arafat wanted to distance Abu Mazen's group, because he realized the agreements were promoting him as his certain successor. The attack of fears he had suffered when the Murphy delegation, in its Tunis talks with Abu Iyyad that same March 1990, had used the technique of the questionnaires under his very eyes, came back and overwhelmed him. Arafat had to make a hard choice; were he to stick with Abu Mazen to carry on with the implementation of the agreements, the Jihadist wing, with the Fatah militant wing at its head, might walk out of the PLO. Abu Mazen would become the strong man in what was left of the PLO, with Arafat turning into a symbolic figure, devoid of authority. The only way out was to carry on with the policy of balances, playing off the two PLO streams one against the other. Accordingly, immediately after the Oslo signing, Arafat again gave the Jihadist wing his support against Abu Mazen.

The Oslo agreements left several injured parties on the ground. In Israel, as is known, the delegation leader, Elyakim Rubinstein, was deeply insulted when he realized that the exhaustive talks in Washington were no more than a diversionary tactic. He wanted to submit his resignation to Rabin, but changed his mind. He refused to continue heading the team to the talks with the Palestinians, because he did not believe the talks with the PLO would bear fruit. Nabil Sha'ath and the heads of the Palestinian delegation, Husseini, Ashrawi, and Abd a-Shafi, also had similar feelings of affront. Arafat lost no time in taking advantage of Nabil Sha'ath's injured feelings to distance him from Abu Mazen. First, he tried to appoint him head of the multinational track teams, replacing Abu al-Ala, but, as far as can be seen, Sha'ath himself had no interest in lending a hand to such a clear split in the Iyyadist camp. He was finally placated by being given the post of head of the negotiating teams with Israel in Taba, thus actually helping Arafat to get rid of the Oslo negotiators.

Arafat's maneuver was, however, designed mainly to put the Fatah organization back in center stage and base the establishment of the Palestinians' national authority in Gaza and Jericho on the Fatah. This was in complete contradiction not just of Abu Mazen's approach, that the organizations should be disbanded; it also conflicted with the positions of his two main partners, the People's Party and FIDA. A strange situation emerged: Abu Mazen and FIDA wanted to further the Oslo agreements and, in contrast to them, Arafat was blocking the process in order to bring the Fatah organization back to his side. What mattered to him was not the success of the agreements' implementation, but foiling the "plot" to use the agreements to crown Abu Mazen leader of the PLO.

The first indication of this came when the process of ratifying the agreements began, toward the White House signing ceremony. It was then that Arafat saw fit to convene the Fatah institutions and did not embark on the process of ratifying the agreements with the PLO institutions. The Fatah Central Council was first to be convened and, as expected, the deliberations were stormy. After three tempestuous sessions this institution, with its 18–21 members, did not succeed in reaching agreement and when the council members were planning to resume the deliberations of the fourth session, and possibly a vote, Bassam Abu Sharif took them by surprise with an announcement that the Council had already ratified the agreements. Arafat hurried to confirm his remarks. Qaddumi, who headed the opponents in these deliberations, explained that the Fatah Central Council had not made any decision and the ratification had not even been put to the vote. It was only after his announcement that Arafat convened the PLO Executive Committee and PLO Central Council, which did indeed ratify the agreements; but not without problems, and with charges levelled against Arafat that the Executive Committee was not a legal quorum.

Arafat's failure at that stage was not that he did not succeed in getting the Oslo agreements through the Fatah institutions, but that he did not succeed in explaining to his arms-bearing colleagues that he had no intention of forsaking them for Abu Mazen and his colleagues. They were convinced that Arafat had reached his last stop – together with Abu Mazen and the Americans – against them. It took a month or two for Arafat to get them to realize their mistake. It was Abu Mazen who grasped Arafat's intentions at once, and as soon as the eve of the emotionally-charged preparations for the trip to the White House, harsh exchanges of words were heard between them.

Under the conclusions between Abu Mazen and Israel, it was only Abu Mazen and Peres who were scheduled to turn up at the White House. At first Arafat tried to send Qaddumi to the signing of the agreements, since he was the head of the PLO's political department, a man from the dogmatic wing of the PLO and one of the leading critics of the agreements. Qaddumi refused, and then Arafat launched a move that would later turn out to be totally new, ignoring all the agreements and secret understandings between Israel and Abu Mazen. Arafat insisted on heading the

Palestinian delegation and delivering the Palestinian speech on the White House lawn.

Israel and the United States did not take kindly to the change, which was not the last. Abu Mazen was skilled at knowing Arafat's moods and found it more difficult to accept the change. It was not the splitting up of the honor that bothered him so much as the realization that Arafat had not abandoned his endless policy of balances and if he were to take over the talks channel, it would not serve the Iyyadist objectives. Abu Mazen reacted to Arafat's invitation to the White House in a way that profoundly injured Arafat's feelings and honor. To stop Arafat turning up on an equal status with the world's great, Abu Mazen forced Arafat not to take his wife Suha with him. By so doing, he demonstrated to the eyes of all that despite the agreements, Arafat's status was not equal to that of the other participants in the ceremony, who were accompanied by their wives, as is customary at historic events of this type. Abu Mazen threatened: if Suha Arafat were to come, he would not. Arafat swallowed the insult and gave in. He had no choice, since he knew that without Abu Mazen there would be no signing ceremony. A cancellation of the ceremony would have put the entire PLO at risk.

The Race to Zero Hour at the White House

The PLO delegation preceded the delegation from Israel and moved into a Washington hotel one day before it, on 12 September. In the plane that carried the PLO delegation – Moroccan King Hassan II's private jet – (another version has it that it was a jet loaned to him by Saddam Hussein and hurriedly painted with Moroccan colors prior to the flight to Washington) there was, of course, euphoria. But Arafat, despite his joy, occasionally looked disturbed. His joy was not complete.

At 0500 on 13 September, Arafat wakened Dr Tibi in his hotel room. He told him they would not be able to sign the agreement without the PLO also being mentioned in the body of the text, not just at the signing. He asked Tibi what was the point of mutual recognition if the decisive document did not mention the PLO. Dr Tibi wondered how to solve this problem at five a.m., when the ceremony was scheduled to commence at eleven, and asked why the matter had not been raised before this. Tibi did not know the original instructions had been for the PLO to give the delegation the green light and wait for its turn to come, after the interim stage. In any event, Tibi called Ambassador Itamar Rabinowitz, who told him he would have to wait until Rabin and Peres landed. At six Tibi called Avi Gil, the head of Peres' office. Half an hour later Tibi rushed to the Israelis' hotel and met with Peres. Tibi told Peres Arafat's stand was unequivocal: if the term "PLO" was not introduced into the agreements, the Palestinians would walk out. Peres was absorbed in the preparation of his speech, so the talk with Tibi was conducted partly through Avi Gil.

Peres expressed his regret at the likelihood that such an important historic opportunity might be missed. He asked him to tell Arafat that the demand for changes after the initialling would make the world say the PLO had not changed and could not be relied on. He believed that the agreements could not be altered after having been ratified by the Israeli Parliament. Tibi commented that, to the best of his knowledge, the agreements had not been ratified by the Knesset, but only by the Cabinet. He proposed conducting a telephone poll among the ministers for this purpose. Peres smiled and went off to Rabin's suite. Rabin and Peres came to the conclusion that Arafat was right and, since there was mutual recognition between the PLO and Israel, there was no reason to ignore the PLO. Ignoring it belonged to the previous era. At the same time, the two decided to bargain and Peres came back with a compromise: the body of the text would not be altered, but the PLO would be mentioned in the signatures. Tibi ran off to the Ana Hotel, where the Palestinians were staying. Arafat was not happy about the compromise and insisted that the text, too, be altered. He demanded that "PLO" replace "Palestinian delegation" in the text. All his aides, as well as Abu Mazen, gathered around Arafat. They were in an aggressive, uncompromising mood. Euphoria had turned into depression. The PLO's non-appearance in the agreements reinforced their basic fears that the entire political process was designed to destroy the PLO and cut the ground from under their feet, and they feared they were going into a trap.

Then began a race against time. Tibi went back to Peres, who expressed his regret. Peres briefed Christopher on the situation and discovered that the Americans already knew about it, since parallel with the contacts with Tibi, Hanan Ashrawi had met with Dennis Ross and the Norwegians.

Peres went back to his hotel and tried to call Tibi. It was already

10:00. Tibi told him they had decided to walk out. Meanwhile Yossi Beilin, Yoel Zinger and Itamar Rabinowitz had also already gathered in the room. An argument sprang up among the Israelis. It was 10:25, and then Peres said Israel agreed that instead of "Palestinian team" the text, too, would say "PLO team." Tibi was excited and there and then he phoned Arafat to brief him. Arafat told Tibi he merited two kisses for this; to Peres he said they would meet in the White House.

Parallel with this, the preparations for the White House ceremony were completed. The text had to be amended in the formulations that were ready for signature. When the Israelis and the PLO agreed on the changes, they forgot that the agreements were actually in the White House and the Americans had to be briefed immediately, so as not to be late for the ceremony. The Palestinians did not agree to the amendments being made in handwriting, and the agreements had to be retyped at the last minute. As it turned out later, the Americans did not address the textual change as being purely technical, and Ashrawi had her work cut out to persuade them to agree; but this was only a partial success, as will be explained later.

Because of the last-minute delays Beilin, Savir and Gil missed the organized transport to the White House. Luckily for them, they managed to get a lift and reached the emotional ceremony on time.

"There is Someone to Speak With": Ammar and Alpher's Security Channel

Hirschfeld and Pundak were not the only academics to precede the negotiations between Israel and the PLO. A no less important role was played by another group of academics, with security backgrounds in Israel, headed by Yossi Alpher, the director of Tel Aviv University's Jaffe Center for Strategic Studies. While Hirschfeld and Pundak thrashed out the political aspects with the PLO, Alpher's group thrashed out the security problems involved in the implementation of the interim period. The two groups did not know about each other. Only Rabin and Abu Mazen knew of all the contacts. The reason why it was Israeli academics who initiated the thrashing out of the security problems with the PLO was that the official security establishment was given no guidelines by the political echelons on this, and did not itself initiate these contacts. It should be recalled that in those years there was an Israeli government which banned any contacts with the PLO.

However, like the members of the "political channel," the members of the "security channel," too, were insufficiently aware of the fact that they were not actually conducting negotiations with the "PLO," but with a very internally-defined group: the Abu Mazen group, and they were not familiar with the group's history and the complexity of the relations between it and the other groups in the PLO. As soon as Abu Mazen's people had concluded the negotiations and led Arafat to the White House, Arafat shut the channel down and, at least in the critical period – which began immediately after the signing of the agreements, with the opening of the talks on their implementation – his channel did not continue. The truth is that the security channel was not the first to thrash out security problems common to Israel and the PLO. This channel had been preceded by contacts between Yossi Ginossar, a Shin Bet man, Brigadier General (Reserves) Shlomo Gazit and Hani al-Hasan, one of the leaders of the Iyyadist group: as far as is known, however, these contacts dealt with specific issues and had no overview of the security problems. The channel conducted by Yossi Alpher from the Israeli side was the first to be encompassing, ongoing, thorough, and formulate understandings, if unwritten, between Israel and the people around Abu Mazen, who had in the meantime become Abu Iyyad's successor, to Hani al-Hasan's great grief.

In times to come, in December 1993, Alpher told me what he had been able to find out of the security channel's history. What will be related below is based mainly on his remarks, but also on snippets of information from Palestinian sources.

At the end of 1989 the following question began to preoccupy Alpher: how could the interim period be actualized from the security aspect? The security aspects appeared to him to be critical. At his own initiative he appealed to security elements in Israel, particularly the Shin Bet, and tried to set up a link with Palestinians who were well-informed on matters of internal security. He went to jails to meet there with Intifada activists and major political figures, considered – mistakenly, for the most part – to be Intifada leaders. Alpher did not find what he wanted with either. The prisoners' security knowledge was limited to the restricted underground activity. The political figures were totally helpless. Even the Black Panthers, Fatah representatives and Shabiba activists had no idea how to operate complex security mechanisms. Nor were they aware of the fact that the issue was problematic and authority for the interim period could not be handed over to them without the joint security problems being agreed. Alpher reached the unavoidable conclusion that the Palestinians in the territories were not relevant interlocutors for joint discussions on security issues.

His next stop was the Palestinian intellectuals in the diaspora who were close to Abu Mazen: Ahmad Khaldi and Yazid Sayegh. At the beginning of 1990 Alpher met with them at academic seminars under the auspices of American and European elements. The first significant meeting at that time took place in a picturesque little village in Oxfordshire, in southern England. The meeting was also attended by Jordanian representatives and Prince Hasan's envoys, Generals Muhammad Shiyab, Shafiq Ajeilat and Fikri Shishani. These were veteran, retired officers close to the crown prince, and of course they briefed the king himself. It was no coincidence that it was actually Prince Hasan who took an interest in these contacts. The crown prince supported the tripartite confederation model with economic connections with the Gulf, and was closer to Abu Mazen than the king, who opposed the tripartite confederation because he feared that Jerusalem would overshadow Amman in importance. In any evet, his agreement to the maintenance of the channel signified the beginnings of a change in his attitude, in favor of Prince Hasan's approach.

These meetings did not satisfy Alpher. The two Palestinian academics specialized in questions of strategic security: arms control, security regimes and so on, but they had never set foot on Palestinian soil and did not have the background to qualify them to discuss problems of internal security in the territories.

In 1991 the Truman Institute, together with Husseini's East Jerusalem Institute for Arab Studies, initiated the writing of papers on various subjects connected with the implementation of the interim period. Various issues were discussed, in the fields of economy, society, and security. The Institute asked Alpher and Khaldi to write papers on security topics, and Alpher was delighted with the opportunity. Khaldi and Alpher wrote papers and Alpher's paper was afterwards used as a basis for the continuation of the deliberations. The document was completed in February 1992, and was the first on these issues. The Israelis and Palestinians discussed the first joint security paper in an Italian townlet overlooking an enchanted lake near the popes' residence in Castel Gandolfo. Ahmad Khaldi sent the document to Abu Mazen.

Up to then the deliberations with the Palestinians had been of an academic, not a practical nature. The turning point came after Khaldi took Alpher's paper to Abu Mazen for his perusal. A genuine Palestinian security man, Brig. Gen. Nizar Ammar from the PLO's internal security mechanism, that is, Force 17, entered the picture. He was a Jordanian Army officer who had transferred to the Fatah after "Black September."

Ammar was incorporated in the talks through the Israeli Palestinian Center for Research and Information (IPCRI), headed by the Israeli Gershon Baskin and the Palestinian Zakariya al-Qaq. The fact that in the course of time al-Qaq became a member of the Palestinian delegation to the arms control committee talks indicates that he was close to Abu Mazen's circles. In any event, the Center proposed getting Nizar Ammar to meet with Alpher and several Israeli figures with security backgrounds: Brigadier General (Reserves) Shlomo Gazit, who had been head of the intelligence branch and the Defense Ministry's Coordinator of Activities in the Occupied Territories, Zeev Schiff, the *Ha'aretz* commentator on security affairs, and also Colonel (Reserves) Arye Shalev and the researcher Gil Feiler. An intensive channel of communications opened in villages in England and around Rome. The first meeting was in London, in October 1992, under the auspices of IPCRI and the US research institute AAAS (the American Academy of Arts and Sciences). The US Administration also kept an eye on the contacts: this may be learned from the fact that the meeting was funded by the Ford Foundation, which does not conceal its activities from the Washington administration. In addition to Nizar Ammar, Dr Khalil Shqaqi, a lecturer on strategic affairs in the a-Najah University in Nablus, a resident of Tulkarm, also went to London. Khalil Shqaqi is a very interesting man: he is the brother of Dr Fathi Shqaqi, a leader of the Islamic Jihad, from the pro-Iranian wing. He is also a devout Muslim, but did not follow his brother's path, but remained faithful to the Fatah. He represented the Fatah at various Islamic congresses in the United States. In any event, the Israeli administration restricted his moves and special intervention by Alpher was needed with the Civilian Administration to enable his departure for London. The Iyyadists – Nizar Ammar and the two academics – kept their distance from him, and did not bring him into their group.

The first discussion in London was based on Alpher's paper. Ammar said that two days previously he had held a discussion on this paper with the Palestinian leadership. He did not go into detail, but introduced himself as one of Abu Iyyad's people, who was now working with Abu Mazen. The Israelis' impression was that Ammar was an out-and-out intelligence man, logical, a general staff member "with no blood on his hands." It was Ammar who had written the entry on Israel's intelligence services for the Palestinian encyclopaedia and it was he who had studied the papers left in the Israeli Embassy in Tehran after the Shah's collapse and Khomeini's takeover of Iran. After his incorporation in the talks, Ammar became the senior man. The two academics helped him in the translation work, because he had no command of English.

Up to the June of 1993 the talks with Ammar were held in England and Italy. It is worth recalling here that it was in June that Rabin sent the Oslo track the sixty questions which presaged the breakthrough toward the crystallization of the agreements. The Israelis and Abu Mazen's people thrashed out many security problems between them. There were no written conclusions, but the Israelis' impression was clear: if these are the people with whom the security arrangements for the interim and permanent periods were to be worked out – there was someone to talk with. Rabin believed there was room for cooperation with the Palestinians on three crucial issues: intelligence and the Shin Bet, border control, and internal control.

The problems were thrashed out patiently and in a mutual desire to learn. Thus, for instance, the understandings on joint patrols were worked out after the Palestinians had proposed opening a police station in the settlements. The Palestinians from the diaspora were not familiar with the special sensitivities in the territories and the particularly hostile attitude of the settlers toward the Palestinian police. Alpher and his colleagues invested many hours in explaining to the Palestinians from the diaspora, far away from the territories experience, what Gush Emunim was and what the settlers' reaction might be in such an event.

Toward the channel's closure in June, Ammar began sending messages from Arafat that if Israel were to speak with him, he would take them by surprise with his moderation. Rabin received the messages and sent the questions to Oslo; but there was one single thing that Rabin and Alpher were unable to foresee: that immediately after the conclusion of the channel, Arafat would replace the entire team, and many things that had been agreed on simply vanished into thin air.

Alpher's Paper: A Tripartite Security Regime

Some sort of an idea of the contents of the deliberations in the security channel may be obtained from an article Yossi Alpher published in the journal on security affairs, *Survival*.[4] Even though the article carries only Alpher's signature, it should be addressed as reflecting the moods and agreements in that channel's deliberations. Alpher does not quote from the minutes of the deliberations, but when he presents the sides' positions there is a high probability that he heard the principal things he wrote down at those deliberations from the sides themselves. In principle, the article is an advanced processing of the paper Khaldi sent to Abu Mazen and reflects what was said at the first discussion in London in October 1992, not what was said subsequently. It should here be recalled that the remarks do not reflect the viewpoints of all the participants, but only Alpher's angle of view. Nevertheless, it is important to know the main points, since from them we may learn of the broad agreements and viewpoints of the other sides, even if they are given solely from Alpher's viewpoint.

If it turns out that the PLO does indeed adhere to these under-standings, Alpher's ruling that "there is someone with whom to speak" on security matters certainly was well-founded. Although this was an Israeli–Palestinian channel of clarifications, the central-ity of the Jordanian participation, through Prince Hasan's envoys, should also be taken into account, since Jordan was to play a major role in the formulation of the security regime with the Palestinians.

The security concept as presented in the article starts out from a dual assumption: Israel's genuine strategic depth is not the West Bank, but Jordan; internal security in the territories should be handed over to the Palestinians and a security regime created, based on demilitarization of the territories and Israeli–Palestinian cooperation against terrorism. From this it follows that a bilateral Israeli–Palestinian security regime would be out of the question, and what was needed was a tripartite regime, together with Jordan, with Jordan as the central, prominent factor in consolidating security in the region.

While the understandings with Jordan touch on Israel's defense against an attack by regular armies, the understandings between Israel and the PLO are based on a common war on terrorism. The understandings with Jordan address consolidating the East Bank as Israel's strategic depth against dangers from the eastern front. A security agreement with Jordan would prevent army forces massing in its territory for an attack on Israel, and enable an IDF withdrawal from the West Bank and its redeployment in security regions overlooking the Jordan River and its bridges. The coastal plain could be only partially defended by a deployment on the ridges of the hills. The genuine defense would be through security arrangements with Jordan. In any event, the West Bank would be demilitarized. The Palestinians would have a gendarmerie for maintenance of internal security. From all this it emerges that the Palestinians would prefer no army at all to a small army, in order to concentrate all their resources on the construction of their political entity under international auspices. A small army would prevent their obtaining such auspices, and expose them to the risk of a military attacks by Israel and Jordan. In all this it is difficult not to identify Abu Iyyad's main points in "Lowering the Sword," written in March 1990.

Jordan's importance as a buffer state between Israel and Iraq and between Syria and Saudi Arabia was proved in the Gulf crisis. Even before that, after the Iran–Iraq war ended in 1988 and Iraq began demanding a regional status that jeopardized Israel and Jordan, the Likud government jettisoned its faith in the actualization of an "alternative homeland" for the Palestinians in the East Bank and recognized Jordan's importance as a stabilizing regional element, and it was actually the Likud government which, immediately after the war, demanded the establishment of a joint Jordanian–Palestinian delegation for peace talks. King Hussein's July 1988 proclamation of his severance of relations with the territories made it easier for the Shamir government to accept Jordan's stance on the Palestinian issue. Alpher did not hesitate to determine that Israel's declaration that any invasion of Jordan would be deemed a casus belli, as well as Jordanian King Hussein's announcement that he would not permit the entry of any foreign army into his kingdom, led to Jordan passing its test as a buffer state and prevented a ground war between Israel and Iraq.

In the article Alpher describe the three sides' existential fears of a common security regime, almost certainly as they were explained at the meetings in Britain and Italy. It transpires that it was not just the Israelis who feared destruction and elimination; the Palestinians and Jordan had similar fears.

The Palestinians feared a transfer, especially in the wake of the great immigration to Israel, and the policies of both Israel and the Arab countries standing in the way of their political independence. In a regional security regime they wanted to guarantee themselves especially against these risks.

The Jordanians were disturbed by the prevalent concept that Jordan was an artificial political entity. It was not just the concept of the Israeli right, that "Jordan is Palestine," which concerned them, but also the views of some central circles in Damascus on a "Greater Syria," the rivalry that developed with the Saudi Arabian dynasty, the sensitive relations with the Palestinian majority in Jordan and the fundamentalist movements. The Palestinians' concern about a transfer, or even normal emigration from the territories to Jordan, disturbed the Hashemite regime, and it defined these aspects by the term: "demographic security."

There were suspicions and fears, then, not just between Israel and the other two sides of the triangle, but between each one and its two future partners. The Jordanians also feared the Palestinians' ambitions for the East Bank, and the Palestinians, Jordan's ambitions for the West Bank. The security regime was, then, designed not to find a solution just for Israel's fears of Jordan and the Palestinians, but also for the fears of each side of the triangle.

The basis for the deliberations was the Camp David agreements, although the Palestinians and Jordanians claimed they had not been partners to them. Those agreements for the first time laid down the principles of the following issues: the transfer to the Palestinians of the authority for security, the establishment of a "strong police force" from among the inhabitants of the territories, and the involvement of Jordan and Egypt in the training of this police force, as well as Israel's withdrawal from the population centers and the deployment of IDF forces in security sites. Nevertheless, in the years that had passed since the Camp David Agreements were signed (September 1978), there had been changes in the territories, mainly in the spread of Israel's settlements. The Likud government claimed that it was because of these changes that it was unable to carry out the redeployment.

The Rabin government, which took over from the Shamir government in July 1992, continued to hold these positions, but changes in its stance gradually became apparent. Alpher does not say so, but the logical reason for this was the existence of the security channel of communications. At first the new government believed there would be a significant deployment in the territories and internal security would be left entirely in the hands of the Israeli army. Only later was the principle accepted of a division between responsibility for internal security, which would be handed over to the Palestinians, with genuine cooperation with Israel, and responsibility for external security, which would remain in Israel's hands.

Since the participants in the various channels of negotiations did not know each other, Alpher did not know that the distinction between internal and external security had been laid down in July 1993, in Ramon and Tibi's channel of contacts. Rabin had then accepted Abu Mazen's alteration to the term "comprehensive security" by dividing it into internal and external security; doubtless from following the deliberations of the security channel.

Since cooperation against terrorism was an essential condition for the transfer of security authorities to the Palestinians, making a goodwill gesture – to improve the atmosphere between the peoples – was essential. This signifies that the foundations of civil cooperation based on open borders and commercial and cultural relations are part of the security regime. The concepts of security borders and going back to the Green Line were unacceptable to most Israelis, Alpher rules.

In actual fact, if the parameters were to be determined for Israel's strategic depth in Jordan and security cooperation against terrorism decided on with the Palestinians, Israel would be able to withdraw from the territories, with an improvement in its security and defense positions. At the same time, it would be Israel that took the risks, because there is no guarantee that the Palestinians would be able to actualize the agreements. There would then be a reversible situation, namely, Israel would be entitled to retract the agreements in the event of their not being honored. This would mean: the re-occupation of the West Bank, or sections of it. The same thing also applies to Jordan: if a new government were to be established in Jordan, or if it did not honor the agreements and were to permit armies to mass in its territory against Israel's will, Israel would be entitled to re-occupy the West Bank and even sections of Jordan, for defensive purposes. Israel must guard against a return to an interim state of security tension, which is not a genuine war, like the War of Attrition or the waiting period before the 1967 war, when Israel was compelled to put its army of reservists on alert for a long time – a situation giving rise to paralysis in Israel's economy and society.

Israel, the Palestinians and Jordan would each reinforce the other's security. The Palestinian would have greater personal security and his national rights would be protected. Alpher does not dismiss the possibility of the establishment of a Palestinian state as part of the permanent arrangement, within the framework of the security arrangements. And, no less important: anchoring these understandings in regional security agreements would greatly decrease the risks of war between Israel and the Arabs.

A series of meetings were held under the auspices of the US Harvard University, far from the spotlights, between Israeli, Jordanian and Palestinian economic leaders, to formulate principles of economic cooperation between the three sides. The agreements in this channel may be said to have complimented the security talks channel headed by Nizar Ammar and Yossi Alpher and given the security cooperation an economic dimension. In June 1993 Harvard University published details of the deliberations, in Arabic, and it is interesting to see the Abu Mazen group among the Palestinian participants, such as the financier Sabih al-Masri, economist Dr Hisham Awartani, Dr Atef Alawna and others.

Winding Up and Shutting Down the Channels

Winding up all the Oslo agreements channels had to produce rapid progress on the track of the bilateral talks between Israel and the Palestinians, leading to a rapid implementation of the understandings in the secret channels. That this did not happen was mainly because at the moment of truth, Arafat did not throw all his weight into the conclusions Abu Mazen and his people had reached with the Israelis, but went back to the endless game of balances, in order to maintain internal balance in the PLO.

After the agreements were signed, the contacts between Israel and the PLO came out into the open, but it was not Abu Mazen, but others, who conducted them. Arafat appointed the offended Nabil Sha'ath to conduct the talks. Sha'ath did not conceal his dissatisfaction with the agreements, reiterating his claim that better agreements could have been attained with Israel.

The nature of the understandings in the different channels on the security issue may be summarized by two basic principles: a permanent mechanism would be established for Israeli–PLO security; there would be a clear division between internal and external security, with internal security being given to the Palestinians, and external security to Israel. Immediately after the signing of the agreements, when the further negotiations were handed over to others to run, the PLO refuted these two agreements. The classic Fatah organization rejected the principle of cooperation, addressing it as though it was betrayal in every sense of the word, nor did the IDF, which was not a partner to the secret channels, feel any commitment to the security conclusions. When Nizar Ammar arrived in Taba for the security negotiations with Israel, Major General Amnon Shahak, the head of the military delegation and later to be Israel's chief of staff, told him he did not recognize Alpher's conclusions. After the channels were exposed, he and the Shin Bet head, Yaakov Peri, lost no time in meeting with Jibrin Rajub and Muhammad Dahlan in Rome and Paris and with them arrived at different security conclusions. Rajub and Dahlan were not members of Force 17, but deportees from the territories, and had connections with Abu Jihad's mechanism. So the conclusions attained by Shahak and Peri were founded on the Intifada activists in the territories, not on Force 17's internal security mechanism on the "outside." Arafat also rejected the economic talks conclusion, to adopt the World Bank's recommendation and set up a common coordination mechanism between Israel, the Palestinians and Jordan. After the establishment of the Palestinian Authority this gave rise to delays in the economic aid for the Palestinians.

On important issues the various channels of communication helped and supported each other, but despite the fact that the security communications channel helped to clear up several important aspects of the Oslo talks, several conspicuous differences in the conclusions among the channels are nevertheless worth noting. First of all, the status of Jordan. In the Alpher– Hammad–Prince Hasan channel, Jordan's security importance is the cornerstone of the strategic system, but immediately after the signing of the Oslo agreements, Israel responded to the PLO's pressures and conceded the formula of the joint Palestinian–Jordanian delegation. Nor did the tripartite economic mechanism get off the ground.

There was an internal upheaval in the PLO on this issue. Over the years, it was actually the Jihadist wing that was close to Jordan, established its bases there and leaned toward cooperation with the government, while the Iyyadists, the successors of "Black

September," were closer to the Israeli right's version, the alternative homeland in the East Bank. Thrashing out the security problems, on the one hand, and the US pressure, on the other, brought this wing closer to Jordan. This also took the form of a rapprochement between Husseini and Jordan. After the Gulf crisis Abu Tayyib, the Force 17 commander, had decided on Amman as his main place of residence. The surprising improvement of relations between Jordan and the Iyyadist wing was of importance from the aspect of the array of forces in the territories: pro-Jordanian Nablus, for instance, went and allied itself with Abu Mazen.

The joint delegation formula did not particularly disturb Abu al-Ala and his people in the Oslo talks. The demand was raised immediately after the signing of the agreements, in the feverish race for time toward the signing ceremony in the White House. In Washington, Israel succeeded in introducing only the changes in the agreements involving the status of the PLO. It was only at the meeting of the supreme liaison committee which met in Cairo immediately afterwards, that Israel gave the PLO its agreement to the disbanding of the joint delegation. This, however, was already a different PLO; not the PLO of Abu Mazen, with whom Israel had conducted the talks in the secret channels.

A most significant difference between the security talks channel and the Oslo channel lay in the status of the PLO compared with the leadership in the territories. A senior Palestinian participant was later to tell us that the Americans insisted on the Palestinian security force being based solely on recruits from the territories. Their idea was that the Palestinian entity would be built up from its foundations, like a foetus in its mother's womb, without any connection with the old PLO, even at the expense of the old PLO. Force 17 people convinced the Americans that they would train the Palestinian security force in the territories, and there was hard bargaining with the Americans over how many Force 17 people would be enabled to enter the territories to train the Palestinian force. Ultimately the Americans agreed to seventy people, with Jordan and Egypt being supposed to provide the major training. When the Americans heard that Israel had agreed to bring in the entire Palestine Liberation Army they were thunderstruck, the Palestinian sources reported.

Israeli security sources have confirmed the above. They reported that Rabin shared the Americans' views before the Oslo agreements, but afterwards told his circle of confidants that it would be better to bring in the Palestine Liberation Army, whose personnel bore no grudges against Israel, such as those of the Intifada activists. Rabin believed it would be easier to work out a formula for cooperation with the external PLO than with the Intifada activists, who had undergone beatings from the IDF soldiers' clubs in the Intifada.

If was not easily – if at all – that the Americans resigned themselves to Israel's decision to give the PLO preference over the territories–Jordan connection. In her memoirs[5] Hanan Ashrawi related that on the day the Oslo agreements were signed in Washington, Arafat ordered the pilot who had brought him from Tunis to ready the plane for a return home, after coming to the realization that the Americans were not prepared to alter the text of the agreement to say the "PLO," instead of the "Palestinian team." Arafat demanded that Ashrawi convince the Americans to accept the alteration (after he had given Tibi the task of convincing the Israelis), but the State Department team was immovable in its opposition and the issue was transferred to President Clinton for decision. As far as can be seen, it was Israel's intervention in Arafat's favor that made Clinton accept the alteration. Washington was only prepared to accept the PLO because of Israel's pressure, but, as matters turned out subsequently, there was no basic change in its policy and, despite its ostensible support for Israel's policy of supporting the PLO, it actually continued to support the encouragement of the link between the leadership of the territories and Jordan, not the old PLO.

Despite the US promise to alter the wordings of the agreements and replace "Palestinian team" with "PLO," they kept their promise to amend the text only on the signature line, not the body of the agreements. Abu Mazen had to alter the wording in handwriting and write P.L.O. over the word "Palestinian" – through which he drew a line.[6] The term "Jordanian–Palestinian delegation" was left unaltered.

Jordan recognized the security talks channels. The publication of the Oslo agreements set off shock waves in Amman, since Jordan's confidence in its own ability to come up with a correct reading of the moods in Israel had been undermined. Amman again suffered, momentarily, an attack of apprehensions of an Israeli coalition with Abu Iyyad's successors – to establish an alternative homeland for the Palestinians in the East Bank.

Syria, too, was shocked by the Oslo agreements. Damascus had thought the peace process was designed, inter alia, to erode the

PLO to the point of its disappearance, in order to encourage the leadership in the territories, and then along came Israel and rescued the drowning Arafat. The shock also accelerated Syria's feeling of urgency about bringing the peace talks to a successful conclusion. Yet it became more and more apparent that foiling the Oslo agreement had become the Syrian policy goal.

It is also noteworthy that, while the security talks channel had the support of such US funding elements as the Ford Foundation, no US elements had been incorporated into the Oslo channel. The agreements in Oslo, which did not take Jordan's centrality into account in the arrangements and opted for the PLO–Tunis over the leadership of the territories, could not, then, be received with sympathy in Washington.

Egypt was not incorporated in the secret security and economic talks, and it reacted with involvement in the Oslo talks, which eventually eliminated both the other channels. Some of the Egyptian anger with the USA. in subsequent years can be attributed to the fact that Washington had tried to keep it away from the Palestinians and encouraged the link between them and Jordan.

Members of the People's Party and FIDA who were incorporated into the Washington talks were not brought in to any secret channel. They, too, were stunned by the Oslo agreements. On the one hand, they were satisfied by Israel having finally recognized the PLO, but, on the other, the agreements conflicted with the direction of the development they wanted to further: that of changing the PLO's appearance to make it more of a civil movement, at the expense of the revolution, and moving the main political weight from Tunis to the territories.

The mounting tension between the inside and outside was accompanied by a new wave of internal Palestinian liquidations, as will be revealed in the next chapter.

17

The Faqahani State Shall Not Pass

The Fatah Kills Its Children

On the morning of 21 October, 58-year-old Palestinian public leader As'ad Saftawi went out to take his 9-year-old son to school. They were ambushed by unidentified persons in a white Peugot car, who aimed their guns at Saftawi, to kill him. Saftawi saw them and tried to flee, but his way was blocked by a stone wall. The death car neared him and its passengers shot him dead under the eyes of his son. According to one eye-witness, they then cold-bloodedly picked up the scattered spent cartridges and disappeared.

Gaza was already accustomed to fierce violence, but this particular murder left it appalled. Saftawi's murder was the third in a packed list of assassinations of major political personalities in Gaza, following directly from the celebrations over that month's agreement between the PLO and Israel: the first to be murdered was Dr Muhammad Abu Sha'ban, a veteran peace activist in Gaza who had been friendly with many in the Peace Now movement's leadership. Unknown persons shot him when he was returning from the celebrations of which he was one of the principal organizers. Then another peace activist, Muhammad Kahil, a confidant of Abu Sha'ban, was murdered and Saftawi made the third. Although the murderers were not found, the word went round Gaza: the Fatah is killing its children!

From many aspects, Saftawi's murder completed Abu Iyyad and Abu Jihad's cycle of murders – the affairs with which this book began. His murder was designed to signal the goal of the other two killings – to maintain the internal balances and, by force, stop either of them reaching the finishing line alone.

The Oslo agreements gave Abu Mazen a flying start to take over the reins of the PLO leadership, after having produced the first realization of the principles of Abu Iyyad's will. A close watch, even if superficial, could have shown that Saftawi was likely to be "Abu Mazen's" man in Gaza. Of all the Gaza figures, Saftawi was the main candidate for promoting the implementation of the Oslo accords, thus establishing a strong leadership position in Gaza for Abu Mazen's group, at the expense of the Jihadist wing.

Saftawi was not just another name in the gallery of "political personalities" who were then coming closer to the "political committees" which had burst out of the obscurity of the Fatah organization's secret activities to take over the overt political activities, but he may have been the most powerful of the "political personalities," one of the only ones from that group capable of "getting people out onto the streets." In Gaza he was known as an upright man, straight as a die. His son Imad, as will be recalled, was one of the leaders of the Islamic Jihad in Gaza and his breathtaking escape from one of the most closely guarded jails in the town was one of the original factors that sparked off the Intifada. What was more, Saftawi came from the Fatah's founding generation, Arafat's close friend from the time the Fatah movement was closest to the Muslim Brotherhood. While Arafat, however, distanced himself from the Muslim Brotherhood and became the Hamas' enemy, the devout Saftawi maintained his good relations with the movement.

Immediately after Saftawi's murder the suffering bereaved ripped Arafat's portrait off the walls of his home. This was not necessarily a sign that it was Arafat who had sent the murderers, but rather, that those close to Saftawi were familiar with the political background and knew how far Saftawi and Arafat had gone since the founding generation.

In their first years, Arafat and the Muslim Brotherhood in Gaza worked against Abu Jihad. This political structure won Arafat Saudi Arabian aid and, to counter Abu Jihad's excess power, Arafat balanced his own, with the protection of Abu Iyyad's Force 17. The Gulf crisis cut Arafat off from the Saudi Arabian aid and took him not only into Saddam Hussein's trench, but also to that of the Jihadists. Saftawi did not follow Arafat into that trench, but maintained his special connections with Saudi Arabia and the Hamas. The Jihadist wing may have had its suspicions that it was Saftawi, more than anybody else, whose power had led to the final Iyyadist wing victory in the struggle for Gaza, and this was why he was murdered.

This is not tantamount to a simple analysis of a theoretically potential risk, since Saftawi himself headed one of the channels in the undercover contacts between Rabin and the Palestinian center in Cairo, that is, the Abu Mazen group and the Egyptian government. Throughout that period he also maintained connections with Saudi Arabia. The impression was that he visited Cairo and Jedda more frequently than Tunis. In those contacts he sounded out his political program, which he first put forward at the peak of the Intifada, and which was designed to bring it to a conclusion, in return for Israeli concessions, the main points of which did not greatly differ from the Gaza first program. What worried the arms bearers was that Saftawi had not worked out his program with Arafat, but with Egypt and Rabin, and briefed Arafat only later. Because of his special prestige among the Palestinian public, Saftawi was one of the only people in the territories capable of doing this.

Saftawi renewed sounding out his initiative in April 1993; at a critical stage of the Oslo talks, and almost certainly without any knowledge of that channel's existence. In Cairo he met with Egyptian figures and the Palestinian ambassador, Sa'id Kamal. As soon as he returned, Rabin visited Gaza and met with Saftawi. The meeting between them aroused attention, because the Palestinian delegation leaders had refused to meet with the heads of the Israeli rule except through the expiring channel of the Washington talks. The meeting between Rabin and Saftawi encouraged Rabin to adhere to the Oslo channel talks, because he had become aware that an agreement could be attained with the Palestinians, even if not through the official delegation, which at that time he considered to be weak.

Saftawi's activity lit up warning lights for the Jihadists. This activity brought with it risks from several directions, principally that of all the anti-Jihadist elements allying themselves into one union which, under Abu Mazen's orchestration, would deliver the coup de grace to the activities of the arms-bearers: the political committees of the Fatah, the Palestinian Party FIDA and the People's Party. This far-reaching alliance could have been perceived by the Jihadists as exhausting all the processes the PLO and the Palestinians had undergone around the Gulf crisis; their goal being to make the Palestinians lay down their arms and make the move to normal political activity, under Abu Iyyad's orders. Arms-bearers have no role in such a process, and they are destined to exit the stage.

Abu Mazen: "The Era of the Revolution is Over"

The storm that rocked Gaza in October may have been the outcome of the severe internal arguments undergone by the PLO-Tunis in September and October. Arafat convened the PLO's Central Council, to continue with the process of ratifying the Oslo agreements. The entire PLO top echelons and members of the central institutions went to Tunis and in the discussion itself, as well as on its fringes, many cards were exposed – including Arafat's. It turned out that Arafat had taken a stand at the side of the Jihadist wing, against Abu Mazen and the Iyyadists. The lines of dispute between them, which had been exposed in the confrontations that surfaced over the signing ceremony in Washington, deepened and took on an ideological dimension in the speeches to the members of the Central Council.

Abu Mazen warned the members of the PLO's Central Council that the Oslo agreements alone guaranteed them nothing; everything depended on how the Palestinians were to realize them. If they applied themselves to building up the infrastructure for the Palestinian state, the agreements would lead to independence, but if they were to actualize them in the wrong way, they might perpetuate the occupation. In this context, Abu Mazen made some remarks that reminded the arms-bearers of old fears:

> We are a clever, an educated people, we built in the world, but as individuals. The proving time has now come, how shall we construct the institutions capable of renewing the scorched earth. What skills and brains are required? And I would like to say: the brain of the revolution is not the brain of the state, and I would like to emphasize: the brain of the revolution is not the brain of the state. We must all don new garb, to enable us to construct the state. As individuals we built states in the Gulf, Jordan, and Syria. Are we, as a group, capable of building [our] state?[1]

It was with a heavy heart that Abu Mazen made his remarks. He did not believe the Palestinians would really be able to pass this test. He had just concluded another argument with Arafat, and almost failed to turn up to deliver his remarks. Previously Abu Mazen had pleaded with the Palestinian billionaire Munib al-Masri, his candidate to head the Palestinian administration, to go to Tunis, but his way was blocked at the entrance to the hall. First he stood with the journalists waiting outside, then he went back to his hotel, from where he took the first plane back to London. Abu Mazen had no doubt that Arafat was behind the arms-bearers who had prevented the entry of the man representing the "new talents," not the "brain of the revolution." The arms-bearers had interpreted his remarks as signifying that it was not they who would head the Palestinian state, not they who would fill the positions when it was established, but new people: Abu Mazen's people. The message they got from Abu Mazen was that, as far as he was concerned, the era of the revolution was over and they were no longer needed. The possibility cannot be dismissed that it was immediately after these remarks were made that the order was given to liquidate Saftawi, whom they suspected of being Abu Mazen's undercover partner in Gaza. From the murderers' viewpoint, whether Saftawi had indeed allied himself with Abu Mazen in any way was of less importance than Saftawi's latent potential from that aspect, and this was what decided his fate.

Sari Nusseiba, whose role paralleled that of Saftawi in the West Bank, understood where the wind was blowing. After coming to the realization that, in the argument between the different sections of the Fatah, Arafat was giving his support to the military wing, he decided to pack his bags. After Saftawi's murder, he took his family for a sabbatical in the United States. In fact, even before that he had made up his mind to leave. In an interview he granted the *al-Quds* daily on 26 October 1993, he ruled that those who had murdered Saftawi, Abu Sha'ban and Kahil, should not be given positions in the new Palestinian administration. These remarks came not only from the exclamation: "Have you murdered and also taken possession?," but also originated in Nusseiba's understanding of what type of regime Saftawi's murderers and their colleagues would impose on Palestine. As will be recalled, back at the peak of the Intifada, Nusseiba wrote that the Palestinians were not just striving for a state, but wanted the establishment of a state in which people could live honorably. In the same *al-Quds* interview, Nusseiba reiterated Abu Mazen's remarks that the agreements as such were no guar-antee of a Palestinian state, and raised the question of whether the Palestinians would succeed in developing the self-rule into a state. He determined that if the Palestinians, in their new state entity, did not succeed in absorbing the values of democracy, pluralism, freedom of faith, human rights, equality and minority rights, they would miss the opportunity to establish the state they had fought for. It is no coincidence that in the argument over cooperation with

Israel, it was Nusseiba who articulated the positions of the political committees, favoring cooperation. He was asked whether, by so doing, the Palestinians would not become agents of Israel, and he replied:

> This is the situation when the benefit is not mutual, or the personal benefit of one of the sides comes at the expense of the benefit of the whole; but the equation I am speaking of is between two peoples, with the benefit one side may draw . . . not harming the benefit resulting to the other side . . . we are speaking of peace between two peoples, two states.[2]

The arguments between the Fatah and the political committees that sprang up from within it – and still regarded themselves as part of it – over the question of Palestinian democracy and the goals of the struggle, were the worst breaking point in Palestinian politics immediately after the signing of the Oslo agreements; for the Fatah organization itself, however, they were only one aspect of the power struggles between the mechanisms and the people, between the inside and outside, and we do not have enough space to detail them all. In the final analysis, the Fatah organization still kept a bullet up the spout and, despite Arafat's undertaking, it did not lay down its arms. Abbas Zaki, the secretary of the Fatah's Intifada committee, summed matters up in the following words:

> The movement is suffering from a profound internal crisis . . . the large number of means of communication between the leadership on the outside and the cadres on the inside, the large number of alliances and axes, the lack of command committees in the occupied land, have imposed a new reality . . . the question of bearing arms, or laying them down, has become a matter of personal viewpoint.[3]

In the last week of March 1994, the Fatah Central Committee met in Tunis for a discussion on the organization's situation in the territories, and decided to close down the political committees' offices altogether. On 29 March, Arafat personally informed the offices of the political committees that this was his decision. On the eve of the decision to close the offices, the militant wing began to publish an underground newspaper in the territories, *al-Istiqlal* (The Independence). Obviously the question arose: if Israel has recognized the Fatah – why publish a underground paper? The message was a return to the underground: the actualization of opposition to the very fact of the political committees' overt appearance. In its edition of 1 March, *al-Istiqlal* discloses something of the internal argument in the Fatah. In a major article headed "The War Goes On," it said:

> Anyone who thinks the enemy will cease his war on us only because of the establishment of a Palestinian authority, or in all our territory that was conquered in 1967, is wrong. Also wrong is anyone who thinks there is a common interest with Israel, as several activists who do not know the minimal facts of the struggle, or who do know, but pretend they do not. The enemy is opposed to the establishment of a Palestinian state and so he will oppose the Palestinian authority's having the ability to establish a state.

Nostalgia for the Occupation?

The months September–October 1993 presaged not only the internal split in the Fatah, but also a profound crisis between Arafat and an important wing of the peace process supporters whose nucleus was in the formerly communist People's Party. The People's Party's critics were joined by many activists from the Fatah organization, who added their signatures to the mass petition submitted to Arafat in December by the delegation headed by Dr Haidar Abd a-Shafi. Arafat rejected the petition and, in reaction, Abd a-Shafi announced his resignation from the leadership of the Palestinian delegation to the Washington talks.

This group's demands were very reminiscent of Abu Mazen's approach, but at that stage this group could not yet be affiliated to Abu Mazen's wing. This may be learned from the circumstances in which the crisis broke out. In October a People's Party delegation met with senior figures from the Fatah organization, including, in addition to Arafat, the heads of the Fatah mechanisms and also Abu Mazen and his people. Abu Mazen sided with the Fatah organization in the argument between the Fatah and the People's Party. Not because he rejected the demand for Arafat to be bypassed through a collective leadership; the People's Party people demanded a leadership committee that would contain representatives of the Fatah, the People Party and FIDA. This was actually supposed to be a supreme committee to supervise the peace process, and was to be a leadership committee in every sense of the term. Abu Mazen thought the leadership committee should be a purely Fatah framework, with the People Party and FIDA being attached to it, not an integral part of it. In any event, when the People Party leaders realized that Arafat's goal was the "foundation of a Fatah dictatorship," they decided to resign from the Palestinian negotiating teams, and launched a concentrated offensive on Arafat.

The FIDA Party's reading of the situation was actually similar to that of the People Party, but it decided not to walk out of the negotiating teams, so as not to foil the Oslo agreements or show the PLO stripped bare. His people turned up for the Taba talks rounds, but, at the same time, were on the alert to further the democratic idea. They had realized where Arafat was heading before anyone else, and even before Saftawi's murder they established the "Independence Guard" – to protect themselves against hard blows from the Fatah organization's secret attack mechanism.

One of the People's Party leaders, Abd al-Majid Hamdan, participated in the deliberations in Tunis and on his return he published a series of articles in the party organ, a-Tali'a, levelling harsh criticism at the PLO leadership. He voiced the fear that the day might come when the Palestinians in the territories would feel nostalgia for the occupation. As early as in the first article, he made it clear: "There is no room for a Faqahani state here," that is, Palestinian terrorism's state that had been in existence in West Beirut and about which Arafat had again begun speaking, with the attainment of the Oslo agreements. This is what he wrote:

> For the first time I have been given the opportunity to get to know and exchange views with many people from the Palestinian leadership . . . and it is my duty to let the reader know the contents of these talks . . . First I told them of the heart's desires of the citizen of the occupied land . . . and what is on his mind . . . and at one of the meetings Abu Ammar (Arafat) confirmed . . . that the citizen in the occupied land has begun saying: "I fear the day will come when we will say: May God have mercy on the occupation." . . . the citizen in the occupied land puts his hand on his heart [incidentally, the phrase with which Abu Mazen concluded his speech to the Central Council in October 1993] and asks hundreds of questions about the possible conduct of those returning, that is, the PLO/Tunis, and their effect, primarily, on his security, the calm of his home and his family . . . the chances of his earning a living and his work, not to mention his welfare

and stability – things he has been dreaming of for many years.[5]

Hamdan quotes Abu Mazen and Qaddumi (!), who said that running a state is not comparable to running the revolution: "We must know that the methods for running the revolution are the absolute reverse of the methods for running a state." He expressed shock at what he had heard from Tunis – that the "Concepts and experience gained in running a Faqahani state in Beirut, with all its details and fine points be transferred to the territories . . . What is so frightening about this proposal is that it goes beyond the differences between a Faqahani state two square kilometers in the Beirut area, with all the negative phenomena we saw in the attitude toward the Lebanese people . . . and a national regime, which has to work for an entire people, containing within it a broad variety of social groups." Hamdan does not conceal why the Faqahani model could bring down disaster: there are differences between the people in the occupied territories who, thanks to the Intifada they conducted, have made achievements, and the outside. Not just the Intifada's achievements, but also the Israeli democracy next door to the Palestinians in the territories; although it was not good to them, they want to build themselves a better model.

There are far-reaching conclusions from these remarks. In an article he published later, Hamdan poured scorn on the PLO's democracy in which Arafat, the head of the executive authority, sits beside the head of the parliament, who is supposed to be the head of the legislative authority, while he, the head of the executive authority, runs the legislative authority's session. Hamdan, then, ruled unequivocally that without a profound reform to the entire Palestinian political system, not only would it be impossible to actualize the Gaza and Jericho agreements, it would also be impossible to plan for the Palestinian state.

Although his remarks are very similar to the criticism levelled at Abu Mazen, there was no political connection at that time between the People's Party and Abu Mazen.

Ashrawi: From Delegation Spokeswoman to Spokeswoman of the Opponents of Oslo

The political committees, FIDA and the People's Party were not attacking the Oslo agreements, but Arafat's intention to establish a "Faqahani State" under his auspices, that is, a Fatah dictatorship. The old Palestinian delegation also shared this criticism, but added an important personal touch of its own: that of finding fault with the Oslo agreements themselves. Dr Hanan Ashrawi, the spokeswoman of the delegation to Washington, rapidly became the most ardent of those who spoke out against the Oslo agreements. In a series of articles and interviews in the period immediately following the signing of the agreements, she did indeed add her voice to those of the supporters, but lost no time in explaining the agreements' drawbacks. For instance, in an interview in *al-Hayat* in December 1993, she said:

> When I read the agreement I was appalled, and some people accused me of being a pessimist. Of course there are positive aspects, such as the recognition of the PLO, approval of matters connected with the permanent arrangements, the connection between the stages and the implementation of 242. But there are matters that conflict with this, such as the agreement to leave the settlements in place during the interim stage. In my view, this is the agreement's greatest Achilles' heel. When we were negotiating in Washington, we insisted that they begin to disband them as soon as in the interim stage. We even agreed that they would remain temporarily, we demanded guarantees of a stop to their expansion . . . and a stop to all the settlement activity.[6]

Despite the relaxed tone of speech, the contents of her remarks are extremely grave, and Ashrawi concludes:

> Had we wanted to propose concessions in Washington, we could have reached an agreement much earlier. We did not arrive at an agreement because we adhered to our initial positions, for several reasons: some, substantive reasons of principle, some political: the political leadership was not aiming at the attainment of compromise solutions . . . because the genuine talks had to be conducted between the sole legitimate representative (the PLO) and Israel. In any event, the negative aspects of the agreement are: splitting the problem, and the people's severance from the land.

It is noteworthy that Ashrawi accuses the "political leadership," that is, the PLO, of having deliberately prevented the delegation from reaching compromises, in order to reserve the compromise for themselves.

The Palestinian diaspora – which was close to the Palestinian delegation, the Husseini–Ashrawi wing – also opposed the agreements. Its most absolute spokesman, Prof. Edward Said, boycotted the White House ceremony. As soon as on 12 October 1993, a day before the ceremony, in an interview to *al-Quds* he ruled that the agreement turned the Israeli-held territories from occupied territories into disputed territories.

In April 1994 he initiated a petition among the Palestinian leadership in the diaspora, containing a demand that dismissal procedures be launched against Arafat. Among the signators' names it was interesting to also find several of the senior Iyyadist wing members of the Palestinian delegation to the multinational track, such as the head of the delegation on refugee affairs, Ilia Zuriq, from Canada.

Said's friend Hisham Sharabi also published a long series of articles in which he did not truly come out against the agreements, but detailed the efforts he believed should be made to guarantee the move's success. In the article he published in the *al-Quds* daily[7] he ruled that the elections should be held at their scheduled date in July 1994, on a democratic basis. This, he believed, was vital, not just because of the need for a Palestinian state to be founded on a democratic basis, but also to encourage investments and create a positive atmosphere for economic development. He determined unambiguously that only general elections in the territories would arouse the international community to take an interest in what was happening in the territories, and without them the Palestinian problem would be no more than a "local dispute, to which the world attaches no great importance."

Following his visit to the territories, Sharabi detailed the essential conditions for the agreement's success,[8] whose salient points – apart from the democratic aspects – were to stop the Palestinian police from turning into a military force under the Fatah's command, and the generation of conditions for economic development; that is: the reverse of the Fatah positions. He demanded the establishment of a professional Palestinian administration for financial affairs and their implementation, the talks with Israel to be conducted professionally and practically, the establishment of a police force "which is non-affiliated," that is, to the Fatah, and for it to be capable of maintaining law and order and running the elections.

Arafat to Christopher: Do Not Make Me the Palestinian Gorbachev

More and more, the argument over the nature of the Palestinian regime took on the image of a profound dispute between the territories and Tunis, because the forces that opposed Arafat's goal of establishing a Fatah rule in the territories were concentrated in the territories themselves. In this argument, the United States backed the personalities in the territories and their supporters in Tunis, such as Abu Mazen and his like. As time went by, it transpired that Washington's support for the Oslo agreements was very limited: the US Administration mainly wanted to avoid rocking the Israeli government, and immediately after the White House ceremony the United States did not throw its weight into furthering the agreements, but gradually went back to the general principles of its original policy. It was hard for it to agree that in the end the Jihadist wing, this time under Arafat's leadership, would defeat the Iyyadist wing, after Abu Mazen had led Arafat to the White House lawn. It gave Husseini's flagging spirits a boost and restored to Orient House, where the Palestinian delegation was staying, its lost honor, by giving it back the model of the political meetings with the world's great who visited Israel. Christopher insisted on resuming the negotiations on elections in the rounds of talks with the Palestinian delegation in Washington; this was despite the other agreements already achieved directly between Israel and the PLO, in which the question of the elections had not been given the major place in the discussion.

One of the substantive differences between the Oslo agreements and the framework of the talks in Washington involved the question of the elections. According to the framework of the talks in Washington, the agreements with Israel would enter into force when the elections were held, while according to the Oslo agreements – the very fact of the signature was the beginning of the agreements' implementation. What this signifies is that under the Washington framework the elections were obligatory, while under the Oslo agreements they were only a privilege. Nevertheless, Washington insisted in viewing elections in the territories as a major issue.

Husseini and his colleagues learned the lesson of their mistakes and when the PLO and Israel were absorbed in negotiations over the implementation of the Oslo agreements, the "internal" leadership was beginning to consolidate a broader public status for itself, no longer basing its power on a small community revolving around the East Jerusalem and Bir Zeit institutions.

Christopher's round of talks in the Middle East in December 1993 was of special importance in clarifying Washington's positions on this matter. When he met with Arafat in the US Embassy building in Amman, he made it clear to him that, despite the Oslo agreements, the financial aid to the territories would be received not by the PLO, but by a central Palestinian economic institution – which had to be sited in the territories, under the management of people from the territories, and under international supervision – to guarantee its non-dependence on the PLO. The institution's name was: PEDCAR: the Palestinian Economic Council for Development and Reconstruction. In his distress, Arafat was unable to restrain his feelings, and told Christopher aggressively: "You will not make me into a new Gorbachev." That is, you will not use me to fulfill your policy of disbanding the PLO, as you disbanded the Soviet Union through Gorbachev. Arafat focused all his fury with the Americans on these remarks and exposed his deepest motives in the crisis of the signature on the White House lawn.

Christopher's talks in Amman in that Middle East round were of importance from yet another aspect. He came to an agreement with Jordan, that its economic interests in the territories would be guaranteed by its banks in the territories being granted exclusivity. Streaming the international aid funds through Jordan's network of banks under the control of the Central Jordanian Bank was designed not only to prevent economic shocks that could stem from the reinforcement of the Palestinian economic entity to the west of the river, but to reinforce the Jordanian economy, which would return to being the channel for the financial aid to the Palestinians. The United States proved to the Jordanians that it was faithful to the old policy lines – those of reinforcing Jordan's strategic depth – in accordance with what had been agreed in the secret security talks track.

From the very beginning Arafat wanted to meet with Christopher in the US Embassy building, not in the Jordanian guest house, so as not to hold the meeting on "Jordanian soil" – as he phrased it to his confidants. He was then scheduled to go to King Hussein's palace to brief him on his talks, but he was so infuriated that he neglected his obligation to honor his host, and went back to his plane in the airfield. This marked another stage in the deterioration in the shaky relations between Hussein and Arafat, which began at the Hussein-Shamir meeting in the Aravah, with the end of the Gulf War.

The "Peace of the Brave," What Next?

Ultimately PLO Leader Yaser Arafat, with breathtaking political maneuvers, succeeded in vanquishing all his opponents and proving that there was indeed nobody to replace him as the only leader capable of signing agreements with Israel and establishing the Palestinian Authority, tantamount to the first Palestinian government in the territories to win recognition by Israel and the nations of the world. In so doing Arafat also displayed enormous courage, and he kept his word that he, together with Rabin, would establish the "Peace of the Brave." From this viewpoint, Arafat merits a place in the pantheon of the world's great. Had Arafat not existed, it would have been necessary to invent him.

At the same time, the Palestinians' fundamental problem has not been resolved. With all the paradox this involves, Arafat's personal decision to confront the challenge of the peace process has not been accompanied by internal Palestinian decisions: Arafat has either not succeeded in giving up the endless balancing maneuvers, or possibly has not even tried, and without any internal decision, it will be hard for the Palestinians to found the infrastructure for the Palestinian state they so long for. Arafat decided to pin his hopes on the United States but, at the same time, he drove away the United States' friends, headed by Abu Mazen and the West Bank leadership, and also rejected the basic US concept of maintaining the ties between the West Bank and Jordan, with openness toward Israel.

Arafat, then, has tied himself to the United States while rejecting its policy; and this is only one example of his convoluted, contradictory pathway. He wanted to establish a national infrastructure, but combatted any attempt to set up national frameworks. He resisted his Fatah colleagues, the members of the political committees, who wanted to turn the combatant organization into a political party, telling them that the revolution was not over. He undertook to combat terrorism together with Israel and, in the same breath, informed his old allies, the Muslim Brotherhood, that the jihad would continue. Arafat, then, is leaving a complex system of internal conflicts to the second generation of the Palestinian leadership; the problem being that after the liquidation of Abu Jihad and Abu Iyyad, the Palestinians have no second generation of leaders of any stature capable of coping with Arafat's legacy.

Our book concludes with the establishment of the Palestinian Authority in Gaza and Jericho, on the eve of its deployment in the West Bank, but history, of course, will not stop with the last page of this book, and it will expose what lies concealed in Gaza's dusty alleyways and the West Bank's mountainous paths.

Notes and References

Part I Ides of March

1 The Revolution Devours its Children

1. Dr Muhammad Hamza, *Abu Jihad – Secrets of his Early Days and the Circumstances Surrounding his Murder* (Arabic), April 1989, no place noted (below: Hamza, 1989). Some time later, in October 1993, Um Jihad herself gave the author further details of the assassination.
2. Ibid., p. 75.
3. Ibid., p. 77.
4. Ibid.
5. Hamza, 1989, p. 80.
6. Such as, for example, *al-Muharer*, Paris, 27 March 1990.
7. According to *al-Quds*, East Jerusalem, 27 March 1990.
8. Abdallah Ghassan, *A Look at the Assassinations of PLO Members* (Arabic), expanded edition, 1992 (below: Ghassan, 1992).
9. Ibid., Publishers' Introduction, Jamil Abu Arafa, p. 5.
10. Ibid., p. 7.
11. Ghassan, 1992, pp. 48–50.
12. Ibid.
13. Muhamad Lafi, "The Palestinian Problem in Arab Summit Meeting Resolutions – the Axioms of the Arab-Zionist Struggle, to Where?" *Ila al-Amam*, 31 May 1990.

2 The Islamic Jihad: Abu Jihad's Fingerprints

1. Reuven Paz, Lecture at the Hebrew University, Jerusalem, 5 February 1993.
2. Dr Iyyad al-Barghuti, *The Palestinian Islamic Movement and the New World Order* (Arabic), East Jerusalem, December 1992, p. 23.
3. Darwish Naser, *The Hadassa House Operation, as its Perpetrators Report* (Arabic), Jerusalem, 1983.

4. Ibid., pp. 33–4.
5. Ibid., pp. 48–9.
6. *Al-Islam wa Falastin*, Edition 31, 23 January 1990.

3 Arafat Goes to Saddam

1. In a conversation with the author in Gaza on 24 May 1995, one of the participants in the meetings, Nizar Ammar, one of Abu Iyyad's people, reported that Murphy had come out of his meeting with Arafat furious and dissatisfied. The meeting with Arafat took two hours, that with Abu Iyyad – three.
2. *Al-Watani*, May 1990.
3. According to Reuter's Agency, 8 December 1990.

4 The Threatening Sword of the Hamas

1. See: Atef Adwan, *Sheikh Ahmad Yassin, His Life and War* (Arabic), Gaza, 1991 (below: Adwan, 1991), p. 138.
2. According to the *al-Muharer* weekly, published in Paris, middle of April, 1990.
3. Robin Wright, "Punishment from Heaven and a Conundrum: The Islamic World Challenges the United States," *Los Angeles Times*, 26 January 1992.
4. Yisrael Altman, "Islamic Opposition Movements in Egypt," in: *Rule and Opposition in Egypt* (Hebrew) (ed. Ami Ayalon), Tel Aviv, 1983, pp. 120–2, 124–35.
5. Adwan, 1991, p. 40.
6. Ibid., pp. 59–60.
7. Ibid., p. 85.
8. Ibid., p. 53.
9. Moshe Maoz, *Assad: The Sphinx of Damascus, a Political Biography* (Hebrew), Tel Aviv, 1988, p. 161.
10. Ibid., p. 181.
11. Major Sections of the Letter translated into Hebrew by Khaled Abu Tu'ama, *Jerushalaim*, 16 August 1991.
12. See Abu Tu'ama's article "Refusing to Die," Jerusalem, 31 January 1992.
13. Adwan, 1991, pp. 111–12.
14. Ibid., p. 56.
15. Ibid., p. 127.
16. Ibid., pp 36, 38.
17. Ibid., p. 47.
18. Pinhas Inbari, *A Triangle on the Jordan River* (Hebrew), Jerusalem, 1982,

pp. 144–5.
19. Adwan, 1991, p. 128.
20. Ibid., pp. 112–18.
21. Ibid., pp. 112–35.
22. Ibid., p. 114.
23. Ibid., pp. 42–3.
24. Ibid., pp. 126–7.
25. Ibid., pp. 136–8.
26. *Al-Fajr*, 3 November 1992.
27. This Hamas leaflet was entitled: "The Islamic Direction." At the beginning of January 1988 the leaflet appeared under the name: "Hams" and it was only afterwards that the name "Hamas" appeared.

5 The Struggle for Control of the Intifada

1. Hamza, 1989, p. 136.
2. Ibid., pp. 98–99. Ibid., p. 76.
3. Ibid., p. 77.
4. Da'ud Ibrahim, *Salah Khalaf – The Teacher and Fighter: His Life, His Struggle, His Death in War* (Arabic), East Jerusalem, 1991 (below: Ibrahim, 1991).
5. Ibid., p. 48.
6. Ibid., p. 49.
7. See: Guy Bechor, *A PLO Lexicon* (Hebrew), Tel Aviv, 1991, pp. 118–21.
8. The Democratic Front for the Liberation of Palestine, Events of the Second World Congress, Session Minutes, Documents and Resolutions, vol. A: *On the Roots of the Internal Crisis, The Lessons and Directions of the Renaissance in our Party's Life* (Arabic), August 1991 (below: Minutes of the Deliberations).
9. Minutes of the Deliberations, pp. 39–49.
10. *Al Hamishmar*, 22 October 1993.
11. Hamza, 1989, p. 87.
12. Ibid, pp. 75–7.
13. Minutes of the Deliberations, pp. 39–40.
14. Bassam a-Salahi, *The Political and Religious Leadership of the Occupied Land, Its Reality and Development, 1967-1991* (Arabic), East Jerusalem, 1993 (below: *Salhi*, 1993).
15. *Al Hamishmar*, 22 October 1993.
16. Oren Cohen, *Hadashot* correspondent, established personal relations with the two families and later was to get the story of the first leaflets from Zaqut and Muhammad Labadi, see: *a-Sinara* (Nazareth), 20 December 1991; and also: Ehud Yaari and Zeev Schiff, *Intifada* (Hebrew), Jerusalem and Tel Aviv, 1990, pp. 94–101.

6 Faisal Husseini and the Palestinian Delegation

1. Hamza, 1989, p. 79.
2. Ibid., p. 79.
3. Ibid., p. 122.
4. David Ronen, *Shin Bet Year, The Deployment in Judaea and Samaria, The First Year*, Tel Aviv, 1989, p. 120.
5. Hamza, 1989, pp. 136–7.
6. Ibid., pp. 156–77.
7. Ibid., p. 120.
8. Prof. Hisham Sharabi, *a-Nahar*, 26–27 January 1990.
9. Rashid al-Khaldi, *al-Fajr*, 16 August 1992.
10. Rashid al-Khaldi, *New Outlook*, July–August 1992.
11. Interview with Faisal al-Husseini, *Al Hamishmar*, 6 December 1991.
12. *Al-Quds* published a curtailed version of the minutes on 1 March 1990. Palestinian sources gave the author the full version.
13. *Al-Quds*, 14 December 1993.

7 The Command versus Force 17

1. Seale, 1992, p. 167.
2. Ibid., p. 168.
3. Sari Nusseiba and Mark Heller, *Without Drums and Trumpets: An Arrangement for the Israeli–Palestinian Dispute* (Hebrew), Tel Aviv, 1991.
4. Ibid., p. 33

8 A Fatal Linkage

1. Interview with Abu Iyyad, *al-Arab* (London), 15 August 1990.
2. *Al-Bayader a-Siyasi*, 23 January 1993.
3. *Kol Ha'Ir*, 6 September 1991.
4. Interview with Nabil Sha'ath in London, according to the French News Agency, 19 February 1991.
5. *Al-Watan al-Arabi*, 3 May 1991.
6. According to *a-Nadwa*, 14 September 1990.
7. A-Nahar, 12 September 1990.
8. According to *a-Nahar*, 12 September 1990.
9. *Falastin a-Thawrah*, 10 February 1991.

9 The Big Bang

1. *Al-Quds*, 25 December 1992.

2. Interview with David Kimche, *Hotam* Supplement, *Al Hamishmar*, 1 January 1993.

Part II   *Window of Opportunities*

10   Moving the PLO to the Territories: FIDA vs. the Organizations

1. Interview with Dr Azmi Shueibi and Zahira Kamal, *Hotam*, *Al-Hamishmar*, 7 May 1993.
2. Interview in *Hotam*, Al-Hamishmar, 9 July 1993.
3. Sari Nusseiba, *al-Quds*, 3 July 1993.

11   Imposing a Delegation on Arafat: in "Dishonorable Conditions"

1. According to *a-Nahar*, 1 February 1993.
2. According to *a-Nahar*, 23 February 1993.
3. *A-Nahar*, 11 June 1993.
4. For example, *Falastin a-Thawra*, 7 April 1991.
5. The article also appeared in the East Jerusalem *a-Nahar*, 11 September 1992.
6. Bashir Barghuti, *a-Tali'a*, 25 May 1991.
7. *Al-Quds*, 17 June 1993.

12   Who Blew Up the New York Trade Center?

1. It is not known who were the members of this committee, but a hint of the identity of some of them may be found in a report published by the Islamic Movement's organ in Israel, which is also affiliated to the Muslim Brotherhood Movement, "*Sawt al-Haq wa al-Huriya*," 16 June 1995. The item reported on various appointments in the Muslim Brotherhood Movement in Egypt and mentions the following names: Muhammad Ma'mun al-Hudeibi, Dr Ahmad Muhammad al-Melet, Mustafa Mashhur, and Hasan al-Hudeibi. These people may be assumed to be members of the Committee of Thirteen in Cairo, along with representatives of other districts, such as Sheikh Yusef al-Azem from Jordan.
2. Islamic Jihad leaflet from 31 August, in the occupied territories. Also: Dr Iyyad Barghuti: *The Islamic Palestinian Movement and the New World Order* (Arabic), Jerusalem, 1992, pp. 82–85.
3. Also published in the East Jerusalem *a-Nahar*, 22 April 1995.
4. According to Israeli sources (15 September 1995), Abu Marzuq was Sheikh Yassin's principal liaison with the Muslim Brotherhood Movement in Egypt, because of his special links with them from the time of

his studies in the Mansura University. The Cairo center did not accept Sheikh Yassin, and at that time – right after the outbreak of the Intifada – Abu Marzuq tried to convince the center in Egypt to recognize Sheikh Yassin. Subsequently he moved to Afghanistan and became one of the confidants of Defense Minister Ahmad Masu'd. During the war in Afghanistan he moved closer to the United States and, with his family, settled in the state of Virginia, becoming involved with the Islamic organization in the United States. After establishing Az a-Din al-Qassam, he moved between Jordan and Egypt, but his permanent office was in Damascus. He tried to set up links with Iran, but his relations with the Iranians did not go well. Jordan had no interest in his visits, since it suspected he had been behind the attempts to attack Israel from its borders. He tried to organize another center in Abu Dhabi, but failed.

5. Interview with Dr a-Zahhar, *Saut al-Haq wa al Huriya*, 18 December.

13 Who is to Succeed Abu Iyyad?

1. *Al-Quds*, 5 September 1991.
2. *Al-Quds*, 11 September 1991.
3. According to *a-Nadwa*, 26 June 1992.
4. *Al-Quds*, 10 September 1991.
5. *Al-Quds*, 5 June 1992.
6. According to *a-Nahar*, 11 September 1993.
7. *Al Hamishmar, 22 October 1993.*
8. According to *al-Quds*, 24 May 1990.
9. *A-Nahar*, 13 May 1993.
10. According to *a-Sha'ab*, 26 September 1992.
11. According to *al-Bayareq*, Arab-Israeli weekly, 19 June 1992.
12. Mentioned in *al-Quds*, 30 April 1992.
13. *Davar*, 8 October 1993.
14. *A-Nahar*, 4 August 1991.
15. According to *al-Quds*, 21 July 1991.

14 Ashrawi or Qaddumi? Washington or Paris?

1. According to *al-Manar*, 2 August 1993.
2. Ibid.

15 The Documents Crisis: Husseini and Arafat on the Brink of a Rift

1. *Al-Quds al-Arabi*, 4 November 1991.

2. WAFA reported on Arafat's rejection in its release of 20 November, 1991.
3. *A-Nahar*, 13 October 1993.

16 The Secret Channels: Guns, Flags and the Economy

1. Ron Pundak, *Politica* (Hebrew) (December 1993).
2. *A-Nahar*, 5 March 1995.
3. Mahmud Abbas, *The Road to Oslo* (Arabic), Beirut, 1994, p. 7.
4. Joseph Alpher, *Security Arrangements for a Palestinian Settlement, Survival*, vol. 34, no. 4 (Winter 1992–3), pp. 49–67.
5. *A-Nahar*, 17 May 1995.
6. *The Road to Oslo*, pp. 349–350.

17 The Faqahani State Shall Not Pass

1. *Al-Manar*, 8 November 1993.
2. Interview with Sari Nusseiba, *al-Quds*, 26 October 1993.
3. The Jordanian *a-Dastur*, 20 January 1994.
4. *Kan'an*, 15 February 1994.
5. Abd al-Majid Hamdan, *a-Tali'a*, 28 December 1993.
6. Quoted in *a-Nahar* on 26 December 1993.
7. Hisham Sharabi, *al-Quds*, 12 November 1993.
8. *A-Nahar*, 16 November 1993.

Index

National Movement, 131–2
national personalities *see* Iyyadist
    political wing
a-Natsha, Mustafa (Mayor
    of Hebron), 149
a-Natur, Mahmud, 105
Nazzal, Muhammad, 164–5
New Outlook, 96, 97
New York Trade Center bombing,
    46, 152–8, 164
Night of the Hang-Glider (1987),
    18–19
Nitzanim operation (1990), 98
Nofal, Mamduh, 15, 70, 76, 171, 215
Nusseiba, Sari, 104–5, 106–7, 136–7,
    137, 144, 149–51, 183, 241–2

occupied territories
    and Abu Iyyad, 80, 89
    and Abu Jihad, 31–2, 73, 79,
        88–9, 106
    call for elections, 169–71, 247, 248
    demilitarization of, 9, 176, 197
    and Democratic Front, 73–5
    and Fatah, 73, 137
    Jordanian–PLO partnership in, 31
    National Guidance Committee,
        32–4
    political committees, 135–7, 138,
        149–51
    Popular Front, 73
    settler's attitude to Palestinian
        police, 227
    and USA, 137, 138, 248, 249
    see also Gaza; Intifada; Unified
        Intifada Command; West
        Bank
Odeh, Abd al-Aziz, 28–9, 51, 52
organizations, 20, 21, 144, 147, 149
    and Abd a-Shafi, 147, 167
    and Abu Iyyad's murder, 120–1
    confidence-building gestures, 196
    and the Fatah, 135
    FIDA challenge to, 130–3
    French support for, 107
    internal relations, 134
    Khaled al-Hasan's criticism of,
        176
    London Forum, 168
    and the outside leadership,

133–5, 137
    and the Palestinian delegation,
        145, 147
    and the political committees, 136
    in the Unified Command, 20,
        75–6, 79, 130, 133–5, 144
Oslo agreements, 179, 191, 193, 200,
    201, 233
    and Abu Mazen, 205–6, 215, 216,
        219, 232, 238, 240–1, 242
    and Ashrawi, 209–10,
        219, 245–6
    Egypt supports, 174, 206–7, 235
    elections in the territories, 248
    establishment of, 205–12
    and FIDA, 219, 235, 245
    Jordan's status, 202, 235
    mutual recognition talks begin,
        217
    and the Palestinian diaspora,
        246–7
    Palestinian ratification, 219–20,
        240–1
    and People's Party, 219, 235
    and Rabin, 206, 208–9, 212, 215,
        226, 239
    signing ceremony, 215–16
    and Syria, 235
    and USA, 202, 235, 248
    winding up, 232–6

Pakistan, 45, 156–7, 157, 158
Palestine Liberation Army, 209, 234
Palestine Liberation Organization
    and Abu Jihad, 4–5
    attempts to eliminate, 145–6
    authority over armed groups, 9
    Al-Azhar University allocation,
        55
    Baker initiative (1990), 98–9
    Cairo dialogue, 86, 118
    Central Council, 220, 240
    Corps of Personalities, 75–6
    document crisis, 190, 193
    economic talks channel, 202, 232
    and Egypt, 22
    establishment of, 22
    Executive Committee, 24, 38,
        132, 220
    FIDA criticism of, 131–3